Police Reform from the Bottom Up

Officers and their Unions as Agents of Change

Edited by
Monique Marks and David Sklansky

Series edited by
Dilip K. Das

Routledge
Taylor & Francis Group

LONDON AND NEW YORK

International Police Executive Symposium

First published 2012
by Routledge
2 Park Square, Milton Park, Abingdon, Oxon, OX14 4RN

Simultaneously published in the USA and Canada
by Routledge
711 Third Avenue, New York, NY 10017

Routledge is an imprint of the Taylor & Francis Group, an informa business

This book is a reproduction of *Police Practice and Research*, volume 9, issue 2, and *Policing and Society*, volume 18, issue 1. The Publisher requests to those authors who may be citing this book to state, also, the bibliographical details of the special issues on which the book was based.

British Library Cataloguing in Publication Data
A catalogue record for this book is available from the British Library

ISBN13: 978-0-415-68679-2

Typeset in Times New Roman
by Taylor & Francis Books

Disclaimer
The publisher would like to make readers aware that the chapters in this book are referred to as articles as they had been in the special issue. The publisher accepts responsibility for any inconsistencies that may have arisen in the course of preparing this volume for print.

MIX
Paper from
responsible sources
FSC® C004839
www.fsc.org

Printed and bound in Great Britain by the MPG Books Group

Police Reform from the Bottom Up

What role can and should police unions and rank-and-file officers play in driving and shaping police reform? Police unions and their members are often viewed as obstructionist and conservative, not as change agents. But reform efforts are much more likely to succeed when they are supported by the rank-and-file, and line officers have knowledge, skills and insights that can be invaluable in promoting reform. Efforts to involve police unions and rank-and-file officers in police reform are less common than they should be, but they are increasing, and there is a good deal to learn about policing, police reform and participatory management from the efforts made to date.

In this pioneering volume, an international, cross-disciplinary collection of scholars and police unionists address a range of neglected questions, both empirical and theoretical, about the place of police officers themselves in the process of reform – what it has been, and what it could be. They provide a fresh view of police reform as occurring from the bottom up rather than the top down. This book will be highly useful for practitioners and scholars who have a serious interest in the possibilities and limits of police organisational change.

This book is based on special issues of *Police Practice and Research* and *Policing and Society*.

Monique Marks is an Associate Professor in the Community Development Programme at the University of KwaZulu-Natal, South Africa. She has published widely about police unions, police labour rights, and police organisational change. She has also conducted participatory action research with police unions in South Africa and in Australia for the past 15 years.

David Sklansky is the Yosef Osheawich Professor of Law at the University of California, Berkeley, USA, and Faculty Chair of the Berkeley Center for Criminal Justice. He has written extensively about policing and criminal procedure.

Police Practice and Research
Series Editor: Dilip K. Das
International Police Executive Symposium

Police Practice and Research is a series of books based on special issues of the pioneering peer-reviewed journal *Police Practice and Research: An International Journal*, which presents current and innovative police research as well as operational and administrative practices from around the world. It seeks to bridge the gap in knowledge that exists regarding who the police are, what they do, and how they maintain order, administer laws, and serve their communities. The journal is published in association with the International Police Executive Symposium (IPES), which brings police researchers and practitioners together to facilitate cross-cultural, international and interdisciplinary exchanges for the enrichment of the policing profession.

Policing: Toward an Unknown Future
Edited by John Crank & Colleen Kadleck

Innovative Possibilities
Global Policing Research and Practice
Edited by Les Johnston &
Clifford Shearing

Police Responses to People with
Mental Illnesses
Global Challenges
Edited by Duncan Chappell

Police Reform from the Bottom Up
Officers and their Unions as Agents
of Change
Edited by Monique Marks and
David Sklansky

Contents

Note on contributors   vii
Series Editor's Preface   xi

1. Introduction: The role of the ranks and file and police unions
   in police reform
   Monique Marks and David Sklansky   1

Part I: The rank-and-file as change agents

2. Police reform: Who done it?
   David H. Bayley   16

3. Police officers as change agents in police reform
   Hans Toch   27

4. From the bottom-up: sharing leadership in a police agency
   Brigitte Steinheider and Todd Wuestewald   39

5. Building the capacity of police change agents: The nexus policing project
   Jennifer Wood, Jenny Fleming and Monique Marks   58

6. Research for the front lines
   David Thacher   74

Part II: Police unions and police reform

7. The neglect of police unions: exploring one of the most important
   areas of American policing
   Samuel Walker   88

8. Strange union: changing patterns of reform, representation, and
   unionization in policing
   Jan Berry, Greg O'Connor, Maurice Punch and Paul Wilson   106

9. No longer a 'workingman's paradise'? Australian police unions and political action in a changing industrial environment
   Mark Finnane   123

10. The human right of police to organize and bargain collectively
   Roy J. Adams   136

Part III: Police culture, police organization and the possibilities of change

11. Why reforms fail
   Wesley G. Skogan   144

12. Enduring issues of police culture and demographics
   Jerome H. Skolnick   156

13. Police and social democracy
   William Ker Muir   167

   Index   172

Notes on contributors

Roy J. Adams is Professor Emeritus of Industrial Relations at McMaster University in Hamilton, Ontario. He was formerly Director of McMaster's Theme School on International Justice and Human Rights and is Steering Committee Chair of the Society for the Promotion of Human Rights in Employment.

David H. Bayley is Distinguished Professor in the School of Criminal Justice at University at Albany - State University of New York. He is a specialist in international criminal justice, with particular interest in policing. He has done extensive research in India, Japan, Australia, Canada, Britain, Singapore, and the United States. His work has focused on strategies of policing, the evolution of police organizations, organizational reform, accountability, and the tactics of patrol officers in discretionary law-enforcement situations.

Jan Berry was the first woman chairman in the history of the Police Federation of England and Wales. After becoming a police officer in 1973 she performed a variety of duties from beat officer to detective, rose quickly through the ranks, and was promoted to the rank of Chief Inspector in 1997. She became a local Federation representative in 1987 and in 2002 was elected Chairman of the Police Federation, a position she held through 2008. From 2008 to 2010 she served as the UK's Reducing Bureaucracy in Policing Advocate. She is currently a professional policing advisor and advocate in the UK.

Mark Finnane is Professor of History and an Australian Research Council Professorial Fellow at Griffith University, Australia. His publications on the history of policing include *Police and Government: Histories of Policing in Australia* (1994) and *When Police Unionise: The Politics of Law and Order in Australia* (2002). Current research focuses on the history of "security policing" in Australia.

Jenny Fleming is Professor in the School of Government at the University of Tasmania, Australia. She is a Member of the Australian and New Zealand Association of Criminology, the Political Studies Association (UK) and the Australasian Political Studies Association. Her research interests include policing, organisational change, women in policing, police/government relations, police labour relations and public policy. Previous publications include *Fighting Crime Together: The Challenges of Policing and Security Networks* (2006; co-edited with Jennifer Wood) and *Government Reformed: Values and New Political Institutions* (2003; co-edited with Ian Holland).

Monique Marks is an Associate Professor in the Community Development Programme at the University of KwaZulu-Natal, South Africa. She has published widely about police unions, police labour rights, and police organisational change. She has also conducted participatory action research with police unions in South Africa and in Australia for the past 15 years. Previous publications include *Transforming the Robocops: Changing Police in South Africa* (2005).

William Ker Muir is professor emeritus of political science at the University of California at Berkeley, USA. He is the author of *Legislature: California's School for Politics* (1985), *Police: Streetcorner Politicians* (1977) and *Prayer in the Public Schools: Law and Attitude Change* (1967).

Greg O'Connor is the President of the NZ Police Association. Greg is a Senior Sergeant of Police seconded full time to the Association National Office. Elected to the position in 1995, Greg is the longest serving president in the Association's history.

Maurice Punch has worked at universities in the UK, USA, and the Netherlands. He has researched corporate crime and police corruption and published widely; in 1999 he became a Visiting Professor at the London School of Economics. He contributes to conferences in several countries, delivers seminars to police officers and executives, and teaches regularly in Criminology programmes at King's College London, UK.

David Sklansky is the Yosef Osheawich Professor of Law at the University of California, Berkeley, USA, and Faculty Chair of the Berkeley Center for Criminal Justice. He has written extensively about policing and criminal procedure. He is the author of *Democracy and the Police* (2008).

Wesley G. Skogan is Professor of Political Science and a Faculty Fellow of the Institute for Policy Research at Northwestern University, USA. He is an expert on crime and policing, and has directed most of the IPR's major crime studies over the past three decades. These include research on fear of crime, the impact of crime on communities, public participation in community crime prevention, victimization, and victim responses to crime. He has written numerous journal articles and book chapters in edited collections, and is the author of *Policing and Community in Chicago: A Tale of Three Cities* (2006) and the editor of *Community Policing: Can It Work?* (2003). His 1990 book, *Disorder and Decline: Crime and the Spiral of Decay in American Cities*, won the 1991 Distinguished Scholar Award of the Section on Crime and Deviance of the American Sociological Association.

Jerome H. Skolnick is Co-Director of the Center for Research in Crime and Justice at the New York University School of Law, USA. His research interests focus on police practice and accountability, and the regulation of deviance. Previous publications include *Crisis in American Institutions* (1997; with Elliot Currie), *Above the Law: Police and the Excessive Use of Force* (1993; with James Fyfe) and *Justice Without Trial: Law Enforcement in Democratic Society* (1993).

Brigitte Steinheider is Associate Professor and Director of the Organizational Dynamics program at the University of Oklahoma–Tulsa, USA. She received her MS in Psychology from the Heinrich-Heine-University, Düsseldorf, her MBA from the University of Applied Sciences in Düsseldorf, and her PhD in Psychology from the

Technical University Dresden in Germany. Her research focuses on shared leadership as well as interdisciplinary collaborations in organizations and research institutions.

David Thacher is Associate Professor of Public Policy and Urban Planning at the University of Michigan, USA. His research aims to develop and apply humanistic approaches to policy research. He is particularly interested in the use of case study and narrative analysis to clarify the ethical foundations of public policy. He has carried out this research primarily in criminal justice policy, where he has undertaken studies of order maintenance policing, the local police role in homeland security, community policing reform, the distribution of safety and security, and prisoner re-entry. Outside of criminal justice, he has also conducted research on urban planning and on adoption policy. He is currently writing a book about humanistic policy research.

Hans Toch is based in the School of Criminal Justice at University at Albany - State University of New York, USA. A social psychologist working in criminology and criminal justice administration, he is a prolific author whose books include *Living in Prison* (1975), *Violent Men* (1969), *The Disturbed Violent Offender* (with Ken Adams, 1989), *Police as Problem Solvers* (with J.D. Grant, 1991), *Mosaic of Despair* (1992), *Police Violence* (with William Geller, 1996), *Corrections: A Humanistic Approach*, (1997) and *Acting Out* (with Ken Adams, 2002). He is an elected Fellow of the American Psychological Association and the American Society of Criminology, and in 1996 he served as president of the American Association for Forensic Psychology.

Samuel Walker is Professor Emeritus of Criminal Justice at the University of Nebraska at Omaha. He is the author of 13 books on policing, crime policy, and civil liberties. Previous publications include *The New World of Police Accountability* (2005). His current research and consulting involves Early Intervention Systems (EIS) for police.

Paul Wilson joined the Metropolitan Police Service in 1979 as a legal clerk and in 1983 became a police officer; in the early 1990s he was instrumental in forming the Metropolitan Black Police Association, and in 1999–2000 became the first elected chair of the National Black Police Association. In 2003 he was awarded a Fulbright Fellowship to research community-policing approaches across the USA. He is currently the Director and Founder of the Safer Global Communities Ltd.

Jennifer Wood is an Associate Professor in the Department of Criminal Justice at Temple University, USA. She is a criminologist with expertise in policing and regulation. Her work has explored how order and security is promoted by mixes of public and private entities including but well beyond the public police. Her co-authored book, *Imagining Security* (2007; with Clifford Shearing), offers an account of 'nodal governance' as a means of explaining this plurality. She has published two co-edited books: *Democracy, Society and the Governance of Security* (2006; with Benoit Dupont) and *Fighting Crime Together: The Challenges of Policing and Security Networks* (2006; with Jenny Fleming). Her current research centers on the connections between security and public health, and in particular the ways in which laws and law enforcement practices contribute to healthy behaviors and environments.

Todd Wuestewald has served as chief of police from 2003 to 2011 in Broken Arrow, Oklahoma, USA. He received his BA from Michigan State University, MPA from the University of Oklahoma, an MS in Criminal Justice from Northeastern State University, and is currently pursuing doctoral studies at Oklahoma State University where his research interests include shared leadership and police workforce development. He serves on the adjunct faculties of several universities and police training foundations.

Series Editor's Preface

Police Practice and Research

I am delighted to write the Series Editor's Preface to the IPES, International Police Executive Symposium, and the Routledge Co-Production, a Book Series, based on the Special Issues of *Police Practice and Research: An International Journal* (PPR). It is an eloquent testimony to the well-known and growing importance as well as global popularity of PPR that a prestigious publishers, Routledge, wrote to me recently to 'confirm that the special issue journals we have agreed upon from *Police Practice and Research* shall be turned into a book series as a joint publication with IPES: International Police Executive Symposium'. They added that 'We are very much looking forward to publishing the special issues of your journal as a book series'.

Police Practice and Research (PPR) is affiliated with the International Police Executive Symposium (IPES) www.ipes.info. PPR is a peer-reviewed, international journal that presents current and innovative academic police research as well as operational and administrative police practices from around the world. Manuscripts are submitted by practitioners, researchers, and others interested in developments in policing, analysis of public order, and the state of safety as it affects the quality of life everywhere. The journal seeks to bridge the gap in knowledge that exists regarding who the police are, what they do, and how they maintain order, administer laws, and serve their communities in the world. Attention is also focused on specific organizational information about the police in different countries and regions of the universe.

A specific goal of the editors is to improve cooperation between those who are active in the field and those who are involved in academic research, as such a relationship is essential for innovative police work. To this end, the editors encourage the submission of manuscripts co-authored by police practitioners and researchers that will highlight a particular subject from both points of view.

PPR publishes special issues on contemporary topics of universal interest. Scrutinizing the titles of the last few special issues will clearly show that these issues are edited by stalwarts in the field. In recent days among others there were special issues such as 'New Possibilities for Policing Research and Practice' (Les Johnston and Clifford Shearing); 'Community Policing, East, West, North and South' (Peter Grabosky); 'Police Reform from the Bottom-Up: Police Unions and Their Influence' (Monique Marks and David Sklansky); 'The Evolving Relationship Between Police Research and Police Practice' (Gary Cordner and Stephen White) and the latest worthy addition is

'From Sorcery to Stun Guns and Suicide-The Eclectic and Global Challenges of Policing and the Mentally Ill' (Duncan Chappell).

As it will be noted, in keeping with PPR's tradition, special issue editors hail from different regions of the globe – Australia, Africa, Europe, and North America. They are renowned researchers like Clifford Shearing, Les Johnston, Peter Grabosky, David Sklansky and Gary Cordner as well as young and emerging ones like Monique Marks. PPR's Guest Editors also hail from the field of practice. Duncan Chappell has just retired after serving as a judge with a long record of academic research and Stephen White, a British Chief Constable, has recently left his position as 'head of the European Union's Integrated Rule of Law Mission for Iraq' to serve as an European Director of the an international strategic consultancy firm, namely, the Soufan Group. Needless to say that the topics they deal with are highly contemporary and in great demand both by practitioners and academics, namely, Community Policing, Police Unions, New Possibilities for Policing Research and Practice or Evolving Relationship Between Police Research and Police Practice, as well as the Eclectic and Global Challenges of Policing and the Mentally Ill.

Policing in today's complex world ranges from horrid to helpful but despite the negative issues raised here, IPES and PPR continue to be on the forefront of democratic policing. It is hoped that this series will help the police in the democratic world meet the challenges that lay ahead.

Dilip K. Das, Ph.D
Series Editor

Produced at the Office of International Police Executive Symposium

Introduction: The role of the ranks and file and police unions in police reform

Monique Marks and David Sklansky

The dominant mindset of police departments, police reformers, and police scholars—the dominant mindset, in short, of nearly everyone who thinks about policing and its problems—is, and always has been, that policing needs strong, top-down management. Good police officers are police officers who follow rules. Rank-and-file organizing is an obstacle to reform and sits uneasily beside the rule of law. Police departments are famously bureaucratic because they are necessarily bureaucratic. Even strong advocates for organized labor often lose some of their enthusiasm when it comes to law enforcement. It was not a great surprise, for example, when the International Labor Organisation (ILO) upheld, in 2003, the Argentine government's determination to curtail the right of the police to unionise and bargain collectively (ILO 2003)—notwithstanding the ILO's general commitment to freedom of association and collective bargaining as basic employment rights for employees in any democratic society (see Braithwaite and Drahos 2000).

And yet suggestions have been made off and on for decades that rank-and-file police officers should have a greater collective voice in shaping the nature of their work. Sometimes the argument has sounded in management theory: participation in departmental decision-making will make officers more engaged and more committed, will lessen their opposition to reform, and will infuse managerial judgments with localized, hands-on knowledge of the day-to-day realities of policing. At other times the argument has sounded in civics: police are citizens and should be awarded the same rights as other citizens; police are most likely to respect and protect citizen rights if they themselves are afforded those rights—not only rights to speech and free association, but also rights to bargain collectively, and to fair and impartial adjudication of disciplinary allegations and workplace grievances. Democratic policing, it has been suggested, should entail a measure of workplace democracy for police officers (see Sklansky 2008; Marks and Fleming 2006b; Birzer 1996).

Those ideas are still outside the mainstream, but there are reasons to think they may be coalescing and gathering strength. A growing number of police executives borrow heavily from the rhetoric and practices of managers in other service sectors (Kiely & Peek 2002), and many of the ideas to which they are attracted call for greater flexibility, less hierarchical rigidity, and more openness to "bottom up" processes of decision-making. Police managers and leaders increasingly demonstrate "a predilection for articulating new philosophies, concepts and approaches to the provision of policing 'services'"; policing, some argue, now "meets the criteria of a 'performance culture', offers 'best value', advocates 'partnerships' with the communities policed, supports the development of a new legal and political culture with 'human rights' at its core and is confident in its 'professionalism'" (Adlam 2002).

A familiar range of political, economic and social changes in policing have cast doubt on previously accepted managerial practices. Community oriented policing calls for more localized and flexible decision-making, which in turn requires recognizing and encouraging greater responsibility and initiative from police officers who work directly with communities (Goldstein 1979; Deukmedjian 2003). New governance arrangements throughout the industrialized world are less bureaucratic (or at least claim to be), and emphasize "partnerships" and "networks" (Fleming & Rhodes 2005). And public sector organizations are expected, increasingly, to have the virtues traditionally expected of large businesses: cost-effectiveness, financial accountability, objectively measured efficiency, and even competition and the marketization of services (Davies & Thomas 2001; Murphy 2004; O'Malley & Hutchinson 2006; Vickers & Kouzmin 2001). As one scholar puts it:

> Police executives are no longer managers of continuing organizational growth and service expansion, they are now confronted with inexorable political demands to find ways to cut costs, increase efficiency, improve productivity and demonstrate what is called "value for money". Pressured to abandon traditional quasi-military, bureaucratic police management models for more contemporary and efficient private-sector service management philosophies and strategies, modern police executives must now provide business-based planning models, argue the cost efficiency of various policing strategies and promote radical organizational change
> (Murphy 2004:2).

Faced with these challenges, police leaders, particularly in English-speaking, established democracies, are increasingly voicing scepticism about traditional, paramilitary organizational structures in law enforcement. A new, "soft HR discourse" emphasizes "a more relaxed, informal, caring and supportive organisation" (Davis & Thomas 2001:8). A range of police services have introduced "team leadership programmes" in an effort to let employees share their experiences and exchange ideas for improving how their jobs are structured (O'Malley & Hutchinson 2007).

Australian police leaders, by way of example, have for some years now been declaring a "new era" in law enforcement management. At a recent police leadership conference, John Murray, the then Chief Police Officer of the Australian Federal Police (AFP), argued for "a more democratic style" of police management (2002:15). He explained that:

> ...police leaders across the developed world have been forced to examine the appropriateness and efficacy of [the] traditional model for at least two reasons. The first is its inflexibility and consequently inability to meet the demands of efficiency effectiveness in an environment described as volatile as any competitive market... The second is the experience of many police leaders that the autocratic style of leadership and the strict enforcement of rules associated with the traditional model is at odds with the expectations of a modern workforce (Ibid.).

The AFP has in fact "flatten[ed]" its organizational structure, in an effort to extend "the concept of empowerment ... to all areas of the organization" and to "increase the authority and decision making power of members from the lowest level up" (*Ibid.*:17). Along similar lines, "corporate governance committees" in the Victoria Police now formulate policy, set performance targets and budget priorities, and monitor organisational behaviour (Victoria Police 2004/2005). And in the United Kingdom, recruitment, selection and training of senior police officers has been completely revamped in an effort to foster "transformational leadership," marked by "participation, consultation and inclusion" (Sivestri 2007:39).

Old assumptions and new directions

All of these "developments" in policing management and organizational restructuring need to be taken with a grain of salt. Most of the evidence suggests that "traditional," "hierarchical," "authoritarian" styles of management persist in policing. (Silvestri 2007:54). Bureaucratic and even autocratic ways of doing things are "alive and well in police organizations" (Fleming & Rhodes 2005:194).

This is the case in both liberal democracies and within more authoritarian countries. It is plainly the case in South Africa, for example, where police leaders have reverted to extremely authoritarian management approaches. While a crucial component of the democratization of the South African Police in the mid 1990s was rank demilitarization, in recent years there has been a complete reversion to militarized ranking (and training) systems. At a symbolic level, the public police in South Africa have shifted from referring to themselves as a "service" to insisting that they be called the South African Police Force. The ranks of the police in South Africa today mirror those of the military, with the leader of the police taking on the title of "General" (see Marks and Wood 2010). All this has been defended in the name of enhancing discipline and effectiveness; the reformative programmes of community policing and more participatory management techniques which were viewed as crucial in the shift to "democratic policing" in South Africa have gone by the wayside.

Clifford Shearing provides an explanation for this easy slide into militarization within police organizations, even in police organizations that aspire to be innovative:

> …resistance to change on the part of traditional police managers is not simply a blind, thoughtless clinging to the known and familiar…Rather it is a statement that the business of management must be concerned with enabling managers to control rank-and-file members at a distance by shaping the inner being of the officers who will be making discretionary decisions. Seen from this perspective, the resistance of traditional managers to the remedial approach is a claim that policing traditions require a style of management that focuses on the identities of rank-and-file officers as 'regulatory regimes' that can be used to control the existence of discretion (1992:22).

Rank-based authority is viewed by police managers as freeing them from the obstacles associated with "dissent, equivocation [and] debate" (Murray 2002:7), and there is a long tradition of thinking this kind of managerial freedom is especially important in policing.

Part of the explanation, particularly in the United States, is historical. At the very point in the twentieth century when interest in workplace democracy reached its zenith

—the late 1960s and early 1970s—American police departments seemed peculiarly inhospitable places for experiments in participatory management. Police officers at that time were almost uniformly white, male, and politically reactionary. Rank-and-file organizing was in fact on the rise, but it took unappealing and often frightening forms. Especially in the United States, a surge in police unionism in the United States was closely linked with fierce opposition to outside oversight, open contempt for civilian authorities, orchestrated brutality against political protesters, vigilante attacks on Black militants, and active membership far-right organizations. As a result, the very scholars and community activists who might otherwise have been most sympathetic to calls for participatory management of law enforcement agencies instead concluded that democracy required tight, top-down control of the police (Sklansky 2008).

By the end of the 1970s, when policing was among the most heavily organized of all public occupations, police unions had joined "the mainstream of American trade unionism," devoting the bulk of their attention to working conditions, job security, and the "bread-and-butter ... issues that have been near and dear to the hearts of U.S. trade unionists for decades" (Delaney & Feuille 1987: 301). But by then the damage had been done. The frightening forms taken by police activism in the late 1960s and early 1970s had dulled the appetite of virtually all scholars and police reformers for bringing workplace democracy to law enforcement. Even after the close of the 1980s, when community policing replaced politically insulated, technocratic "professionalism" as the reigning orthodoxy of police executives and police reformers alike, the "dominant form of policing" continued "to view police officers as automatons" (Goldstein 1990: 27).

It still does today. Encouraging patrol officers to be thoughtful and creative about their work is often said to be part of community policing, and even more so of problem-solving policing, but too often this means little more than placing additional discretion in the hands of individual officers. And the victory of community policing over technocratic, top-down professionalism is itself less than fully secured: recent calls for "intelligence-led policing" and "predictive policing" are, to a considerable extent, calls for a return to something very like the old, much maligned "professional model" (Sklansky 2011). Policing managerial strategies meant to simultaneously build accountability, team work and efficiency such as Compstat have often proved to be extremely top-down in nature (Eterno & Silverman 2006).

Some of the renewed enthusiasm for the professional model has to do with the worldwide economic downturn and the consequent tightening of public service budgets. Those pressures have given additional impetus to preexisting concerns in policing circles for "performance," "efficiency," and "value for money" (Murphy 2004; Gascón & Fogelsong 2010)—concerns that often lead practitioners and scholars, for better or worse, to view traditional, authoritarian patterns of police management more sympathetically. And police unions themselves have had varying, sometimes even contradictory responses to efforts to bring participatory management and other forms of shared workplace decision-making to policing. For all of these reasons, traditional, authoritarian patterns of police management are today competing with a range of less centralized, less hierarchical managerial ideas. What is apparent, however, is that space has been cleared for formulating new workplace arrangements as police leaders along with police unions and other rank-and-file associations struggle to respond to the changes around them (Paoline, Myers & Worden 2000; Kiely & Peek 2002; Marks 2007).

This book grows out of an international, cross-disciplinary conference on "police reform from the bottom up," hosted in 2006 by the University of California, Berkeley, School of Law and co-sponsored by the Berkeley Center for Criminal Justice, the Center for the Study of Law and Society, and the Regulatory Institutions Network at Australian National University. Aimed at reexamining the role of rank-and-file officers and their representatives in police reform, the conference brought together a stellar collection of police scholars, police unionists, police executives, and representatives of identity-based police associations. The participants included well-established academics, justly famed for their path-breaking studies of policing, along with superb younger scholars, bringing fresh perspectives to old controversies.

The discussions in Berkeley were wide-ranging and spirited. There were many areas of disagreement—over the potential for police unions to adopt progressive agendas; over the ability of academics to fully grasp the daily realities of policing; over the degree to which police forces remain racist, sexist, and homophobic; and over the best ways to take advantage of the collective insights of rank-and-file officers.

The Berkeley conference was purposely comprised of academics and practitioners who shared at least some skepticism about the necessity and wisdom of rigid, top-down management in policing, but not all participants were equally resolute about increasing the individual and collective rights of the police. Nor were all the participants equally convinced about the possibility for reform from below or even from within police organizations. There was skepticism voiced, too, about the capacity for police unions to be forces for reform, rather than obstacles. For their part, some of the police unionists at the roundtable criticized existing policing scholarship as uninformed and simplistic. Nonetheless there was also striking consensus on a range of important points. Both the points of common agreement and the areas of disagreement are well illustrated in the contributions to this book.

The rank-and-file as change agents

The first and most important point of consensus is the extraordinary potential of bottom-up approaches to police reform. Outside of policing, three overlapping arguments are commonly made for involving employees in workplace decision-making: it heightens morale and commitment, it develops democratic skills and habits, and it makes for better decisions (see for example Wilms 1996). Each of these arguments can be applied to law enforcement and may, in fact, acquire special force in this context (Sklansky 2008) The morale of officers, and their commitment to the rule of law, are abiding problems in the policing of democratic societies, and the limited experience we have with participatory management in law enforcement suggests that here, as in other sectors, giving employees a say in the shaping of their work strongly increases their job satisfaction and their attachment to the organization's mission.

These points are pursued, in different ways, by each of the chapters in the first part of this book, addressing the potential of police rank-and-file as change agents. In their separate chapters, David Bayley, David Thacher and Hans Toch each emphasize how police decision-making could be improved by securing what John Dewey (1927: 217) would have called the "diffused and seminal intelligence" of the police rank-and-file. Bayley calls it "craft knowledge," Toch calls it "street knowledge," and Thacher calls it "context-specific, situated knowledge." It includes not only the kind of micro-level sociological understanding all good officers acquire about their beats, but also, as Bayley and Toch each make clear, a hands-on feel for best practices, innovative ideas for improving those practices, and a thorough, nuanced understanding of their fellow officers—who can be trusted, who shirks responsibility, who cuts corners, who is prone to violence. Thacher argues, moreover, that line officers can collectively offer not only richer and more nuanced *answers* to central problems of policing, but distinctive and important *questions*—questions different than, and complementary to, the ones typically posed by police executives and typically pursued by scholars.

Bayley notes a handful of successful experiments involving the rank-and-file in police policy-making, in communities that include Madison, Houston, Toronto, Newport News, and Oakland. Yet Bayley makes no bones about his belief that most police reform is initiated from the top or from the outside. Toch expands on the oldest of these experiments, the one in Oakland, in which he himself was involved (see Toch & Grant 2005), and he also discusses a similar, more recent initiative in Seattle. The best way to build on these efforts, and to pursue the broader possibilities suggested by Thacher, may be through cooperative ventures between police scholars and police practitioners—more systematic attempts to foster the kind of collaboration that Toch pursued in Oakland several decades ago.

That at least is the suggestion of the remaining two chapters in Part One, each of which draws extensively on a case study of academic-police collaboration. One, by Jennifer Wood, Jenny Fleming, and Monique Marks, discusses an approach to conducting research with the police in Victoria, Australia, that taps into the knowledge of those police that are the "doers." Wood, Fleming and Marks explore the practical and normative importance of harnessing the dynamism of police officers at all levels in forging new practices and new ways of thinking within police organizations.

This is also a theme explored in the final chapter in Part One, by Brigitte Steinheider and Todd Wuestewald, discussing an experiment with "shared leadership" in the police department of Broken Arrow, Oklahoma. Steinheider, an academic psychologist, and Wuestewald, the police chief in Broken Arrow, collaborated in developing and assessing the program, which has many points in common with the Austrian and British initiatives described earlier. It also resembles isolated, pioneering experiments with participatory management in policing carried out decades ago in the United States, notably in Oakland, California, in the 1970s (Toch & Grant 2005) and in Madison, Wisconsin, in the 1980s (Wykoff & Skogan 1994). But the Broken Arrow initiative was in some ways more thoroughgoing. While Wuestewald, as chief, retained control over operational, day-to-day decision-making, policy formulation is largely delegated to an employee steering committee.

It is an open question how broadly the results from Broken Arrow can be generalized —particularly to larger, more diverse cities and larger, more embattled police forces. But at a minimum the Broken Arrow initiative highlights a series of important questions that must be confronted in any effort to foster "bottom up" police reform, and it suggests some possible answers. First, how can rank-and-file participation in decision-making be harnessed while maintaining appropriate space for managerial flexibility and prerogative?

Broken Arrow provides one model for resolving this conflict—letting the chief decide what issues should be delegated to the "leadership team," but making the team's resolution of those issues binding. There may, of course, be other ways to strike this balance—some involving more radical challenges to management prerogative. Second, what role, if any, should scholars and research institutions play in devising, implementing, and assessing new modes of police management? Again, the Broken Arrow initiative provides an intriguing model that may or may not work elsewhere. Third—a matter to which we will return momentarily—what role should police *unions*, and other organizations of rank-and-file officers, play in a system of "shared leadership"? In Broken Arrow, as in Madison, the police union was brought into the process of participatory management, with union officers sitting on the policymaking committee. Again, there may be other models—purposely preserving the oppositional character of police unions, for example, or drawing more heavily on identity-based police associations. Finally, if police departments and their subunits are viewed as laboratories where theories are tested, new practices are experimented with, and grounded policies are developed, how can those theories, practices, and policies best be evaluated and, where appropriate, exported to other police agencies?

Police unions and police reform

Part Two of this book focuses on one of the issues raised by the Broken Arrow experiment: the role of police unions in police reform. Management-structured exercises in participatory decision-making may compete to some degree with another path toward greater democracy within police organizations: clearing space for collective representation of rank-and-file officers. As Roy Adams suggests in his chapter, basic labor rights, including the rights to freedom of association and collective bargaining, can pose a profound challenge to traditional managerial prerogatives in police organizations. But affording police these basic rights, Adams argues, is important not simply because police are both workers and citizens, but also because it sensitizes the police to the importance of these rights for other groupings.

From the beginning of the twentieth century, police in most Western democratic countries have campaigned for their right to unionize and to bargain collectively. And indeed, in recent decades police unions "have become an increasingly prominent feature of the modern agency and its environment of interested parties" (Magenau & Hunt 1989:547). Despite initial resistance to the unionization of police - even in western liberal democracies - police unions have been remarkably successful in achieving benefits for their members (DeLord et al 2008). Their success has been achieved using what Freeman and Medoff (1984) would refer to as the "monopoly face of unionism": the face that focuses on raising wages over and above the market value and achieving above par conditions of service. Police unions in many countries enjoy membership levels of almost 100%, and they have become prominent "insiders" in the formulation of policing practices (Finnane 2002).

It is worth noting that while the trade union movement across the world is in decline, the police union movement is expanding, gaining strength, and slowly becoming more co-ordinated. Remarkably, these trends can be observed even in countries and regions still characterized by authoritarian rule. Southern Africa offers a particularly striking example. In February 2007, a group of Swaziland police officers came together—in violation of the law—to form a police union. Unsurprisingly, the Swaziland government refused to recognize the union and threatened its organizers with arrest (Nxumalo 2007). Also unsurprisingly, the police unionists turned for strategic and legal advice to South Africa's Police and Civil Rights Union (POPCRU), the region's oldest and most firmly established police union, something of a signifier throughout Southern Africa for the possibilities of attaining social and labor rights for the police. At roughly the same time, the Mauritian Police Association approached POPCRU for assistance and support in their efforts to gain collective bargaining rights similar to those enjoyed by workers in other sectors, both public and private. These Southern African initiatives, while audacious for the region, are mirrored by efforts by police officers around the globe to increase their social and labor rights.

Since September 2006 police unions from Europe, North America, South Africa and Australasia have linked efforts through the International Council of Police Representative Associations (ICPRA). The ICPRA essentially operates as a network, and its member organizations have offered advice and support, for example, to the nascent police union in Swaziland, as well as to police officers from the Guardia Civil in Spain, whose rights have been limited by the Spanish government. The ICPRA is a significant network. The ICPRA was started by the Canadian Police Association (CPA) and now has approximately 1.5 million members affiliated through national police associations and federations. ICPRA membership includes police unions from four continents, speaking over 30 languages, connected through ICPRA. In 2010 the ICPRA was approached by the United Nations Development Programme (UNDP) to develop a proposal for an initiative aimed at assisting police in countries which are in the process of democratizing to form robust police representative organizations. The UNDP is keen to support and partner in such initiatives in order to "test out" whether the democratization of police organizations impacts positively on democratic policing agendas.

Regional and international networks of police unions remain loosely constituted, however, in part because police unions themselves vary widely in their activities, their powers and privileges, and their understanding of their own roles. As Berry, O'Connor, Punch and Wilson explain, the nature of police unionism has been shaped by a range of factors that themselves vary from place to place. These factors include police and labor legislative frameworks; the national labor-management climate; broad police reform programs; the self-perception and external status of police officers as laborer or professionals; and the alliances that local police unions have struck with community groups and the broader trade union movement.

Partly as a result of these varying influences, and partly because members of police unions often are pulled in one direction as police officers and a different direction as unionists, police unions have reacted in complicated and sometimes contradictory ways to efforts to reform police management. They have campaigned for less authoritarian approaches to management, while at the same time opposing the importation of private sector mentalities and techniques. Police officers want to be consulted, they want to be included in organizational decision making and they want their individual contributions to be recognized. Yet, at the same time, police officers at all ranks attach cultural significance to police organizations as havens of discipline, restraint and authority.

In his contribution to this book, Samuel Walker describes the diversity of police unions in the United States as a microcosm of the fragmentation of the public police more broadly. At times, US police unions have pushed for democratic reform not just of the internal management of their agencies but also of police practices on the street. More often, however, they have been obstacles to reform: contesting civilian oversight bodies, for example, or stalling innovative reform projects. In a chapter complementing

Walker's, Mark Finnane argues that state police unions in Australia have become more and more alike, mounting similar challenges, adopting similar strategies, and mouthing similar rhetoric. Paralleling what Walker describes in the United States, though, Finnane observes that while police unions occasionally have been forward looking, for the most part their campaigns have been inward-looking and defensive.

As significant repositories and transmitters of law enforcement culture, police unions have the potential to refashion that culture, and policing along with it. But police unionists have been inclined to take their bearings—structurally, culturally, and normatively—from within the police organization (Marks 2007). There may be moments of dissidence but these are not often sustained. The primary identity of a police union member is as a police officer, not as a trade unionist or a social activist. For the most part, police unions have been fiercely protective both of officers' rights and of the professional distinctiveness of the public police; as a result, they have often served as insular and defensive upholders of the more traditional characteristics of police culture (Reiner 1992).

Police unions will always present a challenge from below, but since union members identify themselves primarily as police officers so too their union culture will always have a strong affinity with the parent culture of the police organization. Managers have experimented with new ways of governing police organizations (Wood & Dupont 2006), but police union leadership has been much less inclined to step into the vanguard of reform. Even so, there is nothing inevitable about the cultural influence of police unions, and simply branding them as "conservative," is a good deal too simplistic, particularly given their steady resistance to orthodox hierarchies. And when they stand up, as they not infrequently do, for the integrity of public policing as a form of public service, their voice can resonate with progressive voices emanating from a range of other public service trade unions and community based organizations.

The discussion of Britain's Black Police Association in the jointly authored chapter by Jan Berry, Greg O'Connor, Maurice Punch and Paul Wilson underscores the growing importance of identity-based associations of police officers, and the dramatic impact these organizations can have on the internal dynamics of law enforcement agencies. This is not a development limited to the United Kingdom. POPCRU's success owes something to its original status as an organization chiefly of *black* police and correctional officers, fully committed to the struggle against racial oppression in South Africa (Marks 2006). In the United States, organizations of minority police officers, women police officers, and—more recently—gay, lesbian and transgendered police officers have loosened up the internal politics of police forces, have made manifest the absence of a unified "police position" on a range of controversial issues affecting law enforcement, and have opened up reform possibilities previously blocked by monolithic police opposition. There are signs, too, that competition with identity-based associations may be pushing police unions to be more inclusive, more forward-thinking, and more open to proposals for police reform (Sklansky 2008).

Police culture, police organization and the possibility of change

The changing demographics within police organizations may offer a measure of hope on another score, as well. One longstanding ground for concern about giving police officers a larger, collective voice in the shaping of their work has been the police occupational culture, long identified as a site of a host of intersecting and reinforcing pathologies, including racism, sexism, paranoia, intolerance, and violence. There are signs that the growing diversity of police workforces has made the workplace culture within police organizations less monolithic, more vibrant, and friendlier to democratic values (Sklansky 2008). But there are grounds for continued concern about the police organization culture, and there are reasons to think that police organizations and police culture still pose serious obstacles to enlisting rank and file officers in police reform.

Those lingering obstacles, and countervailing grounds for hope, are the subjects taken up, in different ways, by each of the three chapters in the third and final part of this book, each written by an extraordinarily influential scholar of policing. Jerome Skonick, in his chapter, focuses on the lingering pathologies of organizational culture, revisiting his own, formative work on this subject (Skolnick 2011), and offering reasons for skepticism about the extent to which the culture has truly changed. The following chapter, by Wesley Skogan, catalogs the hurdles facing any effort at police reform—but especially, perhaps, one based on ideas that come from the bottom, rather than the top, of the law enforcement power structure.

Skogan reminds us, though, that police unions have not always been obstacles to reform. They have offered important support, for example, for community policing in Chicago—a process Skogan has studied in great detail (e.g., Skogan 2006). That experience underscores the capacity, as yet largely unrealized, for police unions and other associations of frontline officers, to be progressive voices for change. Yet there are examples of police unions that have given voice to progressive ideas and have been at the forefront of struggles for equality and justice. When POPCRU was formed in South Africa, its key objective was to tackle (at great cost to their individual members) police brutality and racism. The European Confederation of Police (an association of police unions across Europe) is committed to fairness and equal opportunities within the police service and has charted a democratic policing pathway (Eurocop 2004). The New South Wales Police Association in Australia played a critical role in assisting the Royal Wood Commission's investigation into police corruption. The New South Wales Police Association have also made extensive submissions supporting forward looking change in the New South Wales Police including calls for integrity testing and greater external oversight (Fleming and Lewis 2002).

If most police unions remain less progressive than these examples, that reality may owe something to the way in which rank-and-file officers have been frozen out of departmental decision-making (Kelling & Kliesmet 1996). There are grounds for hope, therefore, that giving officers a larger, collective voice in the shaping of their work may help make not only individual officers but also their bargaining representatives more invested in the overall goals of police reform—at least, again, under the right circumstances. As Marks and Fleming (2006b) remind us, it is important to bear in mind, that the face that police unions present is highly contingent on the political opportunity structures at the local, national, and global level; the characteristics of union members and supporters; the extent to which unions are viewed as valuable within networks of influence; the vision of union leaders; and the frameworks of international regulatory organizations, including the ILO.

While the dominant view may be that the ideal type police occupational culture dims the possibility of progressive police reform from the bottom up, there are aspects of police culture which might indeed spur on forward looking agendas. The shared normative assumption held by many police officers that the world "out there" is a place of incivility could provide the impetus for unions to try develop violence reduction programmes within communities in order to make police work less onerous. And perhaps police work is an especially good place for experiments in workplace democracy, precisely because of the ways in which democratic practices lie latent in much of what we have long valued as good police work. At least this is the view defended by William Ker Muir in his contribution to this volume. Muir's chapter is animated by some of the same spirit found in his classic study of street level policing and the paradoxes of power in a democratic society (Muir 1977), and it closes this book with what we hope is a justified measure of optimism.

Towards a new research agenda

Collectively, the chapters in this book highlight a range of important questions for future research. We have already touched on most of these questions, but they bear repetition and reemphasis.

First, much remains to be learned about participatory management in policing—its successes, its failures, and its untapped possibilities. Steinheider and Wuestewald rightly invite tests of the Broken Arrow model in other police agencies. But other models deserve consideration or reconsideration, too—some implemented by innovative police leaders decades ago but now largely forgotten, others developed in sectors outside policing, and still others, no doubt, as yet unnoticed by scholars. Nor should we assume that past and present efforts, in policing or in other workplace environments, have exhausted the possible ways of structuring participatory management in policing. On the contrary: the tradition of rigid, top-down management remains so powerful in policing, and scholars and outside activists have so rarely mounted serious challenges to that tradition, that the possibilities for "bottom up" reform in policing remain largely unexplored. Fridell (2004) concludes, having conducted a large study of American police agencies very recently, that there has been little "de-layering" within police organizations in the years since the adoption of community policing' hierarchy and top-down control persist. Having said this, as Wood, Marks and Fleming explore in their chapter, it would seem that in Australia the leadership of the Victoria Police, through the nexus project, are committed to team management, partnership approaches to policing, and bottom up solving of policing problems.

There is no avoiding the difficulty of reconciling strong leadership with participatory forms of management, or the murky issue of the limits of "team leadership" in an organization that is operationally dependent on discipline and command responsiveness. But those limits may be far less restrictive than we generally think. Much of the current thinking about best practices in law enforcement, in fact, stresses the need for knowledge generation, responsiveness, and community networking at the bottom of police organizations. Then, too, the potential links between various forms of democracy inside police agencies and the democratic behavior of police officers on their beats deserve more attention than they have received. All of this suggests that policing scholars might profitably pay more attention to localized experiments with participatory management in policing, and to the possibilities for narrowing the gap between the rhetoric and the reality of new management approaches in policing.

It seems clear that bottom-up police reform, when successful, is rarely if ever entirely bottom-up. Rather it depends in part on enlightened leadership and on constructive engagement with outsiders. Bayley, Muir, Skolnick, and Toch all note the important role that progressive police chiefs have played in the handful of American departments that have systematically involved rank-and-file officers in policy-making. Wood, Fleming and Marks find the same thing in Victoria, Australia where innovation in management styles can be linked very directly to the visionary thinking of Commissioner Christine Nixon. The question we are left with as researchers is what happens to these management innovations when forward thinking chiefs exit?

Second, as Walker argues in his chapter, research on police unions remains embarrassingly thin. Given the large and growing role of police unions, it is surprising how little we know about how they operate; how similar or dissimilar they are; how they influence and are in turn shaped by workplace cultures in policing; how they alternately obstruct, facilitate, and redirect reform initiatives; and how they navigate the new fields of pluralized governance within which the police operate, and the simultaneous (even contradictory) pressures on the police to remilitarize and to perform as corporate entities. Berry, O'Connor, Punch and Wilson are right to suggest that unions and employee associations deserve much more attention in the analysis of current changes and future possibilities in policing. Finnane's chapter invites us to find out more about how committed the police unions (in Australia and beyond) are to change and to test out empirically whether or not there is a convergence of police union strategy and rhetoric within and across national boundaries. And Roy Adams plausibly suggests that the belief by many police leaders and policy makers that awarding police basic labor rights will lead to civil disorder and to a breakdown in police discipline may be unfounded; he sensibly calls for more research on the actual relationship between police labor rights on the one hand, and police effectiveness and respect for civil rights on the other.

Third and finally, running through much of this book is a broad set of questions about how the kinds of connections that police scholars, and their academic institutions, can profitably forge with police practitioners and *their* organizations—a broad set of questions, that is to say, about making real the aspiration to combine "police practice and research." The chapter by Steinheider and Wuestewald both discusses and illustrates the potential benefits of a partnership between a police department and a university. Police reform, Steinheider and Wuestewald suggest, can be locally and internally driven with academic researchers providing support, a different knowledge base, and methods for analysis and assessment. These are not novel claims, and the kind of collaboration found in the Broken Arrow initiative, although rarer than it should be, is far from unprecedented (Toch & Grant 2005). Bayley credits most of the successes of American police reform to the openness that law enforcement agencies have shown to outside researchers and to the proposals those researchers have developed, often in collaboration with innovative leaders inside policing.

Recently there has been somewhat of a surge in interest, globally, in the importance of developing research partnerships between police and academic researchers that are based on mutual respect for the knowledge that each partner brings to the collaboration—including, in particular, attention to needs and the insights of frontline officers. Two special criminology journal issues have been devoted to this particular topic. In 2010 Karim Murji was the guest editor of a special issue of *Policing* entitled "Academic-Police Collaborations – Beyond 'Two Worlds'". In his introduction, Murji states that the objective of the special issue is for contributors "to reflect on their working relationships with the police in various jurisdictions, offering pointers about 'what works' in terms of methods, processes, and practices. All take a realistic view about what can be achieved and none try to oversell collaboration as a 'quick fix'" (2010: 92).

The *Policing* special issue follows a special issue of *Police Practice and Research* in 2009 (volume 11, number 2) which aims to break out of what it sees as a "dialogue of the deaf". Murji (2010) contends that discussions on police-academic collaborations have become somewhat of a sub-field of police studies. In both of these special issues, contributors have tried to configure ways in which police and academics can collaborate in ways that benefit both academics and the police, in terms of identifying relevant problems and solutions to policing dilemmas. But getting police and academic researchers to collaborate on somewhat equal terms is not a simple task given the radically different world outlooks (regarding valid knowledge and evidence) between academics and police practitioners. In this book, Wood, Fleming and Marks address the complexity of this research partnership. They make clear that the initiative in Victoria owes much of its success to its purposeful, systematic facilitation of collaboration between academic researchers and rank-and-file officers. And Thacher suggests that rank-and-file officers could have a large and positive effect on police reform simply by helping researchers reshape the kinds of questions they ask.

In contrast, there have been virtually no examples of partnering between academic institutions and police unions. Doubtless this reflects in part a large barrier of mutual mistrust. Scholars view police unions as reactionary, narrow-minded, inflexible bastions of law-and-order conservatism. Unions see academics as arrogant, ivory tower pontificators, insensitive to the reform weariness of police officers or to the real-world constraints that union leaders face in addressing the concerns of their members. We hope this book will help foster research partnerships between police unions and academics. The chapters of this volume illustrate both the robustness and the diversity of the police union movement; they show, too, the key role unions and other associations of rank-and-file officers have come to play in shaping police reform agendas. Forward-thinking police unionists recognize that scholars can help them address, in more reflective and proactive ways, the needs and concerns of their members in the ever-changing field of policing. The chapter in this book by Berry, O'Connor, Punch, and Wilson is, among other things, a provocative, pioneering model for this kind of collaboration.

The Berkeley conference that gave rise to this book was itself exciting and important, in large part, because of the links it forged and the conversations it opened up among scholars, police executives, police unionists, and representatives of identity-based police associations. We hope this volume demonstrates to its readers what the roundtable made clear to its participants: that "bottom up" processes of police reform offer enormous, largely untapped possibilities—but also enormous, largely unexplored challenges —in the continuing effort to make law enforcement fairer, more effective, and more consistent with democratic values; that police unions and other associations of rank-and-file officers have become indispensable, unavoidable, and poorly understood participants in the formulation of police policies and practices; and that police research and police practice both stand to gain from new, more systematic, and more cooperative efforts to understand the police workplace, its management, its increasingly manifold cultures, and its potential to participate in its own transformation.

References

Adlam, R. (2002). "Governmental rationalities in police leadership: An essay exploring some of the 'deep structure' in police leadership practice". *Policing & Society,* 12(1), 15-36.

Birzer, M. (1996). "Police supervisors in the 21st century". *FBI Law Enforcement Bulletin* 65(6), 5-11.

Braithwaite, J., & Drahos, J. (2000). *Global Business Regulation.* Cambridge: Cambridge University Press.

Davies, A., & Thomas, R. (2001). "From passive to active subjects: Gender, restructuring and professional/managerial identities in the UK public sector". Paper presented at the Second International Conference on Critical Management Studies, 11-13 July, Manchester, UK.

Delaney, J.T., & Feuille, P. (1987). "Police". In Lipsky, D.B., & Donn, C.B. (Eds.), *Collective bargaining in American industry: Contemporary perspectives and future directions.* Lexington, MA: Lexington Books, 265.

DeLord, R., Burpo, J., & Spearing, J. (2008). *Police Union Power, Politics and Confrontation in the 21st Century.* Springfield, IL: Charles, C. Thomas.

Deukmedjian, J. (2003). "Reshaping organizational subjectivities in Canada's national police force". *Policing & Society,* 13(4), 331-48.

Dewey, J. (1927). *The public and its problems.* Chicago: Gateway Books (1946 ed.).

Eterno, J., & Silverman, E. (2006). "The New York City Police Department's Compstat: Dream or Nightmare?" *International Journal of Police Science and Management,* 8(3), 218-231.

European Confederation of Police (EUROCOP). (2004). "The voice of police news in Europe". http://www.eurocop-police.org/index.html.

Finnane, M. (2002). *When police unionise: The politics of law and order in Australia.* Sydney, Institute of Criminology, University of Sydney.

Fleming, J., & Lewis, C. (2002). "The politics of police reform". In *Police Reform: Building Integrity,* ed. T. Prenzler & J. Ransley. Sydney: Federation Press.

Fleming, J., & Rhodes, R. (2005). "Bureaucracy, contracts and networks: The unholy trinity and the police". *Australian & New Zealand Journal of Criminology* 38(2), 192-205.

Freeman, R., & Medoff, J. (1984). *What do unions do.* New York: Basic Books.

Fridell, L. (2004). "The defining characteristics of community policing". In L. Fridell (Ed), *Community Policing: The Past, Present and Future.* Washington: Police Executive Research Forum.

Gascón, G., & Fogelson, T. (2010). *Making policing more affordable; managing costs and measuring value in policing.* Washington, DC: National Institute of Justice.

Goldstein, H. (1990). *Problem-oriented policing.* New York: McGraw-Hill.

International Labour Organisation (ILO). (2003). "ILO governing body on freedom of association: 332nd Report of the Committee on Freedom of Association". November. Geneva. Switzerland: ILO.

International Labour Organisation (ILO). (2004). "Organising for social justice. Report of the Director-General. International Labour Conference, 92nd Session, Report 1 (B), International Labour Office", Geneva, Switzerland.

Kiely, J.A., & Peek, G. (2002). "The culture of the British police: Views of police officers". *Service Industries Journal,* 22(1), 167-183.

Kelling, G.L., & Kliesmet, R.B. (1996). "Police unions, police culture, and police abuse of force". In Geller, W.A., & Toch, H. (Eds.), *Police violence.* New Haven: Yale University Press.

Magenau, J. & Hunt, R. (1996). "Police unions and their role". *Human Relations,* 49 (10), 1315-1342.

Marks, M. (2006). "Transforming police orgnizations from within: Police dissident groupings in South Africa". *British Journal of Criminology,* 40(4), 557-573.

Marks, M. (2007). "Police unions and their cultural influence". In O'Neill, M., Marks, M., & Singh, A. (Eds.), *Police Occupational Culture: New debates and directions*. London: Elsevier, 229.

Marks, M., & Fleming, J. (2006). "Transforming police organizations from within: Police dissident groupings in South Africa". *British Journal of Criminology*, 40(4), 557-573.

Marks, M., & Fleming, J. (2006b). "The right to unionise, the right to bargain and the right to democratic policing". *AAPSS*, 605, 178-199.

Marks, M., & Wood, J. (2010). "South African policing at the crossroads: The case for minimalist and minimal policing in South Africa". *Theoretical Criminology*, 14(3), 311-331.

Muir, W.K.M. (1977). *Police: Streetcorner politicians*. Chicago: University of Chicago Press.

Murji, K. (2010). "Introduction: Academic-police collaborations – Beyond 'two worlds'". *Policing*, 4(2), 92-94.

Murphy, C. (2004). "The rationalisation of Canadian public policing: A study of the impact and implications of resource limits and market strategies". *Canadian Review of Policing Research*, 1. http://crpr.icaap.org/index.php/crpr/article/view/11/11.

Murray, J. (2002). "Leaders and integrity in policing: The march away from militarism. Presentation at the Third Police Leadership Conference on Managing Change through Principled Leadership", April 10-12, Vancouver, Canada.

Nxumalo, M. (2007, February 7). "Police union seeks SA help", *Times of Swaziland*.

O'Malley, P., & Hutchinson, S. (2007). "Converging corporatisation? Police management, police unionism and the transfer of business principles". *Police Practice and Research*, 8(2), 159-174.

Paoline, E.A., Myers, S.M., & Worden, R.E. (2000). "Police culture, individualism, and community policing: Evidence from two police departments". *Justice Quarterly*, 17(3), 575-605.

Reiner, R. (1992). *The politics of the police*. London: Harvester Wheatsheaf.

Shearing, C. (1992). *Reflections on police management practices, Discussion paper 6*. Ottowa: Royal Canadian Mounted Police External Review Committee.

Silvestri, M. (2007). "'Doing' police leadership: Enter the 'new smart macho'", *Policing & Society*, 17(1), 38-58.

Sklansky, D.A. (2008). *Democracy and the police*. Palo Alto, CA: Stanford University Press.

Sklansky, D.A. (2011). *The persistent pull of police professionalism*. Washington, DC: National Institute of Justice.

Skogan, W.G. (2006). *Police and community in Chicago: A tale of three cities*. New York: Oxford University Press.

Skolnick, J.H. (2011). *Justice without trial: Law enforcement in democratic society* (3rd ed.). New Orleans, LA: Quid Pro Books.

Toch, H. & Grant, J.D. (2005) *Police as problem solvers: How frontline workers can promote organizational and community change* (2nd ed.). Washington, D.C.: American Psychological Association.

Vickers, M., & Kouzmin, A. (2001). "New managerialism and Australian police organisations". *International Journal of Public Sector Management*, 14(1), 7-26.

Victoria Police. (2004). *Annual Report 2004/2005*. Melbourne.

Victoria Police. (2005). *Delivering a safer Victoria all day every day: Business plan 2005-2006*. Melbourne.

Wilms, W. (1996). *Restoring Prosperity: How Workers and Managers are Forging a New Culture of Cooperation*. Toronto: Random House.

Wood, J., & Dupont, B. (2006). "Introduction: Understanding the governance of security". In J. Wood and B. Dupont (Eds.), *Democracy, Society and the Governance of Security*. New York: Cambridge University Press.

Wycoff, M.A. and Skogan, W.K. (1993) *Community policing in Madison: Quality from the inside out*. Washington, DC: National Institute of Justice.

Police reform: Who done it?[☆]

David H. Bayley

School of Criminal Justice, State University of New York, Albany, USA

This paper examines nine innovations in American policing since the report of the President's Commission on Law Enforcement and the Administration of Justice (1967) - community-oriented policing, problem-oriented policing, signs-of-crime policing, hot-spots policing, mandatory arrest for spouse assault, enhancement of internal discipline, external oversight, COMPSTAT, and increased diversity of personnel. These innovations occurred from the top-down within policing and were not the product of collaboration with the rank-and-file. In all but two cases, innovations were not instigated by the police themselves but were formulated by people outside the police and brought to the police for adoption. I conclude that innovation occurred because of a system of collaboration between police and civil society that is unique in the world and was itself instigated by far-sighted police leaders.

Where did the big reform ideas in policing come from? My answers are contained in two propositions:

First: Police rank-and-file have not been the source of significant reform ideas. Innovation has not been a bottom-up process within police organizations. This is regrettable.

Second: Police organizations themselves have not been the source of significant reform ideas. Police reform has not been self-generated. It has been instigated by people, or events, outside the police themselves. This is not regrettable, however, but a cause for celebration.

In short, significant police reforms have been top-down and outside-inside. Since the conference for which this paper is written is about the role of rank-and-file in police reform, the second proposition might be considered a willful change of subject. I hope, however, it will be accepted as 'lagniappe'.

I will defend these propositions by examining the provenance of the leading American reforms/innovations since the President's Commission on Law Enforcement and the Administration of Justice (1967), which is considered to have instigated the modern, scientific period of police development. The discussion is organized into four parts:

☆ For the Conference on Rank-and-File Participation in Police Reform—Looking Backwards and Forwards, Berkeley, CA, 12–13 October 2006.

1. List of significant reforms, with very short descriptions for the uninitiated.
2. Discussion of the origins of these reforms, with particular attention to whether they were bottom-up/top-down and inside-outside/outside-inside.
3. The regrettable role of the rank-and-file in innovation.
4. The non-regrettable role of outsiders in innovation.

Roster of big reforms

I nominate the following as the big reform ideas since 1967. These are the ideas that have generated real changes in policing. These are the ideas that police themselves consider to be important as well as controversial changes from past practice.

1. *Community-oriented policing* (COP), referring to the recognition that the police must act to encourage the public to share responsibility for public safety, specifically by consulting with them, adapting their operations to local conditions, mobilizing volunteer resources, and problem solving (Bayley 1994; Goldstein 1990; Skolnick and Bayley 1986, 1988; Trojanowics and Bucqueroux 1990).
2. *Problem-oriented policing* (POP). Developed by Herman Goldstein, POP involves developing police programs that ameliorate or eliminate conditions that generate problems of insecurity and disorder that police are repeatedly called upon to prevent (Goldstein 1979, 1990).
3. *Signs-of-crime policing*, where police, drawing on the logic of 'broken windows' (Wilson and Kelling 1982), prosecute minor offences that contribute to the creation of milieu of incivility. This is sometimes mistakenly identified with 'zero tolerance policing,' which I do not consider a major strategic innovation.
4. *Hot-spots policing*, meaning the short-lived or episodic concentration of police resources on areas or situations of repeated criminal activity (Sherman et al. 1989).
5. Mandatory arrest for spouse-assault. (Sherman and Berk 1984).
6. *Enhancement of internal police discipline*, primarily through the explicit articulation of values, the development of policies for problematic situations, and the acceptance of effective internal investigation of complaints against the police (Chevigny 1969; Walker 2003).
7. *External oversight* of the quality of police activity through civilian review, quasi-official independent supervision of management, and professionally driven accreditation (Goldsmith and Lewis 2000; Walker et al. 2002).
8. *COMPSTAT*, for computer-driven crime statistics, is the signature innovation in the development of evidence-based policing (McDonald 2002). Evidence-based policing means evaluating police activity by systematically collecting information about police operations and their effects.
9. *Enhanced diversity of personnel* through the creation of mechanisms to ensure equal opportunity hiring and promotion for women and minorities.

In my view, then, the big reforms of the past 40 years can be grouped under three headings—strategies (COP, POP, broken-windows, hot-spots, spouse-assault), standards (internal discipline, external accountability), and management (COMP-STAT, diversity).

There is a significant but unavoidable problem with an analysis that reasons on the basis of a sample to conclusions about the provenance of police reform. That problem is selection bias. Would other selections lead to different conclusions about the role of the rank-and-file and outsiders in police reform? There are at least four reasons for raising this issue.

First: The reforms in this sample are those that outsiders such as myself have played the biggest role in formulating and advancing. No wonder, then, that this list features top-down and outside-inside patterns of development.

Second: By choosing 1967 as the start of big reforms, the sample neglects the reforms of what Moore and Kelling have referred to as the 'professional era' in police development (Kelling and Moore 1988). In their view, this significant period of reform occurred before the 'constitutional era' (1960s–1980s) and the 'community-policing era' (1980s and after).

Third: The sample focuses on changes in organizational changes and ignores changes in technology and technique, for example, DNA analysis, crime-scene processing, computers and communications, and new technologies of force.

Fourth: It ignores altogether unplanned and often unrecognized changes that have nonetheless been very real. For example, collaboration with burgeoning private security, risk analysis and first-responding planning as part of counter-terrorism, and the hiring of specialists to investigate increasingly complicated commercial crimes as well as crime both by and against computers. These changes represent important adaptations in policing, but do not rise to the level of what are considered reforms.

In other words, the sample I have chosen is biased in favor of innovations that were deliberately undertaken, that were recognized from the outset as constituting reform. These are necessarily top-down and more likely to be pushed by observers outside the police establishment. The sample undervalues, then, changes in policing that loomed larger in the world of working cops than observing scholars.

At the same time, it is an empirical question whether broadening the sample to compensate for the errors listed above would change my conclusions about the process of innovation in American policing. I don't know. I will go as far as I can with this sample, leaving it to others to defend and examine another sample.

The provenance of big reforms

My examination of the route from idea to change with respect to the nine big reforms listed is idiosyncratic. Well informed, I think, but necessarily partial. I have been closely involved with some of them; hardly at all with others. It is very likely that my own interests have limited my understanding of the trajectories of all these reforms. Hence, it should be understood that these are my opinions about provenance, based on my personal involvement and perspective. If I have got the stories wrong, people who are better informed must correct me.

(1) *COP*. COP was inspired by the research of the 1970s that demonstrated that the core strategies of effective policing were not as effective as claimed. These studies examined the hiring of additional personnel (Loftin and McDowall 1982; Krahn and Kennedy 1985; Koenig 1991; Walker 1989), increasing uniformed patrol visibility

(Kelling et al. 1974; Morris and Heal 1981), rapid response to calls for service (Tien et al. 1978; Bieck and Kessler 1977; Spelman and Brown 1981), and relying on forensic evidence in criminal investigations (Greenwood et al. 1977; Eck 1982; Royal Commission on Criminal Procedure 1981). These 'debunking' studies were carried out by scholars outside the police and their findings were often challenged by the police. Interestingly, the foundational studies of this sort were sponsored by the Police Foundation, supported by the Ford Foundation, but inspired and led by Pat Murphy, a former and very influential insider. I shall comment more about the role of people like him later.

This research led to the conclusion formulated by the scholarly community that the police posture of being able to control and prevent crime through their own efforts, even with higher levels of material support, was false. To be truly effective, the argument went, the police needed a public that would notify them of crime, identify likely suspects, undertake self-protection, and mobilize informal opinion against potential law-breakers (Bayley 1994). The first clear translation of this into police action was by Robert Trojanowics who inspired and organized in Flint, Michigan, what subsequently became community policing (Trojanowics and Bucqueroux 1990). The Flint precedent was developed into doctrine and given professional attention within policing through the discussions and publications of the Executive Session on Policing at Harvard University, 1985–1988. The Executive Session was led by the Kennedy School, supported by funding from the Department of Justice, and involved a carefully selected mix of knowledgeable academics and influential police chiefs. Its activities put COP on the police map of reform, even though its adoption was to prove uneven and often superficial.

Clearly, COP was outside inspired and largely outside-led, with no discernable input from the rank-and-file. Indeed, the general response from the rank-and-file was active skepticism and resistance.

(2) *POP*. The second reformulation of basic police strategy arising out of the evaluations of standard operating procedures came from Hermann Goldstein (Goldstein 1979). He argued that police strategies were too generic and applied too broadly throughout jurisdictions. What was needed was the focusing of police resources on recurrent problems that accounted for a disproportionate amount of police attention. This required the police to analyze the nature of their work, to isolate recurrent issues that might yield to a focused approach, to determine whether the conditions that generated these problems could be ameliorated through police activity, and, if so, to develop multifaceted strategies for doing so. This methodology became SARA—scanning, analysis, response, and assessment. Problem solving became institutionalized through the activities of the Police Executive Research Forum (PERF).

POP, like COP, was clearly an outside-inside reform with substantial resistance from rank-and-file police. In fact, almost 30 years after Goldstein's introduction of POP (1979), the methodology of POP is still difficult to implant, deflected by unquestioned faith among police in their standard operating procedures, top-down management, unsupportive reward systems, and clumsy and imprecise measures of achievement. At the same time, it is important to note that Goldstein was a kind of insider, having worked as executive assistant to Superintendent O.W. Wilson in the Chicago Police Department from 1960 to 1964.

(3) *Signs-of-crime policing*. Although many police deplored the decriminalization of public-order misdemeanors in the 1970s, largely because it deprived them of control over the unruly, it was two scholars (Wilson and Kelling) who developed the theory that serious crime was encouraged by allowing activities that created the impression in particular places that standards of civility were in abeyance, that no one cared, that 'anything goes.' The primary indicators of such 'free-fire' places were signs of physical deterioration (broken windows) and disorderly behavior (panhandling). Interestingly, 'Broken-windows' policing has taken on new life in Great Britain with the recent development of 'reassurance policing' (Fielding and Innes 2006; Herrington and Millie 2006).

Not only was 'signs-of-crime policing' developed by outsiders, admittedly very knowledgeable ones, it was resisted by police executives who thought it diverted resources from deterring more serious crime. Rank-and-file officers too thought this was 'penny ante' law enforcement and not worth their time. When 'signs-of-crime policing' has become operational policy, as in New York City in the mid-1990s, it has been because of the leadership of a determined chief or the desire of a department to appear to be progressive. Clearly 'broken windows,' as well as contemporary 'reassurance policing,' is top-down and outside-inside innovation.

(4) *Hot-spots*. The National Research Council's recent panel on police research concluded that the hot-spots strategy was one of very few promising strategic crime-control innovations to emerge since 1967 (Skogan and Frydl 2004). Because this strategy is associated with the research of Lawrence Sherman and David Weisburd, one might conclude that it is a clear example of outside-in and top-down innovation. This would be a mistake. Uniformed patrol officers have known for generations that crime and disorder are not evenly distributed in any jurisdiction. Police have shown pin maps to visitors displaying the clumping of crime as long as there have been police stations. Hence, the insights of hot-spots analysis and its attendant crime mapping are not new to police. What is new is the institutionalization of these insights, shared by rank-and-file and scholars alike, into the strategic methodologies of contemporary policing. In effect, outsiders validated internal knowledge and assisted the police to act in accordance with it.

The credit for strategic innovation here must be shared between insiders and outsiders and between rank-and-file and senior commanders.

(5) *Spouse-assault*. This is as clear a case as any of innovation being driven by research carried out by people outside the police. Its findings quickly led to the passage of legislation requiring police to arrest suspects in cases of serious domestic violence. Rank-and-file officers welcomed it, on the one hand, as simplifying their lives, but had doubts, on the other hand, that it accounted sufficiently for differences in situations. In this respect, subsequent research proved them right (Sherman 1992).

(6) *Internal discipline*. The modern period of police reform, commonly accepted as beginning in 1967, was inspired by the research of William Westley into the prevalence of police violence and by Kenneth Culp Davis and Jerome Skolnick into the use of police discretion (Westley 1970; Davis 1969; Skolnick 1966).[1] It was the founding concern of the police research movement, abetted by the dramatic events of the civil rights struggle and the anti-Vietnam war movement. The need for standards for police behavior was dramatized by the findings of the Governor's Commission on the Los Angeles (Watts) Riots (McCone Commission, 1965) and the National Advisory Commission on Civil Disorders (Kerner Commission, 1968). The Supreme

Court created important new legal rules for the police, for example, Miranda v Arizona (1966) concerning interrogations and Garner v Tennessee (1985) concerning the use of deadly force. In short, the police did not become 'constitutional' on their own initiative (Walker 2003). They were forced into it and resented it every step of the way.

The police began their own effort at self-regulation in 1979 through the creation of the Commission on Accreditation for Law Enforcement Agencies, Inc. (CALEA), managed by the International Association of Chiefs of Police (IACP), the National Organization of Black Law Enforcement Executives (NOBLE), the National Sheriffs Association (NSA), and the PERF (Klockars 1983).

Altogether, the improvement in police discipline, which has been substantial in the past 40 years, was driven from the outside and then institutionalized from the top-down, very often over the objections and legal challenges of the police rank-and-file represented by their unions.

(7) *External accountability.* The same is true for this mode of regulating police behavior. The most dramatic initial impetus was probably the demand by African-Americans in northern California, Oakland and Berkeley, for neighborhood control of the police. This was part of campaign for 'power to the people' in the 1960s. On the other coast, allegations of police abuse of force also led to the creation of a Civilian Review Board in New York City in 1966. Although these initial forays into popular control and oversight of the police failed, the underlying message began to get traction (Chevigny 1969; Sklansky 2005), leading not only to police-directed COP but also to police-resisted civilian review of public complaints against the police. As Walker has documented, civilian review in some form now exists in over 100 American cities, over the strenuous and often well-organized objections of the police (2005).

More recently, the federal government has intervened to hold American police departments to account through consent decrees obtained under the US Civil Rights Act (Walker 2005). Although government to government, these decrees, which are often quite detailed, are clearly an example of change foisted on police departments from outside rather than being generated from within.

(8) *COMPSTAT* and *evidence-based policing.* COMPSTAT is a management device for connecting strategic decision making by mid and senior-level commanders to accurate, up-to-date information about the effects of their decisions on public safety. The model was developed first in the New York City Transit Police by Commissioner William Bratton with the help of Jack Maple, 1990–1991 (McDonald 2002). The model was refined when Bratton and Maple returned briefly to Boston. Bratton became Commissioner of the New York City Police Department in 1994 and COMPSTAT developed as an observable management-rite shortly thereafter.

Although Bratton was unusually open to advice from knowledgeable outsiders, notably George Kelling, who had been a seminal figure in the evaluation of police strategies, full credit should be given to Bratton and Maple for creating a management mechanism for providing timely and reasonable accurate information to responsible commanders. Therefore, I score this reform as being insider-driven but determinedly top-down. It wouldn't have happened without the previous two decades of evaluation research, but it also wouldn't have happened without the willingness of these police executives to find a way to introduce information about outcomes into the management system of the police.

(9) *Diversity.* The increase in both women and minorities into American police agencies is entirely due to legal mandates in the form of affirmative action. Quotas and standards for selection and promotion were imposed on the police from outside. They were and still remain controversial within the police and have been the subject of numerous legal challenges by police unions.

Considering the nine reforms together, all but two have been driven from the outside in. The exceptions are COMPSTAT and, to a lesser degree, hot-spots targeting. Without exception, however, none of them were inspired by rank-and-file pressure. All were met with some degree of resistance by the rank-and-file, notwithstanding the fact that rank-and-file police officers often had insights on which some of these reforms were based, such as COP, 'broken windows,' and hot-spots deployments.

The regrettable role of the rank-and-file

Although it may be that the dissatisfaction of rank-and-file police officers with standard operating procedures encourages reform, the fact is that they are very rarely consulted about the kind of changes needed. This is a pity. Police officers at the 'coal face,' as the Australians say, often have important insights into the impediments to more effective policing (Toch et al. 1975; Toch and Grant 1991). In my experience of trying to 'sell' community policing to police personnel, I have often found that although they regard it an imposed obligation—a new 'flavor of the month'—they often spontaneously suggest its core elements when asked to suggest ideas for controlling and preventing crime more successfully, namely, enlisting the support of respectable people in making communities safer through consultation, adaptation to local needs, encouraging community self-protection, and attending to recurring problems of disorder that cause anxiety and inhibit normal life.

Lower-ranking officers have a wealth of unorganized and under-utilizing knowledge about which police activities are not working and why. Some of this knowledge is about social conditions. Police officers have more first-hand knowledge of the pathologies of modern societies than battalions of sociologists. They also have a rich fund of what I call craft knowledge, that is, an understanding of the tactics needed to achieve control, justice, amelioration, and legitimacy in daily encounters with the public (Bayley and Bittner 1984). Sadly, this kind of knowledge is not exploited either in shaping strategies or training other police. Although FTO programs serve as conduits of this kind of knowledge, training in craft skills is haphazard, depending on the quality of patrol partnerships or the unpredictable tutelage of first-line supervisors. Policing does not provide sufficient space for sharing tactical 'best practices,' especially about problematic encounters, even though such encounters may be career threatening and officers welcome opportunities to talk about their accumulated street knowledge. They believe that experience teaches valuable lessons, as in other crafts, and they are willing to learn from their peers.

Rank-and-file police are also shrewd observers of the conduct of one another. They know who is hard working, reliable, trustworthy, and law-abiding (Bayley and Garafolo 1989). Police officers are especially judgmental about colleagues who unfairly exploit the organization by, for example, shirking work, claiming false sick leave, and appropriating supplies for personal use. Informally, the opinions of colleagues powerfully influence the behavior of police officers, both for good and ill. Police organizations have not, however, organized the informal social control to enhance adherence to high standards of behavior. This has been recommended since the early 1970s, notably by Hans Toch. The idea seems now to have been rediscovered and is expanding as programs of early supervision and intervention (Walker et al. 2005).

Unfortunately, however, police officers and sergeants, which is what is generally meant by rank-and-file, are regarded by senior officers as the source of unhelpful complaints rather than of useful insights. A few progressive police leaders have involved them in analysis and planning—Charles Gain in Oakland (1967–1973), Lee Brown in Houston (1982–1990), Darrell Stephens in Newport News (1983–1986), David Couper in Madison, WI (1972–1993). At least one divisional commander in Toronto in the early 1990s appointed small management committees of all ranks to evaluate and improve programs concerning audit, budget, office automation, and community policing. By and large, however, systematic attempts to develop bottom-up contributions to police management and strategic decision making, such as team policing and more recently POP, have been announced with fanfare, struggled, and disappeared.

Various reasons have been cited for the failure to involve lower-ranking police systematically in policing planning, for example, the preoccupation of police organizations with discipline, their traditional quasi-military management practices, and managers unskilled at collaborative problem solving. In my view, these are symptoms of a deeper problem. Despite the talk of policing being a profession, police are a public-service bureaucracy with the ethos of blue-color factory workers. They work in a rule-bound world that discourages initiative and is preoccupied with conditions of service. As I observed several years ago, 'They never lose track of what the organization owes them for their effort in terms of days off, vacation, meal breaks, sick leave, and overtime payments' (1994). Unions compound the problem by focusing entirely on conditions of service, placing management and the rank-and-file in a permanent adversarial relationship.

Police organizations must learn that involving patrol officers and sergeants in diagnosis and planning of both strategic and managerial programs is not incompatible with maintaining necessary discipline in carrying out decisions once made. Indeed, such involvement is an important way to obtain acceptance of new ways of doing business. The irony is, as many observers have noted, that American police officers have enormous amounts of street-level discretion. Increasing their involvement in setting organizational plans would not undercut operational discipline, but would ensure that directives and goals were more closely connected, with both serving the interests of public safety.

The non-regrettable role of outsiders

From the finding that the major police reforms of the past 40 years were instigated largely by outsiders, one might conclude that American policing lacks self-awareness and creativity. To some extent, this is true. The designated agencies of public policing are not willing to evaluate rigorously the success of their core activities and to change accordingly. At the same time, the outsider–insider system of innovation in the

United States is an enormous source of strength and is a tremendous credit to American police.

The United States has been the source of most of the big new ideas in policing in the past half century. Internationally, the innovations described in this paper constitute what other countries regard as the leading edge of innovation in law enforcement, along with a variety of technical innovations. This has happened, I believe, precisely because the United States has developed a unique paradigm for developing policing. It consists of three elements. First, the United States has explicitly harnessed science, in the sense of empirical evaluation, to policing. Second, studies of the police focus on behavior, that is, on police activities in real life, and not on jurisprudence, which is the norm in all but a handful of developed, democratic countries. Third, study of the police, in particular whether it is achieving its goals both of efficacy and fairness, is carried out largely by people not employed by the police, indeed, by people who are independent of government altogether (Skogan and Frydl 2004). In other words, American policing has been unusually creative precisely because it has allowed outsiders access to policing and accommodated their opinions. The essence of the American paradigm is insider–outsider collaboration.

Moreover, this paradigm, which implies criticism of the police establishment, is exactly what far-sighted American police executives wanted. It was created by serving and retired chiefs of police, such as August Vollmer (Berkeley), O.W. Wilson (Chicago), Charles Gain (Oakland), Edward Davis (Los Angeles), Pat Murphy (New York), Lee Brown (Houston), Darrell Stephens (Newport News), and Bill Bratton (New York). Supported by private foundations such as the American Bar Foundation and the Ford Foundation, they developed the outsider–insider paradigm and made it acceptable to American police (Walker 1977). In so doing they created a culture within policing that is almost unique in the world—a culture that is open to outside evaluation and accepts outsiders as collaborators in the design of policing.

In an interesting twist to the story, the outsiders are now trying to implant evaluation within police organizations, making them less dependent, one might think, on outside instigated reform. This is being done under the rubric of turning police agencies into 'learning organizations' capable of determining for themselves what works.

The American reform paradigm constitutes a new and generally unrecognized mode of public accountability. It has allowed America's intellectual elite to monitor policing by becoming 'embedded' in police departments. This is remarkable when you consider that the norm in the rest of the world is for professional intellectuals to be hostile to the police.

In short, the reforms of the past 40 years have been developed from the outside-inside, and that is precisely the way police leaders wanted it to be. Particular reforms have developed outside police agencies, but the system of reform was developed at the invitation of the police. In the United States, outsiders have become part of the police establishment. Viewed this way, the outsider–insider distinction is becoming less meaningful.

Note

1. Westley first published the work cited here as a PhD dissertation in 1951, 'The Police: A Sociological Study of Law, Custom and Morality.' University of Chicago. A short

version of his findings also appeared as 'Violence and the Police,' 1953, *American Journal of Sociology* LIX (July): 34–41.

References

Bayley, D.H., 1994. *Police for the Future*. New York, NY: Oxford University Press.

Bayley, D.H. and Bittner, E., 1984. "Learning the skills of policing". *Law and Contemporary Problems*, Fall, 53, 35–59.

Bayley, D.H. and Garafolo, J., 1989. "The management of violence by patrol officers". *Criminology*, 27 (1), 2–24.

Bieck, W. and Kessler, D.A., 1977. *Response Time Analysis*. Kansas City, MO: Board of Police Commissioners.

Chevigny, P., 1969. *Police Power: Police Abuses in New York City*. New York, NY: Random House.

Davis, K.C., 1969. *Discretionary Justice: A Preliminary Inquiry*. Baton Rouge, LA: Louisiana State University Press.

Eck, J.E., 1982. *Solving Crimes: The Investigation of Burglary and Robbery*. Washington, DC: Police Executive Research Forum.

Fielding, N. and Innes, M., 2006. "Reassurance policing, community policing and measuring police performance". *Policing and Society*, 16 (2), 127–145.

Goldsmith, A. & Lewis, C., eds., 2000. *Civilian Oversight of Policing: Governance, Democracy, and Human Rights*. Oxford, UK: Hart Publishing.

Goldstein, H., 1979. "Improving policing: A problem-oriented approach". *Crime and Delinquency*, 33, 6–30.

Goldstein, H., 1990. *Problem-oriented Policing*. Philadelphia, PA: Temple University Press.

Greenwood, P.W., Petersilia, J., and Chaiken, J., 1977. *The Criminal Investigation Process*. Lexington, MA: D.C. Heath.

Herrington, V. and Millie, A., 2006. "Applying reassurance policing: Is it 'business as usual'?". *Policing and Society*, 16 (2), 146–163.

Kelling, G.L. and Moore, M.H., 1988. *The Evolving Strategy of Policing*. Washington, DC: National Institute of Justice.

Kelling, G.L., *et al.*, 1974. *The Kansas City Preventive Patrol Experiment: A Summary Report*. Washington, DC: Police Foundation.

Klockars, C., 1983. *Thinking About Police*. New York, NY: McGraw-Hill.

Koenig, D.J., 1991. *Do Police Cause Crime? Police Activity, Police Strength and Crime Rates*. Ottawa: Canadian Police College.

Krahn, H. and Kennedy, L., 1985. "Producing personal safety: The effects of crime rates, police force size, and fear of crime". *Criminology*, 23, 697–710.

Loftin, C. and McDowall, D., 1982. "The police, crime, and economic theory: An assessment". *American Sociological Review*, 47, 393–401.

McDonald, P.P., 2002. *Managing Police Operations: Implementing the New York Crime Control Model—CompStat*. Belmont, CA: Wadsworth/Thompson Learning.

Morris, P. and Heal, K., 1981. *Crime Control and the Police: A Review of Research*. London: Home Office Research Study 67.

President's Commission on Law Enforcement and the Administration of Justice. 1967. *The Challenge of Crime in a Free Society*. Washington, DC: Government Printing Office.

Royal Commission on Criminal Procedure. (1981). Research Study 17, HMSO, London.

Sherman, L.W., 1992. *Policing Domestic Violence: Experiments and Dilemmas*. New York, NY: Free Press.

Sherman, L.W. and Berk, R.A., 1984. "The specific deterrent effects of arrest for domestic assault". *American Sociological Review*, 49, 261–272.

Sherman, L.W., Gartin, P.R., and Buerger, M.E., 1989. "Hot spots and predatory crime: Routine activities and the criminology of place". *Criminology*, 27, 27–55.

Sklansky, D.A., 2005. "Police and democracy". *Michigan Law Review*, 103 (7), 1699–1830.

Skogan, W.G. & Frydl, K., eds., 2004. *Fairness and Effectiveness in Policing: The Evidence*. Washington, DC: National Academies Press.

Skolnick, J.H., 1966. *Justice Without Trial: Law Enforcement in Democratic Society*. New York, NY: John Wiley and Sons.

Skolnick, J.H. and Bayley, D.H., 1986. *The New Blue Line*. New York, NY: Free Press.

Skolnick, J.H. and Bayley, D.H., 1988. *Community Policing: Issues and Practices Around the World*. Washington, DC: National Institute of Justice.

Spelman, W. and Brown, D.K., 1981. *Calling the Police: Citizen Reporting of Serious Crimes*. Washington, DC: Police Executive Research Forum.

Tien, J.M., Simon, J.W., and Larson, R.C., 1978. *An Alternative Approach in Police Patrol: The Wilmington Split-Force Experiment*. Washington, DC: Government Printing Office.

Toch, H. and Grant, J.D., 1991. *Police as Problem Solvers*. New York, NY: Plenum Corporation.

Toch, H., Grant, J.D., and Galvin, R.T., 1975. *Agents of Change: A Study in Police Reform*. New York, NY: John Wiley and Sons.

Trojanowics, R. and Bucqueroux, B., 1990. *Community Policing: A Contemporary Perspective*. Cincinnati, OH: Anderson.

Walker, S., 1977. *A Critical History of Police Reform: The Emergence of Professionalism*. Lexington, MA: Lexington Books.

Walker, S., 1989. *Sense and Nonsense About Crime*. 2nd edn. Pacific Grove, CA: Brooks/Cole Publishing Co.

Walker, S., 2003. "The new paradigm of police accountability: The U.S. Justice Department 'pattern or practice' suits in context". *Saint Louis University Public Law Review*, xxii (1), 3–52.

Walker, S., 2005. *The New World of Police Accountability*. Thousand Oaks, CA: Sage Publications.

Walker, S., Archbold, C., and Herbst, L., 2002. *Mediating Citizen Complaints Against Police Officers: A Guide for Police and Community Leaders*. Washington, DC: U.S. Department of Justice, Office of Community Oriented Policing Services.

Walker, S., Milligan, S.O., and Berke, A., 2005. *Supervision and Intervention Within Early Intervention Systems: A Guide for Law Enforcement Chief Executives*. Washington, DC: Police Executive Research Forum and the Office of Community Oriented Policing Services.

Westley, W.A., 1970. *Violence and the Police: A Sociological Study of Law, Custom, and Morality*. Cambridge, MA: MIT Press.

Wilson, J.Q. & Kelling, G.L., 1982. "Broken windows: The police and neighborhood safety". *Atlantic Monthly*, March, 29–38.

Police officers as change agents in police reform

Hans Toch

School of Criminal Justice, University at Albany, State University of New York, NY, USA

The organization of police departments along hierarchical, classic management lines makes it difficult for departmental leadership to tackle commonly-experienced internal problems, so as to improve performance and enhance morale. The main reason for this fact is that top-down reform invites resistances from rank-and-file officers who feel that their views have been disregarded. By contrast, interventions can gain considerable credibility if officers are enlisted as change agents, encouraging them to get involved in the design and implementation of change. This approach not only reduces opposition to innovation but results in congruent change by harnessing the experience of officers who are targets of reform. As a case in point, we review a pioneering effort to reduce the use of excessive force in a metropolitan police department which was successfully implemented by a group of patrol officers, prominently including problem officers.

The pragmatic virtues of organizational democracy

The most common arguments for organizational democracy do not generally lie in the abstract realm of rarified idealism but have to do with the bread-and-butter premise that participatory involvement may be the best way of getting an organization's job done. This particularly a view held in the US, where pragmatic considerations tend to be heavily valued.

Thirteen years ago, I tried to summarize the perspective for a group of prison administrators in Scotland. I told the Scottish wardens that

> [As we have defined it,] the goal has fit most neatly under a heading such as human resource management. The premise of this approach is that people work more effectively when they are involved in making decisions that govern their work, and that organizations are more effective when they deploy the intelligence, wisdom and judgment of all their members—particularly those in the front line of the organization. A second premise is that involvement brings a sense of ownership, and buys loyalty, dedication and commitment ... [A] recent version of this argument sees organizational democracy as the only means to achieve quality of products or services. (Toch 1994: 65)

In retrospect, it might have been silly of me to discuss the issue of democratization in relation to prison governance. And it might be just as silly for me to make a case for participatory involvement in policing if we did not have a wealth of documented experience showing that rank-and-file initiatives in community policing have generated a great deal of exemplary quality service.

The subject for this paper is probably a bit more esoteric. I shall be arguing that police departments could be well advised to encourage participatory involvement as *a vehicle for organizational reform*. My argument is based on the premise that some features of the average police organization are, or have become, dysfunctional. Attributes of police organizations that come particularly to mind in support of this contention are the following:

1. The paramilitary arrangement of police work is in practice mostly a fiction, which can occasionally be mobilized and sprung on officers, creating resentments.
2. The monitoring of officer behavior and the disciplinary responses to infractions, reliably provoke displeasure about perceived inequities.
3. Where police administrators formulate policy decisions without advance consultation, this frequently invites resistance to implementation.
4. Police work has often been described as stressful, but police officers universally nominate administrators as their principal source of stress.
5. Police managers tend to be promoted from the ranks, but a cultural divide separates the administration of police departments from the rank and file.
6. The responsiveness of police leaders to external constituencies can be interpreted as insensitivity to the concerns of their subordinates.
7. A code of conduct can evolve in the locker room that appears to tolerate transgressions and discourages 'snitching' on peers.
8. Other agencies in the criminal justice system can come to be regarded as sources of obstruction rather than partners.
9. Quality police work (other than arrests) is imperfectly recorded and in practice is rarely rewarded.

Most importantly, from my perspective about the process of reform,

10. The specification of problems to which police officers are asked to respond, and the analyses on which these specifications are based, are generally not tasks that are shared within the organization, despite the advertised emphasis in police departments on educational attainment in the recruitment of officers.

Some of the above-cited observations are in practice interrelated, because any grievances of police officers can generalize beyond their origin, or transfer from one source of resentment to another. And once an officer becomes completely alienated he is unlikely to encounter a great deal that pleases him at work, and the task of rekindling his allegiance and enthusiasm can become formidable (Toch 2002).

What does it mean to be a 'paramilitary' organization?

Police officers across the world are issued uniforms, which define their function and advertise their authority, and serve to distinguish the officers from mere mortals or 'civilians.' The uniform serves as a symbol of demarcation, differentiating the ingroup from the outgroup, the empowered from the disempowered, and the service deliverers from the clients or targets of their services. The blue of the uniform (wherever the uniform is blue) is the 'color of law' under which the officers act.

The uniform is finally a deterrent message, an invitation for the more cautious or guilt-ridden citizens to be wary, and a prescription for respectful social distance.

The uniform also concretizes the definition of police organizations as 'para-military,' with whatever the word implies by way of connotations and baggage. The prefix *para* tells us that professions to which it is appended are substitutes for or auxiliary to other professions. Although a military-handmaiden role is not usually assigned to police departments (as is, say, the paralegal role in law) the police are somehow expected to emulate the military. 'Para' means 'closely related to.' If we have two sets of organizations, this obligates one to share key attributes of the other.

However, which 'military' attributes would one expect to be adopted by police departments? Putting aside a literal warfare analogue (as favored by Theodore Roosevelt as police commissioner), features that readily come to mind are standard hyper-bureaucratic military organizational attributes—those of formal rank, formal hierarchy, and a chain of unquestioned and unquestioning command. Such is the shape of police organizations enshrined in tables of organization and motivational sermons. These features are, however, hard to reconcile with militant unions and civil service rules. In practice, moreover, these austere attributes become attenuated. They do not, for instance, accommodate prevalent live-and-let-live collusions between front-line supervisors and their subordinates. They do not accommodate many of the standard carefree arrangements of policing. They do not provide for individuals who work mostly on their own between radio calls, or groups that operate in the field on a virtual freelance basis, disengaged from any chain of command.

An insightful, experienced officer who entered the force after service in the military has observed in this connection that

> Even as a rookie patrolman, I was very aware that my sergeant did not run my police squad. How could he possibly? He was responsible for up to a dozen officers scattered over roughly one-fifth of fifty-plus square miles of densely populated, urban area where heavy traffic induced time separation to exacerbate the separation by space. With the sergeant's time and space disconnection from us, the day-to-day direction of my squad, from both a social and working perspective, was in the hands of the peer group, influenced rather loosely but ever so powerfully by the most dominant peer leaders—some "good," and others, "not so good." (Murphy 2006)

Given the uninhibited routines of policing, tensions are bound to arise where the chain-of-command model is disinterred or reinstituted. Where attempts are made to reassert abrogated leadership or to monitor autonomous activities, such efforts can be resented. Resentment can, for instance, be acute at organizational crisis points, where decisions have proved controversial or judgments problematic. Such junctures can raise concerns such as 'which side are they [the politicians who run this organization] on?' Among disaffected officers, the command structure may be suspected of serving some foreign interest, at the expense of the rank and file. Where productivity concerns have become an issue, for instance, officers may envisage themselves at the end of a stressful transmission belt in a numerical pressure game (never to be alluded to as one of 'quotas'), in which a public-relations-oriented demand for penny-ante arrests is passed on from one layer of the hierarchy to the next.

There are obviously junctures in any officer's life that require his or her participation in quasi-military rituals, such as roll calls and performance reviews. Most such junctures are bureaucratic routines that are regarded with good-humored equanimity. However, some demands can come to be seen as gratuitous hurdles (or proliferating red tape), and may come across as petty and demeaning. At extremes, there are organizational routines that send emasculating messages about the range and scope of the officers' role or responsibilities. One such juncture is that of 'stress training' in recruit academies. The timing of infantilizing treatment at entry into the system is arguably unfortunate, but so is the pairing of boot camp routines with academic components in training. It is hard to see how an organization can inculcate its officers with a readiness to exercise wise and informed discretion when the officers are being barked at, marched about, and treated like recalcitrant children.

Playing cops-and-robbers with cops

Because police officers in practice engage in considerable discretionary behavior, their supervisors have had to grapple with the question, 'Can we really trust those bums to be honest and law-abiding, dispassionate and evenhanded, punctilious and dedicated?' The response to this question has often been cautious and guarded, and laced with translucent suspicions. This dilemma is as old as the police profession, and its resolution has often been messy, undignified, and discordant. Actions inspired by mistrust tend to breed resentment, which fuels obduracy and resistance. Resistance reinforces suspicion, which incites intrusive monitoring moves, which breed resentment. And so the cycle continues, and can spin out of control.

During the era of 'police reform' at the turn of the last century, police leaders were obsessed with the question of whether officers were assiduously attending to their obligations while they were out of sight. Early technology provided the supervisors with some capability for periodically communicating with their officers in the field. The officers were correspondingly challenged to work around or to circumvent these intrusions into their familiar routines. A 'cat-and-mouse' game between supervisors and their subordinates ensued (Walker 1977: 13). The details of this contest have undergone transformation over time, keeping pace with progress in information technology. However, mutual suspicion and mistrust have contributed to the development of divergent officer and supervisor cultures, which have been eloquently described by some students of policing (e.g., Reuss-Ianni 1983).

The infamous cup of coffee

Inspired by allegations of political corruption, early police leaders subordinated their concern with indolence to an obsession with dishonesty. Their anxiety about deviations from 'integrity' by officers has retained its salience over time. The attention has focused throughout the period on a wide spectrum of misbehaviors ranging from accepting discounts for lunches (or stray cups of coffee), to participation in robberies or thefts. Police policy manuals covering the subject frequently discuss it in totalistic fashion, and include wholesale injunctions warning officers that they may be embarking on a slippery slope, in which accepting a cup of coffee can be the seductive prelude to serious transgressions. Where police departments buy into this 'Broken Windows' view of corruption, some of the edicts they issue (such as 'thou shalt never accept discounts at lunch counters') are bound to inspire limited credibility in the locker room, which can compromise the entire campaign.

Officers not only are able to discriminate between inconsequential minutiae and serious unprofessional behavior, but they also can be put off when the difference is obfuscated by generic proscriptions and promiscuous interventions. Officers can be further put off when interventions cast their nets too widely, resort to stings, entrapment, or other uses of deception, and treat targeted officers (as the cop saying goes) 'like criminals.' Such actions can mobilize solidarity in the locker room and generate support for peers who are subjects of corruption-related allegations.

Most officers do not condone egregious lapses of integrity, nor will most officers object to the sanctioning of colleagues who have seriously transgressed. Klockars et al. (2000) conducted a comprehensive study in which they used a wide range of vignettes of officer misconduct, and they report that

> The more serious the officers considered a behavior to be, the more likely they were to believe that more severe discipline was appropriate, and the more willing they were to report a colleague for engaging in that behavior. (p. 1)

In relation to less substantial transgressions covered in the vignettes, officers sometimes felt that the penalties they anticipated were overly harsh, and most of the officers indicated that they 'would not report a police colleague who had engaged in behavior described in the four scenarios considered the least serious' (p. 6). This pinpointed reluctance-to-inform is far from an all-encompassing 'Code of Silence,' and it is not a stance designed to protect crooked cops. If there are misapprehensions about the scope of locker-room resistances, police managers may resort to needlessly intrusive interventions that serve to antagonize potential informants. The result may be to exacerbate conflicting feelings such as those reported in another study (Weisburd et al. 2000), which found that

> Some of the strongest and most varied opinions expressed by respondents concerned the difficult question of whether officers should report other officers' misconduct. Responses on this subject suggest the possibility of a large gap between attitudes and behavior. That is, even though officers do not believe in protecting wrongdoers, they often do not turn them in. (p. 3)

The alternative officers have to the unthinkable option of finking can be silent disapproval. However, if direct questions are subsequently raised (such as in the course of internal investigations), they may feel free to reveal the truth. The much-maligned Code of Silence calls for loyalty to the group, but it does not prescribe perjury to protect brutal or dishonest men who commit egregious offenses.

Does decentralization increase the prevalence of misconduct?

An interesting issue touched upon in the study cited above was the question of whether decentralization enhances the risk of rank-and-file misconduct. In other words, when the cat is back at headquarters, would the mice act irresponsibly? The authors of the study (Weisburd et al. 2000) report that the officers they surveyed felt 'that a close relationship with the community, such as that resulting from community-oriented policing did not increase the risk of police corruption' (p. 7), and the authors go on to indicate that many of the officers 'said that community policing reduced the number of incidents involving excessive force, and ... [many] thought that it decreased the seriousness of incidents' (p. 8).

These beliefs counter an assumption that is sometimes made by critics of police reform, which is that the decentralization of police organizations and the expansion of neighborhood autonomy create a breeding ground for unlawful conduct and unlicensed behavior. It may even be tempting for some police executives to buy into this cautionary view of opponents because it raises questions about a strategy they may suspect is a passing fad and because it reinforces a command-and-control conception of management.

The concern about dangers of democratization, however, goes beyond worrying about what brutal or corrupt officers may do when they are afforded expanded discretion. This concern also reflects a lack of trust in local citizens and their capacity to pursue the common good. The dangers envisaged are those of collusions in which (1) citizens are snowed or buffaloed by irresponsible officers; or (2) officers are snookered by citizens into supporting illegitimate or parochial concerns. Occasionally, stories appear in the press suggesting that scenarios such as these may have unfolded. Officers may be described eagerly sundowning marginal miscreants, earning encomia from residents and complaints from the ACLU. Such resolutions of sectarian demand and legalistic restraint, of course, are not limited to local neighborhoods in decentralized police departments. These are precisely the sort of dilemmas experienced on a daily basis by police executives, who have to respond to a variety of constituencies, and deal with the consequences of their responses. One of the unappreciated side benefits of decentralization in policing may be that it provides community-oriented officers with a scaled-down managerial role—allowing them to negotiate the force field within which their organization must operate. The question is, should officers as managers be expected to be less honest and evenhanded than executives who face comparable situations?

Decentralized and centralized data-driven policing

Police departments frequently take pride in the capacity they have evolved to consider updated information about problems in their communities in planning their activities on a day-by-day basis. This capacity is not unrelated to a decentralized perspective because the problems to which any police department must respond vary from one part of town to the next. Disaggregated statistics therefore have to be collected, and familiarity with local conditions becomes an asset in interpreting the data and planning appropriate action.

This advantage of decentralized planning was highlighted in a 2002 Annual Report of the Seattle Police Department, which focused on a restructuring move that was described as follows by Seattle Chief Gil Kerlikowske:

> The most important shift has been to decentralize command and control at the headquarters level and place additional responsibility and decision-making at the precinct level. There are five distinct geographical precincts within the city, each commanded and led by a veteran police captain. These captains know the special character of their precincts and the people they command better than anyone else in the organization. By providing them limited additional resources but far greater control

over their piece of the city, we have increased accountability and the speed at which operational decisions are made. (Seattle Police Department 2002: 2)

The Seattle Report noted that as a result of the decentralization, the precinct commanders had been accorded 'a significant increase in responsibility to become acting 'chiefs of police' for their respective areas' (p. 24). One of those involved in the move was Captain Fred Hill, who commanded Seattle's East Precinct. In describing the East Precinct, Captain Hill wrote, 'we have old money, new money, little money, ultra-left wing politics, ultra-right wing politics, people living in high rises and people living in houseboats ... and everything in between' (p. 32). Among specific attributes, according to the Report,

> The East Precinct is predominantly residential. As the smallest precinct geographically, it has far less space than the others, and consequently it has much high-density urban housing. ... The East Precinct also serves the largest number of Seattle schools in the smallest physical area ... Captain Hill sees the large and diverse student community as a primary constituency of the Precinct. The Precinct provides School Resource Officers to work actively with the schools. ... This is an example of neighborhood-based policing at the individual school level, where officers get to know the students and the issues at a school so well that often they can avert problems before they start. ... One of Capt. Hill's goals for the future is to provide more officers to work directly with schools (p. 32).

Local data can be supplied to precinct commanders such as Captain Hill to help them to further delineate the problems in their precincts. Precinct commanders can share such data with their subordinates, including rank-and-file officers. Data-driven policing, however, started out being conceived of as a centralized process, directed from a digital war room in which large maps displayed the latest crime statistics in living color for the edification (or alarm) of top management and technically savvy staff members. By way of response to any given set of data, the managers in charge of the areas in which mapped incidents appeared aggregated would be summoned for review sessions. The outcome of such sessions tended to be a resolve to intensify targeted enforcement activities. This resolve would be subsequently communicated to rank-and-file officers, who were instructed to do the targeted enforcing.

The paradigm in its top-down form (called Compstat, after a computer program) was credited with contributing to hefty crime reductions in New York City. The model consequently became popular, and many departments claimed to have emulated the idea or replicated it. Because slippages occur between resolves and implementation steps, it is hard to say how many Compstat-equivalents were actually instituted. And it is even harder to know how much the average Compstat offspring resembled the UrCompstat model, or differed from it.

Reforming compstat

It would be nice to assume that transmutations had in fact occurred, because the original Compstat regime deviated from most organization-management prescriptions. The process did not encourage participation, teamwork, feedback, or creative thinking, and—especially at its inception—relied on threats or intimidation to motivate compliance (Swope 1999). Fortunately, the proliferation of Compstats provided an opportunity to experiment with refinements, and especially modifications of the process that could improve the way human resources were deployed. Ideally, one could eventually envisage a Compstat model that would harness the thinking of the entire police chain of command, very much including that of rank-and-file officers now enlisted in the process without serious consultation. Such reform at the front lines would make data-driven enforcement (or other) activities more mindful and meaningful.

This possibility was recognized in some localities years before Compstat was invented. Ron Oznowicz, a veteran officer running for mayor of Oakland, thus recalled that

> Many years ago we had personnel assigned, civilian and police, to place colored pins in huge maps to indicate how crime patterns were emerging. The cop was there to make "sense" of it. They could see where the car thieves were located by the dumping grounds of the stolen cars. They could see that most burglaries were committed within four blocks of certain thieves. They could see robberies with similar patterns. Any beat cop could visit Crime Analysis and see what was happening. (Oznowicz 2006).

The reform process of Compstat could be participatory in nature. Through the use of task forces, Compstat could be redesigned by those who knew it best, and who had to live with its less-than-felicitous edicts and problem definitions. These problematic junctures will inevitably be experienced in any top-down sequence, such as Compstat. This is the case because consequences of decisions can rarely be anticipated in 'war rooms,' and because statistical compilations provide imperfect guides for action in the field. In real wars, the extrapolations of command staff are frequently (and belatedly) refuted by experiences in the trenches, where men can be ordered to assault impregnable fortifications. The front-line experiences of the survivors of such charges can obviously provide useful feedback, if attended to.

Interpolating street wisdom

Any top-down process can benefit from feedback loops that serve to ensure that expectations conform to reality—especially at the key juncture where the organization's rubber hits the road. The ultimate source of feedback can thus be that of personnel involved with the targets or consumers of services. It is patrol officers who encounter the wide range of full-blooded incidents, and the protagonists who are involved in the incidents represented in war room maps. In the course of doing their work, the officers become the repositories of considerable first-hand information. Officers can and do draw their own personal inferences from this reservoir of information. This street wisdom is admittedly different in kind from the ruminations inspired by the data recorded in war room maps. Street knowledge is stubbornly particularistic. It centers heavily on specific problem locations and individual events. It invites disdain because it sounds anecdotal, and appears oblivious to questions about the reliability of potentially unrepresentative experiences.

The limitations of street wisdom, however, can be readily compensated for. If officers are to be invited to relay their views, they could first be offered the opportunity to compare notes with each other, to pool their experiences or review records relating to their experiences, and pose questions about the patterning of the incident attributes they had observed. If one did this carefully and systematically, the analysis would approximate that prescribed by problem-oriented policing (Goldstein 1990). This approach envisaged a reconfiguration of police goals and objectives, a concern with the communalities among incidents that help us to understand and address their causes. By focusing on patterns of incidents, the approach compensates for the unreliability (and sterility) of offense-incident-based thinking or planning. At the other end of the spectrum, problem-oriented thinking offers an intervening level of analysis for managers planning strategies in war rooms, adding flesh and concreteness to statistically based ruminations, helping to bridge from the sand box to the trenches.

Implementing participatory reform

A variety of means can be used to promote the study of problems and initiate proposals for change. Such vehicles can range from task forces that are assigned specific topics to examine, to groups that have broader mandates, and more freedom to study and explore. To consider comprehensive reforms, 'parallel organizations' can be created that are both bureaucratically informal and relatively autonomous (French and Bell 1999).

As a vehicle of empowerment, 'units' can be fielded which exercise specialized skills or pursue special interests in areas relevant to the organization's mission. The Seattle Department's 2005 Report lists a number of enterprises that fit this general description. The Department had thus instituted a Force Options Research Group, described as 'an internal study group that evaluates and makes recommendations on less lethal options for use by Departmental officers' (Seattle Police Department 2005: 18). In the field of domestic violence, 'the Department has developed specialized expertise in the areas of stalking, elder abuse, custodial interference, and abuse in the homeless and sexual minority communities' (p. 22). Some of the units involve teaming of officers with members of the community. A Victim Support Team (VST) program thus 'works directly with citizen volunteers ... [who] provide crisis intervention, and emergency resources referrals to domestic violence victims' (ibid.).

The most direct way of facilitating rank-and-file input is by being hospitable to proposals for change from front-line personnel, and being willing to implement their proposals. Seattle's 2005 Report provides a case in point of some historical interest:

> In 1987, former Seattle Police Officer Paul Grady was sitting in his patrol car, stuck on traffic, in the congested downtown city core. As he watched bicycle messengers weave back and forth through traffic to get to their destination, he had an idea that would revolutionize modern policing. With permission from his commander, he and his partner, Officer Mike Miller, began to patrol downtown Seattle on their own personal mountain bikes. While it took a while for the public to get used to seeing officers on bicycles, the quick but quiet bikes soon proved themselves invaluable in catching criminals in the act of open-air drug buys and other street crimes. ... One idea almost 20 years ago has now spearheaded the widespread use of bicycle patrols nationwide. (p. 8)

A problem-oriented approach to officer misconduct

As I have noted, an obdurate dilemma that has been challenging the ingenuity of police leaders is how to go about preventing, controlling, and discouraging incidents of police misconduct—including uses of excessive force. The quandary arises from the fact that much vociferous grousing by officers relates to the way police organizations try to prevent, control, or discourage incidents of misconduct—including uses of excessive force. This is an obdurate dilemma that has been challenging the ingenuity of many police administrators. Monitoring and disciplinary sanctions that are intended to be proportionate, legitimate, and fair often seem to appear to come across as unfair, discriminatory, disrespectful, tinged with favoritism, and politically tainted. Resentments experienced by officers and frustrations experienced by administrators can create insurmountable communication problems.

An intervention called the Peer Review Panel, instituted in the Oakland (California) Police Department 35 years ago, was designed to remedy this situation. The concept had been formulated by a member of a group of seven patrol officers, and presented to his colleagues for discussion. This action had been preceded by weeks of research by members of the group. It was followed by extensive deliberations and additional research, and culminated in a formal proposal submitted to the Chief of Police for implementation. After a period of operation, the Panel operation was also evaluated by the officers, with help from resident consultants.

The group was part of a project that included four groups of officers that met for two days a week for several months. All meetings ended with recorded summaries. On the day the Panel concept was introduced, the officer who invented the Panel described the inception of his idea as follows:

> And I started making little notes about maybe coming up with trying to work up some sort of system where we can have line patrolmen or the peer group meet in some sort of order review or some sort of review unit where you can analyze the problems that the specific officer might be having on the street when it becomes apparent: Recommendations from superior officers, numerous trips up to Internal Affairs, just numerous violent incidents on the street. This would not be a disciplinary unit or anything like this and it wouldn't really come up with any particular finding pro or con about the officer's action. (Toch and Grant 2005: 166–167)

In a subsequent session, after his group's midnight lunch (the project convened mostly at night) the officer reemphasized what he saw as the goal of his intervention. He said,

> And what you're going to try to do then is review the behavioral patterns of the person and analyze what he is doing and somehow make him, in this process, come up with some self-critique, like we do here. You know, after he reads the report somebody asks the questions, ... And [the Panel subject] would have to stop and think, "Do I do that very often?". (p. 170)

This statement alludes to continuity between the activities of the group of officers ('like we do here') and those being envisaged for the Panel ('review behavioral patterns' and 'self-critiques'). These pairings were not coincidental, because the Oakland study was premised on the assumption that personal development and organization development could be linked. The participants in the project had been tasked with studying problems of violence between officers and civilians, but most of the participants had been selected (by fellow participants using statistics) because they had been repeatedly enmeshed in conflicts with citizens. For the officers, the subject of inquiry carried personal significance. Having been part of a problem, the officers were concerned with understanding the nature of the problem and contributing to its solution.

The Oakland legacy

The Action Review Panel may have been a significant reform, but the groups of officers made other contributions to the operation of their department. As was pointed out by Oakland's Chief of Police,

> Possibly more important than the project's impact on police-citizen contacts is the fact that this program has resulted in a series of significant organizational changes which touched such diverse activities as communications, patrol and training. It conditioned departmental procedures for dealing with family and landlord-tenant disputes, and it may eventually bring about a significant change in performance evaluation techniques. (Gain 1975: iv)

I was a direct participant in the Oakland project, though I am not a police officer. The project was entirely officer-based and officer-run. However, the operation did require a measure of coordination, and external support. An NIMH-sponsored group of civilians provided the coordination and support.

The key ingredient of the project was an enlightened Chief of Police, Charles Gain, who empowered the officers, encouraged them in their work, buttressed their efforts and implemented their suggestions for reform. The function of resident academics was to facilitate the research involvements of the officers, and provide them with technical assistance, as needed. We also chaired the initial group of officers, before leadership devolved to the group. Such assignments of functions did not produce hard-and-fast delineations of roles. We became honorary members of the groups, inter-disciplinary relationships developed, and some friendships that have endured the test of time.

It would be nice if I were able to claim that the manifold changes instituted through the Oakland project had survived as handily as have our personal relationships. For the most part, however, they have not. This fact is in retrospect not particularly surprising, because the Oakland department has gone the way of many settings that were once headed by leaders far ahead of their times. In such settings, the successors of the innovative leaders frequently do not share their readiness for risk taking and reform. It has also appeared to me that in some instances wheels have to be reinvented from time to time because organizations have limited staying power. And if such is the case with police reform, it would be delightful if a juncture for the reinvention of participatory strategies were impending.

References

French, W.L. and Bell, C.H., 1999. *Organization Development: Behavioral Science Interventions for Organization Improvement*. Upper Saddle River, NJ: Prentice-Hall.

Gain, C.R., 1975. Foreword. *In*: H. Toch, J.D. Grant and R. Galvin, eds. *Agents of Change: A Study in Police Reform*. Cambridge, MA: Schenkman.

Goldstein, H., 1990. *Problem-oriented Policing*. New York: McGraw Hill.

Klockars, C.B., Ivkovich, S.K., Harver, W.E. & Haberfeld, M.R., 2000. The measurement of police integrity, *National Institute of Justice Research in Brief*. US Department of Justice, Washington, DC, May.

Murphy, L., 2006. Personal Communication, 21 June.

Oznowicz, R., 2006. Where is crime analysis? *Ron Oz Latest Issues.* Available at: www.ronoz.com

Reuss-Ianni, E., 1983. *Two Cultures of Policing: Street Cops and Management Cops.* New Brunswick, NJ: Transaction.

Seattle Police Department. 2002. *Annual Report.* Seattle, WA: Seattle Police Department.

Seattle Police Department. 2005. *Annual Report.* Seattle, WA: Seattle Police Department.

Swope, C., 1999. "The Compstat craze", *Governing*, September, pp. 40–43.

Toch, H., 1994. "Democratizing prisons". *The Prison Journal*, 73, 62–72.

Toch, H., 2002. *Stress in Policing.* Washington, DC: American Psychological Association.

Toch, H. and Grant, J.D., 2005. *Police as Problem Solvers: How Frontline Workers Can Promote Organizational and Community Change.* 2nd edn. Washington, DC: American Psychological Association.

Walker, S.A., 1977. *A Critical History of Police Reform: The Emergence of Professionalism.* Lexington, MA: Lexington.

Weisburd, D., Greenspan, R., Hamilton, E.E., Williams, H. & Bryant, K.A., 2000. Police attitudes toward abuse of authority: Findings from a national study, *National Institute of Justice Research in Brief.* Washington, DC: US Department of Justice.

From the bottom-up: sharing leadership in a police agency

Brigitte Steinheider[a] and Todd Wuestewald[b]

[a]Department of Psychology, University of Oklahoma–Tulsa, Tulsa, OK, USA; [b]Broken Arrow Police Department, OK, USA

Police work has become intensely community and crime-prevention oriented, demanding high commitment and discretionary activity from police officers. Collaborative leadership practices that involve employees in workplace decision-making have been shown to increase commitment, but have not been widely adopted within law enforcement organizations. This case study examines the effects of a shared leadership initiative in a suburban police department. Twenty-four months after implementation of an employee steering committee (called the Leadership Team) quantitative and qualitative data indicate significant improvement in employees' perceptions of work conditions, labor–management relations, commitment, and community-oriented policing, as well as increases in discretionary police productivity.

Contemporary policing has moved from reactive to proactive strategies, such as community-oriented policing (COP) and intelligence-led policing. The focus has shifted from leadership at the top to leadership at the bottom, where the discretionary activities of front line officers can make a real difference in terms of community engagement, prevention, and interdiction. However, modern police organizations remain largely centralized in their decision-making, structurally vertical, rule bound, and mired in power relationships (e.g., Mastrofski, 1998; Sklansky, 2007). These limitations are seen as impediments to the development of adaptive, learning organizations capable of leveraging their human assets and appropriately responding to the dynamics of modern social expectations (Alarid, 1999).

Research suggests that inclusive decision-making practices can foster greater rank-and-file commitment to organizational initiatives, particularly with regard to community-oriented policing (e.g., Fridell, 2004; Skogan & Harnett, 1997; Taylor, Fritsch, & Caeti, 1998). Traditional hierarchical police management is often cited as a major hindrance to line officer empowerment, which community policing and problem-oriented policing (POP) seem to require (Goldstein, 1990; Kelling & Coles, 1996; Skogan, 2004). In addition, the top-down nature of most community-oriented crime control initiatives have tended to generate resistance from both line officers and first line supervisors.

This issue is further complicated by the inherent discretionary nature of police work. The basic paradox of police hierarchy is that autonomy tends to be greatest at the lowest levels of the law enforcement organization where police officers make fundamental decisions on the street, far removed from their supervisors (Wilson, 2000). They deal with ambiguous situations that often fall into the gray; their decisions frequently influenced by a variety of extra-legal considerations (e.g., Bittner, 1967; Kelling, 1999; Wilson, 1968).

In addition to these supervisory challenges, contemporary civil service protections and the growing influence of police unions further council for negotiation and inclusion over authoritarian management (Flynn, 2004; Skogan, 2004). Instead of commanding and controlling, modern police administration is more about 'winning the hearts and minds' of the police workforce (Skogan & Hartnett, 1997). Participative management strategies that bring together the major stakeholders in police organizations in collaborative decision-making seem to offer promise for labor–management relations, building employee commitment, improving public service, and reducing rank-and-file resistance to police reform initiatives (Skogan, 2006). In this paper, we will describe a representative participation scheme which was implemented within a suburban police department and its effects on the agency. We will begin by reviewing what is known about participative management from various organizational studies, move to a review of related research in the law enforcement field, and then discuss the impact of the implementation of a shared leadership concept in terms of work conditions, employee commitment, labor relations, and productivity. We will conclude by considering the potential impact of such management approaches for law enforcement agencies.

Participative management and shared leadership

Participative management approaches have been widely adopted in organizations as a strategy for increasing workforce commitment and enhancing organizational performance. Participative management is defined as any power-sharing arrangement in which workplace influence is shared by individuals who are otherwise hierarchical unequals (Locke & Schweiger, 1979). Participative management usually involves some form of collaborative decision-making between employees and supervisors and can entail co-determination of working conditions, shared information processing, problem solving, and goal-setting (Wagner, 1994).

The body of research concerning participative management is quite large and has been carried out in a variety of workplace contexts. This research suggests a wide array of potentially positive outcomes, including increased job satisfaction (e.g., Cotton, Vollrath, Froggatt, Lengnick, & Jennings, 1988; Kim, 2002); organizational commitment (e.g., Meyer & Allen, 1997; Mowday, Porter, & Steers, 1982); organizational citizenship behavior (e.g., Eisenberger, Fasolo, & Davis-LaMastro, 1990); perceived organizational support (e.g., Armeli, Eisenberger, Fasolo, & Lynch, 1998); labor–management cooperation (e.g., Ospina & Yaroni, 2003), as well as job and organizational performance (Huang, 1997; Keller, 1997).

Participative management schemes can vary from informal suggestion systems to direct involvement at the policy and administrative level. Lawler's typology (1988) distinguishes among three types: *suggestion involvement* or the capacity for employees to offer information and suggestions (e.g., Quality Circles); *job involvement* wherein systems provide a degree of autonomy to employees regarding day-to-day work conditions (e.g., semi-autonomous work groups); and *high involvement*, which encompasses both suggestion and job involvement and adds a significant management and policy-setting function. High involvement of employees in company-wide policymaking is rare, however. For instance, Lawler, Mohrman, and Ledford (1992) found that while 80% of the Fortune 1000 companies practiced either suggestion or job involvement, only 1% utilized high involvement strategies. Significantly, the companies that utilized high involvement schemes were also found to be among the most profitable.

High involvement participation, with its emphasis on collaborative management, is similar to the concept of Shared Leadership (SL) where power is divided among co-workers rather than concentrated in the hands of one or a select few superiors (Pearce & Conger, 2003). Models of Shared Leadership distribute tasks and responsibilities up, down, and across the hierarchy; view leadership as a social process; and focus on collective learning. Shared leadership is prevalent within companies that utilize team-based problem solving and decision-making. While participative management in its various forms has been well researched in the private sector, studies in the law enforcement field have been more narrowly defined.

Participation and the police

In large measure, police administration has been defined by the need to gain control of police discretion rather than liberalize it (Sklansky, 2007). Historically, American policing has gravitated toward paramilitary command structures as a bulwark against corruption, political influence, and abuse of authority (Klockers, 1985). However, even authoritarian approaches to police management have failed to allay concerns about police abuse of authority, thereby periodically generating interest in alternative approaches. For example, there were attempts in Oakland, California in the 1970s (Muir, 1977; Toch, Grant, & Galvin, 1975) to experiment with internal democratic processes in policing in the hope that such reforms might foster greater respect for civil liberties and a higher degree of officer commitment. The results seemed to support this view that training in democratic values, use of participatory supervision techniques, and involvement of rank-and-file officers in decision-making and problem solving could improve police–citizen interactions and address issues of police violence. Despite the encouraging results, these innovative approaches were not sustainable because reactionary police activism at the same time counseled against the idea of officer empowerment (Sklansky, 2006).

The community policing era renewed interest in officer autonomy. This movement spurred considerable research into the connection between participative management and the philosophy of community-oriented policing. Continuing to the present, a number of studies have explored the degree to which participatory styles of supervision can affect line officer acceptance of, confidence in, and satisfaction with community policing (e.g., Adams, Rohe, & Arcury, 2002; Skogan & Hartnett, 1997; Wycoff & Skogan, 1994). The results suggest quite convincingly that participation is conducive to COP initiatives. Yet, this research has had little impact on police hierarchical structure (Fridell, 2004) because police administrations are still reluctant to grant line officer autonomy (Vito, Walsh, & Kunselman, 2005).

Beyond COP, there has been some research of other workforce impacts of participative decision-making in criminal justice contexts. A notable case study of a Quality Leadership initiative within the Madison, Wisconsin Police Department in the early 1990s demonstrated that participative management could contribute to significantly higher job satisfaction and task identity in an experimental group of officers as compared to a control group (Wycoff & Skogan, 1994). Beck's research (1999) with police officers in Australia and New Zealand established a positive correlation between organizational justice, perceived organizational support, and commitment, with officer participation in decision-making acting as a mediator. Studies by Farkas (2001), Simmons, Cochran, and Blount (1997), and Slate, Wells, and Johnson (2003), suggested that participatory approaches can decrease stress and burnout symptoms among probation and correctional employees.

Most research on participative management in law enforcement, however, has emphasized informal police officer participation at the suggestion level or examined line officer discretionary decision-making on the street (e.g., Bittner, 1967; Wilson, 1968). There have been few studies concerning strategic decision-making within police agencies (Morreale, Bond, & Dahlin, 2003) and, with the possible exceptions of the Madison Quality Policing project (Couper & Lobitz, 1991; Wycoff & Skogan, 1994) and the Oakland P.D. Peer Review Panel (Toch et al., 1975), little research on high involvement participation of rank-and-file police employees in policy decisions.

Besides employees, labor unions have also been excluded from strategic decision-making processes in police agencies, particularly in the USA. Even though their growing influence in law enforcement have made unions a major player in the administration of many agencies (Flynn, 2004; Skogan, 2004), administrators are reluctant to grant them formal authority, partly because of traditional notions of police hierarchy and partly due to the often self-interested nature of union activism. Frequently, legalistic and fixated on the traditional role of law enforcement rather than the service side of policing (Fleming, Marks, & Wood, 2006; Magenau & Hunt, 1989, 1996), union leaders have done little to endear themselves to agency administrators. DeLord (2006) notes that in the USA union and agency leaders often seem to be traveling in parallel universes, with little common ground to bring them together.

Analyses of labor–management cooperation in the public sector indicate that the relationship between management and union does not have to be adversarial and can, in fact, be cooperative. Based on 50 successful labor–management cooperative arrangements, the US Department of Labor Task Force concluded that collaborative problem solving and decision-making are associated with improved service, greater responsiveness to citizens, and higher cost-effectiveness in the delivery of services (US Department of Labor [DOL], 1996). Additionally, employees' ratings indicate higher quality of life and job satisfaction, as well as overall improved work relations.

In a study by Ospina and Yaroni (2003), three formal labor–management cooperative (LMC) projects were qualitatively examined. All involved LMC arrangements in which union and management leaders were jointly tasked with making collaborative decisions about their organizations. The authors report critical shifts in the roles of stakeholders, with managers becoming team players with their employees and labor representatives taking on managerial perspectives. Participants described changes in information sharing as striking, contributing to better communications and incrementally growing levels of trust. Both groups developed close relationships resulting in changes in their perspectives and mental models: a greater appreciation of the service nature of work; an enhanced ability to identify with the other side; and an understanding that cooperation involves a partnership with shared goals, costs, risks, and benefits.

Given the formal and informal power of police unions, participative LMC arrangements may be important options for reforming police organizations by facilitating the development of trust between administrators and union leaders. It appears that the formal inclusion of union leaders in agency policy decisions, as well as inclusion of rank-and-file employees as individuals, has the potential to improve work conditions and increase organizational commitment. Increased commitment, in turn, could potentially improve service delivery and even productivity.

Therefore, this study examined the internal workforce impacts of a shared leadership concept as well as the potential effects on the community. Specifically, the following research questions guided the inquiry:

Research Question 1:	Does participative management improve police officers' perception of work conditions, labor–management relations, and sense of organizational commitment?
Research Question 2:	Does participative management improve police officers' attitudes toward community-oriented policing?
Research Question 3:	Does participative management improve police officers' productivity and service delivery?

Implementing and assessing shared leadership

This case study was conducted in a suburban police department in northeastern Oklahoma. The initial research took place over a two-year period between 2003 and 2005, while the assessment of long-term effects is ongoing. One of the authors serves as the chief executive of the agency and authorized the study in order to assess organizational development efforts.

The Broken Arrow Police Department (BAPD) currently employs 176 full-time personnel and provides a full spectrum of police services to a metropolitan community of 95,000. The top-down autocratic management style of the previous administration had alienated employees and strained relationships between the administration and the labor union. Further, line officers and supervisors displayed significant resistance towards efforts to implement community-oriented policing. In 2002, the police union circulated a questionnaire among sworn officers to assess and document resentment toward the former administration. Results indicated low morale and poor communication between the administration and line officers. In July 2003, a new Chief was selected from the ranks of the department's senior administration.

Seeking participation: design of the Leadership Team

In August 2003, the BAPD formed a representative employee steering committee, called the *Leadership Team*, to assist senior management in running the agency. Comprised of 12 individuals representing the labor union, management, and most of the divisions, units, ranks, and functions within the department, the goal of the *Leadership Team* was to directly involve a cross-section of all employees, and particularly the police union, in important policy and strategic decisions for the agency. It was hoped that such a team could solve problems, improve processes, facilitate communication, and build unity within the department. The concept of fostering employee input through an empowered team was based on examples of high involvement semi-autonomous work groups found in the private sector (see Teerlink & Ozley, 2000), as well as various European work counsel models (Punch, 2006). In order to balance the power between the administration and union, leadership of the Team was divided between two chair persons. One Chairman was appointed by the Police Chief; the other was designated to be the police union President. Each Chairman then selected two additional Team members.

The remaining Team members, both sworn and non-sworn, were either elected by peers or were placed on the team by virtue of their function or experience. For instance, the Department's policy writer was placed on the team since much of the Team's work was to involve drafting formal policy. Overall, the intent was to ensure an equal representation of the various units and functions within the agency. This was not always possible since team size was limited initially to 12 persons.

The *Leadership Team*'s power and responsibilities constitute a 'high involvement' (Lawler, 1988) structure within the organization, meaning it possesses policymaking authority and the ability to direct the activities of various other components of the organization. The Team's bylaws establish it as an independent body, with authority to effect change and make binding decisions on a wide range of policy issues, working conditions, and strategic matters. In many respects the Chief's authority is subservient to that of the *Leadership Team* since all Team decisions are final and binding upon the rest of the agency, including the Chief. By policy, the only Team decisions that can be vetoed by the Chief are those that violate labor law, exceed budgetary constraints, or might expose the agency to undue civil liability. Specific personnel matters, such as individual questions of misconduct, never fall within the purview of the *Leadership Team*, although the generic policy governing such issues can be considered.

Any member of the Department can submit items for consideration by the Team which can be forwarded via email, inter-office memo, or verbally. Issues can also be suggested anonymously through the chain-of-command or through *Leadership Team* representatives. Although the Chief does not sit on the Team, he maintains control of its agenda thus serving as a gate-keeper of what they can consider. However, once an item is approved and referred to the Team, the Chief is committed to accept the Team's decisions.

The gate-keeper function was judged to be critical for the Chief so that appropriate control and accountability could be maintained and since he is ultimately responsibility for the performance of the police department. If things go wrong, either internally or externally due to poor decision-making by the *Leadership Team*, the Chief's Office is answerable to municipal government. Thus, before referring items to the *Leadership Team* the Chief conducts a 'risk assessment' wherein worst-case scenarios are considered; if the potentially least desirable outcomes are not expected to adversely impact service delivery to the community, negatively affect the political environment, or hinder the overall effectiveness of the agency, then the issue will be duly referred to the *Leadership Team*. Typically, 95% of issues coming to the Chief's Office are referred to the Team for consideration. An example of an item that was declined for the Team's agenda concerned a request for a work schedule that, if approved, would have provided more desirable schedules for officers, but would also have reduced available staffing and therefore service to the community.

The *Leadership Team* primarily deals with overriding policy matters and not day-to-day operational issues. In this respect, the traditional hierarchy of a police organization is fully maintained with watch commanders running their shifts, division commanders managing their divisions, and the Chief's Office maintaining authority over the agency's operations. Similarly, while the Leadership Team drafted policies that guide how disciplinary matters should be handled, the enforcement of these actions was left up to the respective supervisors. For example, in cases of employee misconduct the Team created a policy that set up a matrix of potential penalties tied to given types of violations. Final determination of where on the matrix an offense (and therefore punishment) should fall was left up to the supervisory chain-of-command.

Team operations and decision-making

Contrary to typical police hierarchy, rank and seniority play no part in *Leadership Team* proceedings and all members maintain equal voting rights. The chairpersons have a facilitative rather than a directive function in heading up the team. A loose set of guidelines for the *Leadership Team* were drawn up and then later refined and codified into formal departmental policy by the Team itself. The Team established a two-thirds majority democratic vote as its means of decision-making. In some cases, ad hoc voting members serve temporarily to provide technical expertise on a given issue or to bring a particular viewpoint to bear. In the beginning, the *Leadership Team* met once a week for two hours to work on the policies or issues given to them by the Chief. Typically, they would hold an opening discussion of the issue in question and then assign all Team members to conduct applicable research, which usually consisted of gathering a cross section of information and policies from other police departments. At a follow-up meeting the Team would then assimilate this information and develop a policy or recommendation on the matter.

Method: Assessing shared leadership

In February 2005, 18 months after implementation of the *Leadership Team*, a first assessment of the program was carried out utilizing quantitative survey data, qualitative interviews, and archival data to assess potential outcomes of the SL interventions. The study employed a pre-/post-test design with the implementation of the *Leadership Team* as the independent variable and perceptions of work conditions, motivational factors, and commitment as dependent variables. In addition, changes in productivity and citizen satisfaction with police services were assessed. Survey data gathered from sworn officers in 2002 by the police union was used as a baseline for comparison against identical data gathered in 2005. The same questionnaire items were used in both surveys, except that civilian employees were added to the 2005 database.

In 2002, 59 out of 100 distributed surveys were returned by sworn officers, equaling a response rate of 59%. However, 27 contained only qualitative comments, so that only 32 questionnaires could be quantitatively analyzed. However, purely qualitative responses tended to be even more negative in their evaluation of agency leadership than the quantitative data, thereby suggesting consistency throughout the entire data set. Forty-five percent of the sample had been employed at the agency up to 10 years, 47% had the rank of officer, 3% were corporals, 30% sergeants, 13% captains, and 7% majors. Age and gender of the respondents were not assessed.

In 2005, 103 questionnaires were given out to sworn officers, and 40 to civilian employees, of which 129 were returned, equaling a response rate of 90%. New probationary employees, part-time employees, and those on military duty were not included in the 2005 survey sample. The average age of the respondents was 36.4 years (SD = 9.0 years), 73% of the sample were male, and 18% were either current members of or had worked with the *Leadership Team*. Sixty-four percent of the sample had been employed by the agency for up to 10 years. Sixty-four percent of the sworn employees had the rank of officer, 10% were corporals, 16% were sergeants, 6% were captains, and 3% majors. Forty percent of the civilians worked in communications, 26% in the jail, 20% in administration or the records department, and 14% in animal control.

The original 2002 union questionnaire was comprised of demographic data and 43 items with 5-point Likert scales ranging from 1 (*strongly disagree*) to 5 (*strongly agree*). The survey instrument assessed officers' attitudes concerning the general administration of the police department, and included items on internal communications, work conditions, motivational factors, competency of administrative personnel, and relations with the community.

The 2005 questionnaire consisted of 32 items drawn from the original union questionnaire, demographic data, and an additional 18 items designed to assess affective organizational commitment, perceptions of empowerment, and the performance of the *Leadership Team*. Results presented here will concentrate on those items which were assessed at both times. Non-sworn civilian employees were administered a slightly different survey instrument.

Statistical analysis of sworn employee questionnaires compared the differences between 2002 and 2005 using a MANOVA procedure, with work conditions, labor–management relations, and motivational factors as dependent variables, and the implementation of Shared Leadership as the independent variable. For the 2005 sample, additional ANOVA/MANOVA procedures were carried out to compare sworn and non-sworn results and to assess the influence of rank on survey answers.

In addition to the quantitative analysis, from August to December of 2005 semi-structured interviews were carried out with 28 employees of the agency, equaling roughly 17% of the total agency workforce. Interviewees were selected to cover a broad spectrum of criteria such as different ranks, union or administration affiliation, elected vs. appointed team positions, status as civilian or sworn, as well as *Leadership Team* members or non-members. All interviews were tape recorded with the consent of the respondents and transcribed. The length of the interviews varied from 20 minutes to over an hour.

Interviews began with direct questions soliciting explanations for any perceived changes within the agency and the effects of the *Leadership Team* either on the agency or on the role of the respondent. The emphasis of the qualitative interviews was on interviewees' perceptions of the situation, reported changes in emotions and behaviors, and individual reasons given for such changes. Further, interviews were sifted for descriptions (stories, metaphors, examples) of the situation before, during, and after the implementation of shared leadership. Recurrent themes and concepts were analyzed in order to support or explicate analysis of the quantitative data.

Self-report questionnaires are useful measures to gage whether Shared Leadership can influence affective workforce indicators, but the agency was also interested in studying whether SL could impact productivity. Archival data on citations, arrests, and field interview reports are fairly traditional measures of police discretionary productivity (Armeli et al., 1998; Cordner & Kenney, 1999). Therefore, aggregate data on these indicators, as well as data on investigative cases cleared, were collected to assess officer performance for the period from January 2004 to January 2007 (post-SL implementation) and were compared with the previous years from 2000 to 2003 (pre-SL implementation). In addition, BAPD officer turnover was examined from 1996 through 2006 as an additional indicator of work conditions and workforce morale.

As a final consideration, the study looked indirectly at whether the implementation of Shared Leadership might have any discernable effect on public perceptions of the police department or other benefits for the community. Customer satisfaction was analyzed by comparing longitudinal data from citizen surveys. Crime rates were also examined for a 10-year period. Like productivity data, citizen surveys and uniform crime report (UCR) crime rates are affected by many variables and causal relationships to the new collaborative management approaches cannot be definitively established without a control group design. Consequently, these data sources were examined primarily for discussion purposes.

Beginning in 1998, and replicated in 2000, 2004, and 2006, the BAPD Citizen Crime Survey was mailed out to all city water customers, a sample that ranged from 28,000 to 32,000 homes. Response rates ranged from 8 to 9% per survey. The 2004 and 2006 surveys were also posted on the police department website. All responses were voluntary and anonymous. While none of the survey samples were random, the same methodology was employed in each case so that samples are statistically comparable. Although the questionnaires contained a variety of questions concerning crime issues, our analysis focused on items concerning citizen satisfaction with police services. As a corollary to the crime surveys, Broken Arrow's Part I and Part II UCR data was analyzed from 1996 to 2006.

Results: Work conditions, commitment, and labor relations

Research Question 1 examined whether the implementation of Shared Leadership improved police officers' perceptions of work conditions, organizational commitment, and labor–management relations. Generally, the 2005 survey data indicate that officers' perceptions of the higher echelons of the department improved dramatically, vertical communications improved, critical employee relations were stronger, and employees displayed more motivation and greater pride in the agency.

Comparison of the 2002 and 2005 surveys revealed that officers' perceptions of their Chief and division commanders had drastically improved, while evaluation of direct supervisors remained good (see Table 1 and Figure 1). In terms of their perceptions of work conditions and motivational factors, employees felt significantly more recognized for their work, more rewarded for good service, and perceived incentives to be available. Equally important, employees seemed to appreciate the work of the *Leadership Team* because policies it had created concerning performance, disciplinary, hiring, and promotional matters also improved significantly. Employees noted that organizational processes were far more predictable and transparent.

With regard to empowerment, officers felt that they had significantly more opportunity to participate in agency decisions and that their input and opinions were seriously considered. Their sense of pride in and commitment to the agency was also extremely high. Correlation analyses revealed medium associations between participation and commitment. Perceptions of empowerment correlated positively with pride in the agency ($r = 0.26, p < 0.01$) and feeling recognized for their contributions ($r = 0.45, p < 0.001$).

Lower officer turnover rates also indicate improved morale and continuance commitment within the agency. Between 1996 and 2003 (traditional management) the voluntary attrition rate of sworn personnel in the BAPD averaged 3.75 officers per year. This attrition rate dropped to zero between 2004 and 2006 (Shared Leadership). Interviews with several former officers who had left prior to 2004 indicated that the authoritarian management style

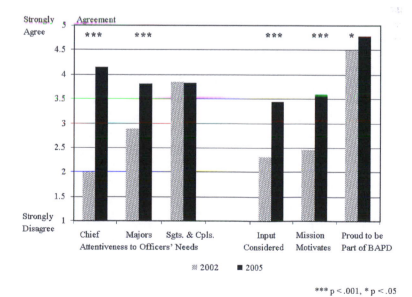

Figure 1.   Sworn employee differences: 2002–2005.

47

Table 1. Comparison of survey results 2002–2005.

Item	N_{2002}	M_{2002}	SD_{2002}	N_{2005}	M_{2005}	SD_{2005}	df	F	η^2
The Chief of Police is committed to ensuring officers' needs are met.	32	2.00	1.08	91	4.15	0.70	1,121	166.44***	0.58
The Division Commanders are committed to ensuring officers' needs are met.	32	2.88	1.04	91	3.81	0.73	1,121	31.01***	0.20
First Line Supervisors are committed to ensuring officers' needs are met.	32	3.84	0.85	91	3.82	0.77	1,121	0.02	−0.01
BAPD recognizes employees who do a good job.	32	2.94	1.13	91	4.15	0.71	1,119	48.14***	0.28
BAPD rewards officers for providing good service.	32	2.53	1.02	91	3.76	0.78	1,119	48.26***	0.28
Sufficient incentives are available to encourage good job performance.	32	2.47	1.11	91	3.34	0.91	1,119	18.45***	0.13
Discipline is administered impartially.	32	2.00	1.05	89	3.57	0.92	1,119	64.31***	0.35
The current hiring process ensures the most qualified applicants are hired.	32	2.69	1.12	91	3.62	1.02	1,119	17.92***	0.12
Promotional decisions are made in a fair and equitable manner.	32	2.97	1.18	91	3.51	0.97	1,119	5.92*	0.04
When I provide input, my opinions are seriously considered.	32	2.31	1.03	91	3.44	1.04	1,119	28.14***	0.18
I am proud to work for BAPD.	32	4.50	0.80	91	4.78	0.44	1,119	5.98*	0.04
BAPD's mission motivates employees to do their best work.	32	2.47	1.05	91	3.59	0.75	1,121	43.25***	0.26
The relationship between BAPD and the citizens of BA is good.	31	3.90	0.83	91	4.33	0.58	1,121	9.93**	0.07

*$p < 0.05$; **$p < 0.01$; ***$p < 0.001$.

of the former administration influenced their decisions to leave the agency and that the new inclusive culture would have actually enticed them to stay.

The qualitative interview data support the conclusion that SL contributes to improved employee perceptions of work conditions and sense of organizational commitment. The changes in the agency before and after implementation of the *Leadership Team* were described by participants as '*night and day*' or '*almost too many to describe.*' Respondents' perceptions of the situation under the old administration were characterized by '*a climate of fear*' and '*a lot of tension.*' In the eyes of the participants, decisions previously were made '*above at the Command Staff level*' and '*filtered down and implemented*'; and in a deprecating tone: '*we were treated like a bunch of drowning people that needed saving.*' Another respondent summarized the situation by describing it as a '*battle of wills.*'

Asked to describe the situation after the change of administration and the implementation of Shared Leadership in 2003, participants mentioned dramatic effects both on an emotional and administrative level. Emotionally, participants felt '*a lot happier, more comfortable*' and reported to be '*proud to work for the Department now versus in 2002.*' Participants perceived that they were involved in the administration of the agency; that the *Leadership Team* was '*freeing up the upper management of this Department to do other things.*'

Interview respondents consistently referred to their greater identification with and commitment to the department, for example: '*I have an extreme commitment to my organization, to my Department, to my Chief, and I've never had that before*' and '*I've had headhunters call me, you know and try – and I'm like no, I'm happy at BAPD.*' Responses reflected a theme of participation and inclusion, having '*restored morale,*' and increased job satisfaction. Respondents also expressed a more holistic appreciation of and commitment to the organizational context, '*I definitely learned what it was to work in a true Team setting where everybody had to participate and put forth the effort if there was anything that needed to be done.*'

Leadership Team members internalized their mission and developed a high sense of responsibility and accountability. Qualitative interviews revealed recurrent themes of Team members expressing a high degree of sensitivity to the well-being of the agency and to their constituents in the organization. As one member put it, '*Your voice matters, your opinions matter ... not necessarily just for you, but for those you represent.*' There were also instances where the *Leadership Team* referred agenda items back to the Chief for final decision '*in the overall interests of the Department.*' The *Leadership Team* was then prodded into their decision-making responsibility when the Chief refused to take the item back and expressed his trust in their judgment. Events such as this were milestones for the concept in that they fostered reciprocal trust and made it evident that the empowerment was genuine.

The three major reasons given by participants for the changes they perceived and experienced were all associated with empowerment-related factors: (1) participation of all ranks in the decision-making process ('*Chief* [name]'*s philosophy is to allow participation from all levels*' and '*There's more input from Officer level on up*'); (2) management asking for feedback from all levels ('*He* [the Chief] *wants feedback from every employee [...] good or bad*'); (3) consistent and reliable support of employee decisions by management ('*He has backed us on every issue that we have come across with*'; '*the fact that he's gone with the decisions has given the credibility to the Team*'). A general theme that emerged was that, in contrast to the situation before, '*everyone's encouraged to speak their opinion, give their ideas and their input.*'

These results suggest that Shared Leadership can make officers feel more empowered and committed to their organization. Research shows that participative decision-making is often perceived by employees as being fair and an expression of trust (e.g., Lau & Lim, 2002; Rhoades & Eisenberger, 2002). This sense of empowerment and organizational trust may, in turn, elicit a degree of reciprocal employee commitment.

Participants indicated that the previous adversarial relationship between the administration and the union improved as a by-product of the *Leadership Team*. Regardless of their rank, job assignment, union affiliation, or *Leadership Team* association, interviewees indicated that the relationship between labor and management had become more of a partnership. Specifically, factors such as improved communications, role reversal, and global organizational perspectives were cited by participants as outcomes of the new management style. One participant mentioned '*better understanding*,' '*better communication between the two*,' and that he '*learned a lot about, you know, the different relationships within this Department*.' A major factor for this improvement was attributed to the inclusion of the Union President in the *Leadership Team*. The direct and consistent contact between the union and administration that this entailed also seemed to be a major factor: '*It (Leadership Team) fosters a very positive attitude between the two of them ... it helps in carrying on a positive attitude from Union standpoint toward management*.' These findings affirm research by Kearney and Hays (1994), Nurick (1982), and Ospina and Yaroni (2003) that cooperative management–union decision-making can produce positive outcomes and extends this concept to the law enforcement arena.

Shared Leadership and community-oriented policing

Research Question 2 examines the potential for Shared Leadership techniques to improve police officers' attitudes toward community-oriented policing. The 2002 and 2005 questionnaires contained one item that related directly to the community policing mission of the agency, and two which referred to overall relations and communication with the community. Mean comparisons show statistically significant improvement in officers' evaluation of the department's community policing mission in 2005, as well as better relationships with citizens and better communication with the community (see Table 1 and Figure 1). Medium to strong correlations were found between items related to empowerment and community-oriented policing.

Qualitative data supported this finding with regard to COP even more strongly. Though the agency's community policing mission did not change before or after the implementation of Shared Leadership, all participants perceived improvement in their attitudes toward COP. Interviewees cited empowerment as a key factor, that is, '*Community policing as a goal has not changed here; it's the way it was presented to the officers. It gives the officers more freedom, more creativity, and they have more say in how they're getting to accomplish those goals*.'

Officers explained their higher acceptance of COP with the more collaborative leadership style; '*I would have to say it's because it's not really being pushed on us like it was previously*.' Under the previous administration, '*officers felt like we were being treated as children*' and were told what to do with regard to COP initiatives: '*We kind of lost our dignity there*' and '*Officers were way down on the food chain*.' Consequently, they did not buy into the agency's mission. Once SL and an empowering approach were introduced, COP as a philosophy became more '*user friendly*' and '*more appealing to the officers than before*.' The substitution of participative for authoritarian management styles appears to have been critical: '*The administration treats us as adults*' and *once that changed and it wasn't forced at us and it was more of a decision that could be made by people who were actually out there and seeing what was going on – I think it greatly changed the attitude toward that [COP].*

The indication here is that police officers feel more motivated when they are empowered to implement community-oriented policing as they see fit. Our results therefore support previous studies suggesting that participatory approaches can promote officers' acceptance of community policing or other programmatic change initiatives (Adams et al., 2002; Skogan & Hartnett, 1997; Wycoff & Skogan, 1994). The qualitative data also provide strong evidence of the reverse effect when COP or other change initiatives are implemented through autocratic management styles, as typically occurs in traditionally vertical police organizations.

Productivity and service delivery

In order to assess the effects of Shared Leadership on productivity, we included data in our study to complement quantitative and qualitative self-reports. Discretionary police productivity was assessed by gathering archival data on citations, arrests, field interview reports, and investigative cases cleared. Comparison of archival data revealed significant increases in all measured activity indicators (see Table 2): in 2004 which was the first full year of the new Shared Leadership management system, patrol officers made 24% more arrests of all types, issued 6% more traffic citations, and carried out 51% more field interviews compared to the preceding four-year mean. These numbers increased again in 2005 compared to 2004 and remained fairly stable in 2006. With respect to investigations, detectives cleared 34% more cases in 2004 compared to the mean of the preceding four years and this total continued to rise in 2005 (+9%) and 2006 (+11%) (compare Table 2).

Such increases in proactive, discretionary police activity suggest that officers may be displaying greater motivation to engage in discretionary conduct when not otherwise busy with routine call response. Interestingly, these general increases in police productivity occurred while the FBI UCR Part I & II crime rate for Broken Arrow dropped dramatically. The UCR Part I crimes of Homicide, Rape, Robbery, Aggravated Assault, Burglary, Larceny, and Auto Theft dropped 32% between 2003 and 2006. The total of Part I and Part II crimes combined fell 14%. During 2006 major crime was reduced by 18%, bringing the city's crime rate to its lowest level in 10 years. Remarkably, the city grew at the same time at a rapid rate, from 83,000 in 2000 to 95,000 in 2006 (US Census figures).

In addition, a comparison of citizen survey data from 1998 to 2006 indicated steadily increasing levels of citizen satisfaction with police services. The proportion of residents who reported satisfaction with police services rose from 58% in 1998 to 93% in 2006 (2000: 60%; 2004: 87%). Interviews with various department representatives reflected a theme of higher morale accounting for greater productivity and better quality interactions with the community, that is: *'Now that whenever you come to work and you're happy or you're motivated, you like where you are at, that's going to reflect positively with the community.'*

Inclusion of lower ranks and civilian employees

Despite the generally positive outcomes of SL for police employees, significant disparities between civilian and sworn personnel were evident concerning affective commitment. Type of employment was significantly associated with organizational commitment, with sworn

Table 2. Patrol and investigative activities 2000–2006.

Activity	Year							Difference 2004 – before[a]	Difference 2005 – 2004	Difference 2006 – 2005
	2000	2001	2002	2003	2004	2005	2006			
Arrests made	1807	1939	1778	2110	2359	2656	2584	24%	15%	−3%
Citations issued	13,240	18,046	13,511	12,353	15,090	17,871	17,686	6%	18%	−1%
Field interviews	675	332	445	445	549	590	581	51%	7%	−2%
Investigated cases cleared	1757	1836	1861	1861	2369	2572	2857	34%	9%	11%

[a]Calculated as 2004 (mean 2000–2003).

officers exhibiting more pride to work for BAPD compared to civilian employees ($F_{1,127} = 4.47, p < 0.05, \eta^2 = 0.03$). To some degree, this might be expected in that civilian employees generally enjoy less career track, receive less compensation, and tend to have less autonomy than officers on the street.

Similarly, lower perceived levels of empowerment were detected from baseline officer vs. supervisory ranks. Among sworn personnel, rank was inversely correlated with a sense of participation and empowerment ($F_{4,82} = 4.14, p < 0.01, \eta^2 = 0.13$) but was not associated with commitment ($F_{4,82} = 0.99, p = 0.42, \eta^2 = 0.00$). However, effect sizes for both variables were rather small compared to the other results.

This suggests that police participation models can be improved by expanding representation of the lower ranks and civilians when implementing interventions such as the *Leadership Team*. With this issue in mind the makeup of the BAPD *Leadership Team* was subsequently altered in 2005 to allow for even greater representation of the lower ranks and civilians. In addition, a number of standing *Leadership Team* subcommittees at the unit level have been established. Essentially functioning as Quality Circles, these subcommittees operate under the auspices of the *Leadership Team* to provide greater representation and involvement throughout the workforce. As this practice expands, the BAPD may develop into a 'webbed organization' with a *Leadership Team* of rank-and-file employees at its center. No follow-up data is yet available on the impact of these changes.

In a similar move to provide opportunities for involvement, rotating positions of short duration have been added to the *Leadership Team*. To fill these positions, the Team has reached out to the most outspoken members of the department; those most likely to play a devil's advocate role. Initial feedback from these temporary Team members has been positive.

The role of executive leadership

Although the study did not set out to investigate the role of executive leadership in Shared Leadership, its importance was consistently evident in both the quantitative and qualitative data. Recurrent interview themes referenced the impact of the Chief Executive on perceptions of empowerment, boundary management, facilitation, and sustainability. Members of the *Leadership Team* described the Chief's role as being critical to their empowerment; the '*Lighthouse*' in defining their agenda and purpose. Further, their Chief Executive's commitment to Shared Leadership was crucial to winning over the doubters and sustaining the process: '*I didn't understand the passion towards what he said he was going to do and the commitment he had to make it work.*'

This is in accordance with Locke's notion (2003) that, even in Shared Leadership contexts, leadership starts at the top. A parallel could be drawn here with the Madison Quality Leadership initiative wherein the most positive effects of the experiment tended to dissipate following retirement of the Chief who helped initiate the program (Skogan, personal information, 11 November 2005).

Top leadership has a strong effect on employees' identification with the agency and their perceptions of empowerment, suggesting a transformational role (Bass, 1985) for chief executives in participative schemes. It may be that even as executive leaders relinquish some aspects of decision-making, they might concentrate more intently on strategic planning, defining mission and values, facilitating change, promoting communication, and building leaders around them (Manz & Sims, 1989). The intersection of vertical and horizontal models of leadership deserves more study, particularly as regards organizations with a traditionally authoritarian orientation.

Police reform: from bottom-up to inside-out

David Bayley (2006) notes that, historically,

> ... police organizations themselves have not been the source of significant reform ideas. Police reform has not been self-generated. It has been instigated by people, or events, outside the police themselves ... In short, significant police reforms have been top-down and outside-inside. (p. 1)

The Broken Arrow case study represents an exception to this view in that the administrative reforms occurred primarily through an internal initiative, without benefit of external precipitating events, mandate, or funding. In addition, while instigated at the top of the organization, it drew its energy from the bottom where theory and design were put into practice, with top leadership falling into a facilitating role once participants internalized the concept.

A recent evolution of the *Leadership Team* involves formation of a Citizens Subcommittee to provide direct input and community perspective to the *Leadership Team* as it undertakes its decision-making process. Staffed by civilian graduates of the agency's Citizens Police Academy, the mission of this subcommittee is to provide an inside-out sounding board for departmental and *Leadership Team* initiatives and vice versa. Still under construction, this phase is a first step toward Shared Leadership with an external focus.

Limitations and further research

The design of this study and the specifics of the situation within the BAPD are important limitations that bare discussion and that point to opportunities for further research. Unlike the Madison, Wisconsin Quality Policing project (Couper & Lobitz, 1991; Wycoff & Skogan, 1994), which involved a control group design, the SL initiative within the BAPD was an agency-wide intervention. Lacking a control group design, we cannot establish causal relationships between Shared Leadership practices and the observed outcomes. On the other hand, triangulation of subjective and objective data from different sources and using a pre-/post-test design does provide some robust support to our findings.

Another important potential limitation of this research is the possibility of rebound effects. This case study revolved around an agency that was admittedly suffering from labor–management problems at the time of the new chief's appointment and the implementation of SL. Officers even stated during interviews that the agency '*needed heeling.*' Some of the outcomes may be due to a rebound effect associated with a simple change of administrative personality rather than a shift in management philosophy. Interestingly, it is possible that organizations have to be in serious crisis situations before management and union representatives are willing to cooperate with each other (Ospina & Yaroni, 2003), as was the case here.

The question of how an intervention like the *Leadership Team* would work in other police agencies is as yet unexplored and therefore generalizing conclusions may be unreliable. Certainly, factors such as size, complexity, and culture can all be expected to affect both implementation and outcomes. The study should therefore be replicated in organizations of both similar and dissimilar characteristics. This, in fact, is in progress at the present time, but as yet no data is available for comparison. Longitudinal research is also needed to determine the sustainability of Shared Leadership in policing.

The study also points out the potential for policing to benefit by collaborations with academia. With relatively little financial commitment, the Broken Arrow initiative was carried out in cooperation with university resources in the way of consultation, training, and ongoing evaluation services. This is an external asset which is generally available in police circles, but often overlooked. Collaborations of this kind reinforce the advisability of conducting rigorous, data-based evaluation of police programs.

Conclusion

This study assessed the effects of a high involvement Shared Leadership initiative within a medium-sized police agency. The results suggest that workforce involvement strategies in police departments can improve employee attitudes about working conditions and labor–management relations. The findings extend the research on labor–management cooperation to the law enforcement field and hold important implications for the growing issue of police labor relations. Confirming previous research, the data also indicate that empowerment has the potential to elicit line officer commitment to community-oriented policing, as well as to other organizational goals. Enhanced commitment may even translate into greater discretionary officer productivity and better service delivery. Participation also seems to improve communications at all levels and can help bridge the typical schism between senior management and line officers. Finally, the study suggests that bottom-up democratic reform of police organizations is not only possible, but in fact, may already be at hand.

References

Adams, R.E., Rohe, W.M., & Arcury, T.A. (2002). Implementing community-oriented policing: Organizational change and street officer attitudes. *Crime & Delinquency, 48*(3), 399–430.

Alarid, L.F. (1999). Law enforcement departments as learning organizations: Argyris's theory as a framework for implementing community-oriented policing. *Police Quarterly, 2*(3), 321–337.

Armeli, S., Eisenberger, R., Fasolo, P., & Lynch, P. (1998). Perceived organizational support and police performance: The moderating influence of socioemotional needs. *Journal of Applied Psychology, 83*(2), 288–297.

Bass, B.M. (1985). *Leadership and performance beyond expectations.* New York: Free Press.

Bayley, D. (2006, October 12–13). Police reform; Who done it? *Proceedings of the UC Berkeley/ Australian National University Conference on Police Reform from the Bottom-Up,* Berkeley, CA.

Beck, K. (1999). *Optimizing the organizational commitment of police officers: Background and summary of the research and guidelines for management.* Payneham, SA: National Police Research Unit.

Bittner, E. (1967). The police on skid-row: A study in peace keeping. *American Sociological Review, 32*(5), 699–715.

Cordner, G.W., & Kenney, D.J. (1999). Tactical patrol evaluation. In D.J. Kenney & R.P. McNamara (Eds.), *Police and policing: Contemporary issues* (pp. 127–155). Westport, CT: Praeger.

Cotton, J., Vollrath, D., Froggatt, K., Lengnick, M., & Jennings, K. (1988). Employee participation: Diverse forms and different outcomes. *Academy of Management Review, 13*(1), 8–22.

Couper, D., & Lobitz, S. (1991). *Quality policing: The Madison experience.* Washington, DC: Police Executive Research Forum.

DeLord, R. (2006, October 12–13). *Police unions and police reform.* Paper for the University of Berkeley/Australian National University Conference on Police Reform from the Bottom-Up, Berkeley, CA.

Eisenberger, R., Fasolo, P., & Davis-LaMastro, V. (1990). Perceived organizational support and employee diligence, commitment, and innovation. *Journal of Applied Psychology, 75*(1), 51–59.

Farkas, M.A. (2001). Correctional officers: What factors influence work attitudes? *Correction Management Quarterly, 5*(2), 20–26.

Fleming, J., Marks, M., & Wood, J. (2006). 'Standing on the inside looking out': The significance of police unions in networks of police governance. *The Australian and New Zealand Journal of Criminology, 39*(1), 71–89.

Flynn, J. (2004). The merits of community policing in the twenty-first century: The view from the street. In L. Fridell (Ed.), *Communicy policing: The past, present, and future* (pp. 141–149). Washington, DC: Police Executive Research Forum.

Fridell, L. (2004). The defining characteristics of community policing. In L. Fridell (Ed.), *Community policing: The past, present and future* (pp. 3–12). Washington, DC: Police Executive Research Forum.

Goldstein, H. (1990). *Problem-oriented policing.* New York: McGraw-Hill.

Huang, T. (1997). The effect of participative management on organizational performance: The case of Taiwan. *International Journal of Human Resource Management, 8*(5), 677–689.

Kearney, R., & Hays, S. (1994). Labor–management relations and participative decision-making: Toward a new paradigm. *Public Administration Review, 54*(1), 44–51.

Keller, R. (1997). Job involvement and organizational commitment as longitudinal predictors of job performance: A study of scientists and engineers. *Journal of Applied Psychology, 82*(4), 539–545.

Kelling, G. (1999). *'Broken Windows' and police discretion.* Washington, DC: US Department of Justice.

Kelling, G., & Coles, C. (1996). *Fixing broken windows: Restoring order and reducing crime in our communities.* New York: Touchstone.

Kim, S. (2002). Participative management and job satisfaction: Lessons for management leadership. *Public Administration Review, 62*(2), 231–241.

Klockers, K. (1985). *The idea of police.* Beverly Hills, CA: Sage.

Lau, C., & Lim, E. (2002). The intervening effects of participation on the relationship between procedural justice and managerial performance. *The British Accounting Review, 34*(1), 55–78.

Lawler, E.E., III. (1988). Choosing an involvement strategy. *Academy of Management Executive, 2*(3), 197–204.

Lawler, E.E., III, Mohrman, S.A., & Ledford, G.E. (1992). *Employee involvement and Total Quality Management: Practice and results in Fortune 1000 companies.* San Francisco: Jossey-Bass.

Locke, E.A. (2003). Leadership: Starting at the top. In C.L. Pearce & J.A. Conger (Eds.), *Shared Leadership: Reframing the hows and whys of leadership* (pp. 271–284). Thousand Oaks, CA: Sage.

Locke, E.A., & Schweiger, D.M. (1979). Participation in decision-making: One more look. In B.M. Staw (Ed.), *Research in organizational behavior* (pp. 265–339). Greenwich, CT: JAI Press.

Magenau, J., & Hunt, R. (1989). Sociopolitical networks for police role-making. *Human Relations, 42*(6), 547–561.

Magenau, J., & Hunt, R. (1996). Police unions and the police role. *Human Relations, 49*(10), 1315–1343.

Manz, C., & Sims, H., Jr. (1989). *Superleadership: Leading others to lead themselves.* Englewood Cliffs, NJ: Prentice Hall.

Mastrofski, S.D. (1998). Community policing and police organizational structure. In J. Brodeur (Ed.), *How to recognize good policing: Problems and issues* (pp. 161–189). Thousand Oaks, CA: Sage.

Meyer, J., & Allen, N. (1997). *Commitment in the workplace: Theory, research and application.* Thousand Oaks, CA: Sage.

Morreale, S., Bond, B., & Dahlin, L. (2003). *Strategic decision-making in police organizations.* Paper presented at the Academy of Criminal Justice Sciences Conference, Boston.

Mowday, R., Porter, L., & Steers, R. (1982). *Employee–organization linkages.* New York: Academic Press.

Muir, W. (1977). *Police: Streetcorner politicians.* Chicago: University of Chicago Press.

Nurick, A. (1982). Participation in organizational change: A longitudinal field study. *Human Relations, 35*(5), 413–429.

Ospina, S., & Yaroni, A. (2003). Understanding cooperative behavior in labor management cooperation: A theory-building exercise. *Public Administration Review, 63*(4), 455–471.

Pearce, C., & Conger, J. (2003). All those years ago: The historical underpinnings of shared leadership. In C.L. Pearce & J.A. Conger (Eds.), *Shared Leadership: Reframing the hows and whys of leadership* (pp. 271–284). Thousand Oaks, CA: Sage.

Punch, M. (2006, October 12–13). *'Get back in your kennel!': Representation, consultation and 'voice' in policing.* Paper for the University of Berkeley/Australian National University Conference on Police Reform from the Bottom-Up, Berkeley, CA.

Rhoades, L., & Eisenberger, R. (2002). Perceived organizational support: A review of the literature. *Journal of Applied Psychology, 87*(4), 698–714.

Simmons, C., Cochran, J.K., & Blount, W.R. (1997). The effects of job-related stress and job satisfaction on probation officers' inclinations to quit. *American Journal of Criminal Justice, 21*(2), 213–229.

Sklansky, D. (2006). Not your father's police department: Making sense of the new demographics of law enforcement. *The Journal of Criminal Law and Criminology, 96*(3), 1209–1243.

Sklansky, D. (2007). Seeing blue: Police reform, occupational culture, and cognitive burn-in. In M. O'Neill & M. Marks (Eds.), *Police occupational culture: New debates and directions.* Oxford: Elsevier Science.

Skogan, W.G. (2004). Community policing: Common impediments to success. In L. Fridell (Ed.), *Community policing: The past, present, and future* (pp. 159–167). Washington, DC: Police Executive Research Forum.

Skogan, W.G. (2005, November 11). Personal communication.

Skogan, W.G. (2006, October 12–13). *Why reforms fail.* Paper for the University of Berkeley/Australian National University Conference on Police Reform from the Bottom-Up, Berkeley, CA.

Skogan, W.G., & Hartnett, S.M. (1997). *Community policing, Chicago style.* New York: Oxford University Press.

Slate, R.N., Wells, T.L., & Johnson, W.W. (2003). Opening the manager's door: State probation officer stress and perceptions of participation in workplace decision-making. *Crime & Delinquency, 49*(4), 519–541.

Taylor, R.W., Fritsch, E.J., & Caeti, T.J. (1998). Core challenges facing community policing: The emperor still has no clothes. *ACJS Today, 17*(1), 3–5.

Teerlink, R., & Ozley, L. (2000). *More than a motorcycle. The leadership journey at Harley-Davidson.* Boston, MA: Harvard Business School Press.

Toch, H., Grant, J., & Galvin, R. (1975). *Agents of change: A study in police reform.* New York: John Wiley.

US Department of Labor (DOL). (1996). *Working together for public service: Report of the U.S. Secretary of Labor's Task Force on Excellence in State and Local Government through Labor–Management Cooperation.* Washington, DC: Government Printing Office.

Vito, G.F., Walsh, W.F., & Kunselman, J. (2005). Community policing: The middle manager's perspective. *Police Quarterly, 8*(4), 490–509.

Wagner, J.A. (1994). Participation's effects on performance and satisfaction: A reconsideration of research evidence. *Academy of Management Review, 19*(2), 312–330.

Wilson, J.Q. (1968). *Varieties of police behavior: The management of law and order in eight communities.* Cambridge, MA: Harvard University Press.

Wilson, J.Q. (2000). *Bureaucracy: What government agencies do and why they do it.* New York: Basic Books.

Wycoff, M.A., & Skogan, W.G. (1994). The effect of a community policing management style on officers' attitudes. *Crime & Delinquency, 40*(3), 371–383.

Building the capacity of police change agents: The nexus policing project[1]

Jennifer Wood[a], Jenny Fleming[a,b], and Monique Marks[a,c]

[a]Australian National University; [b]University of Tasmania; [c]University of Kwazulu-Natal

This paper argues that police members from all ranks possess potential to challenge the beliefs and meanings that inform their daily practices, and are able to alter their routines when innovative practice and new ideas assist them in responding to new dilemmas. The paper suggests that both scholars and practitioners pay insufficient attention to nurturing rank-and-file police as change agents and to building their capacity as knowledge workers and ideas generators in forging change. In response to this gap, the paper discusses the Nexus Policing Project in Victoria, Australia, which is based on a police–university partnership aimed at realising new ways of seeing and doing in the field of policing. The participatory action research method is utilised as a way of overcoming the traditional gap between research and practice. The paper discusses some of the challenges associated with this kind of collaborative endeavour.

Introduction

A question that is often not addressed in the policing literature is how ways of theorising police reform and police culture inform methodological choices in researching the police. This paper explores this line of inquiry. We write this paper as academic researchers who are interested in advancing both theory and practice, but who believe that this is only possible to achieve when practitioners (in this case police officers) are actively involved in the research process and in finding solutions to practical problems.

We adopt a modest understanding of police reform. We do not regard it as a parabolic leap in organisational structure, managerial style and strategic direction. We propose rather, that change occurs through new ways of thinking and acting. This paper is concerned with identifying and establishing the conditions that allow for the introduction of new perspectives and practices on the part of individual and group members of the police, regardless of rank. We focus in particular on change from a micro-cultural perspective, and suggest that ways of seeing and doing are mutually constitutive. We propose that in thinking of police as individual agents it is important to employ research methodologies that promote the capacity of police

---

[1] An earlier version of this paper was prepared for the workshop on *Police Reform from the Bottom Up* held in Berkeley, CA, 12–13 October 2006.

officers to resist, accommodate and shape police organisational reform (see Marks 2004).

Although it is now commonplace to suggest that police culture is neither monolithic, universal nor unchanging (Reiner 1992: 109), it is a notion that continues to be deployed without nuance and specificity. 'Culture' is used to paint a brush over broad social patterns, rather than to illuminate the individual practices of individuals as they go about deriving meaning from, and ascribing meaning to, the situations in which they find themselves every day. David Sklansky refers to this broad brush depiction of police culture as 'the Police Subculture Schema' which he says 'makes it hard to see differences between officers, new complexities of police identity, and dynamic processes within the police workforce' (2007: 21). In order to identify such differences a more 'hands on' approach to research is required.

Police researchers who wish to conduct research with police organisations are usually directed to senior management to discuss their proposals and ideas about new ways of doing business. Arguably it is easier to introduce such ideas and innovative practice at this level because management see such issues as central to their role. At the same time, operational officers spend much of their working life seeking creative solutions to the daily problems they face on the street, and discussions with them reveal a wealth of knowledge about policing styles and strategies that have great potential to shape organisational reform.

Although change in policing undoubtedly hinges on more effective ways of integrating the realities and experiences of 'street cops' and 'management cops' (Reuss-Ianni and Ianni 1983), we focus rather on the notion of a more fragmented, micro-level view of police culture, which helps us to move away from thinking about cultural change as necessitating major changes to traditional organisational practices, norms and belief systems. Culture changes as individual members 'struggle to resolve conflicts and negotiate new understandings that tie together (sometimes loosely) heterogeneous elements' (Foote Whyte et al. 1991: 43). Change can occur in small shifts in ways of seeing and acting. Taking this view of organisational change requires us to think about research approaches that allow individuals to explore and construct, then assess and reconstruct their concerns (Grundy 1986: 28). What we propose is a methodology whereby academic researchers bring police officers directly into the process of solving practical problems as part of the research process. We advocate participatory action research (PAR).

PAR is a methodology where creating a positive social change is the predominant driving force. PAR grew out of social and educational research and exists today as one of the few research methods that embrace principles of participation and reflection, and empowerment and emancipation of groups seeking to improve their social situation. The approach is not new. Kurt Lewin first talked about action research 60 years ago (Holter and Schwartz-Barcott 1993: 298–304). However, the nature of the methodology has changed markedly since then and prominent writers including McTaggart (1991), Grundy (1986), Foote Whyte (1991), McKernan (1991) and Jordan (2003), to name a few, have progressed the method considerably.

In this paper, we focus on the Nexus Policing Project in Victoria and the emphasis Nexus places on the importance of collaborative partnerships between police and academics in pursuit of innovative ideas and practice that may inform new ways of seeing and doing from the bottom-up, as well as from the top-down. At the time of writing, Nexus is one of the 17 projects—funded by the Australian

Research Council—that Victoria Police is undertaking with various university partners on a wide variety of subjects (see Bradley et al. 2006). Our paper is thus concerned more broadly with the relationships between agendas of reform, cultural change and research, and uses the case of Nexus to illustrate our optimism for the capacity of small groups of police officers to engage positively with new possibilities and reconfigured social arrangements. In policing more generally, the shift towards collaborative projects like Nexus do, however, involve challenges associated with carving out a new place and role for research (and academics) in what is a historically pragmatic and task-oriented institution of law enforcement. We discuss some of these challenges, drawing on key debates in the literature.

Agency and change in police organisations

Bevir and Rhodes propose an 'interpretive' approach to studies of governance, one that focuses on 'meaning in action' (2006: 1). In stressing the importance of the mutually constitutive relationship between people's actions and the meanings that surround them, the authors argue that beliefs inform practices, and practices reinforce and rework beliefs. 'To explain an action', they say, 'we cannot merely correlate it with an isolated attitude. Rather, we must interpret it as part of a web of beliefs and desires' (2006: 3).

This interpretive view supports a micro-level understanding of culture. If we want to understand cultural expressions we must examine *all* practices, and the 'webs of meaning' that surround them, from the 'bottom up'. In other words, individual beliefs cannot be taken in isolation. Beliefs are sustained and supported by colleagues with similar beliefs and the institutional environment that informs them.

Bevir and Rhodes make clear that although the everyday practices of individuals are informed by wider webs of meanings, they are not pre-determined by them. People are able to reflect on the beliefs that shape their behaviour and adjust those beliefs based on the ideas circulating around them as well as the ones that they themselves generate. Individuals do not exist outside of a particular social context(s); they are 'situated' in that context rather than fully autonomous agents (Bevir and Rhodes 2006: 4).

It is therefore essential to think about human agency as central to change in policing. Change is vitally contingent on the capacity, and opportunities for individual police members to exercise this agency. 'To accept agency' Bevir and Rhodes argue, is 'to imply people have the capacity to adopt beliefs and actions, even novel ones, for reasons of their own. In so doing they can transform the social background' (2006: 5). Individuals have the capacity to respond innovatively to new ideas, problems, or dilemmas. Even when individual agents are confronted with new ideas that do not sit comfortably with existing ones, they can be, and indeed must be, given the space needed to reflect upon established ways of thinking and acting.

Studies of change in policing have revealed the important place of agency on the part of police members, although the focus has tended to be more on the agency exercised by police leaders, rather than on rank-and-file members. Police leaders are often viewed as the innovators within police organisations—certainly more so than the rank-and-file (see Bayley 2008). Wood's study of change in policing in Ontario (Wood 2000) highlighted the capacity of police leaders to exercise agency in addressing a series of contingent, and sometimes unrelated, factors in their internal and external environments. The study revealed that police leaders were not simply colonised by a new way of thinking imposed by those in higher levels of political authority. Rather, they configured new management paradigms to suit their own public policing environment. The end result was the introduction of new managerial models which were never completely convergent with the model that 'originated' in the private sector (see Poole et al. 2006). In actively playing with new ideas, individual police members—or in the case of the above study, individual police leaders—exercised a form of 'situated agency' (Bevir and Rhodes 2006: 5).

If *all* police officers are to be considered as change agents, the challenge before us is to identify and then to establish the conditions that build this capacity, not exclusively from the 'top', but also 'from the bottom up.'

Bradley, Nixon and Marks identify some of the conditions required for police organisations and for police members in particular to evaluate their everyday practice and ritual against the 'web of meanings' that shape and determine the world of public policing. These conditions include, 'equal partnership', 'dialogic engagement' and the creation of an environment that empowers officers to access innovation and put that innovation into practice. The opportunity for reflection on this practice, for both individuals and the organisation itself is crucial (Bradley et al. 2006: 190).

The Nexus Policing Project has sought to apply a PAR philosophy as a way of 'partnering' with the police in reflecting on existing traditions and in forging new ideas and practices. The PAR approach is centred on notions of collaboration. It tries to overcome the traditional gap between research and practice (Whyte Foote 1991) through an interactive involvement of researchers and research subjects (Geva and Shem-Tov 2002: 192). Practitioners are directly involved in the research process from problem identification, to research design, to data collection and analysis, and thereafter dissemination and uptake of research findings. The action research encounter is one where 'equal partners meet, enter into dialogue and share different kinds of knowledge and expertise . . .' (Jordan 2003: 190). Rather than the traditional research model where there is a rigid distinction between researcher and subjects and a quest for objectivity, PAR focuses on a 'dialogical relationship between theory and practice' (Jordan 2003: 188) where knowledge is generated within the everyday world of participants. PAR thus 'contrasts sharply with the conventional model of pure research in which members of organisations and communities are treated as passive subjects with some of them participating only to the extent of authorising the project, being its subjects and receiving the results' (Foote Whyte et al. 1991: 20).

In the remainder of this article we discuss the Nexus Policing Project, its research approach and the challenges associated with fully adopting such a method. The Nexus Policing Project is one of many partnerships that Victoria Police has created with Australian universities. The word "nexus" refers to a binding or linking together—a connection. In the context of research it refers to the linking together of different forms of knowledge and capacity in the propagation of new ideas about police policy and practice. It refers specifically to the connection between all those who in some way work with the police towards knowledge generation, validation, diffusion and adoption. It is this latter linkage that we will focus on in this paper. In discussing this we will provide some insight into the kinds of outcomes that have been achieved and which are likely to inform new practices in Victoria Police.

The nexus policing project: building agency through participatory research

Historically, police have been regarded as generally anti-intellectual in their outlook and considerably hesitant about exposing themselves to the beliefs and assumptions of outsiders (Young 1991). At the same time, academic researchers have found it difficult at times to collaborate with police (Fleming 2005). There is of course research being conducted between police and academics. Police in both the United Kingdom (UK) and the United States (US) have begun to commission pieces of research from universities and indeed, act upon existing policing research in pursuit of evidence-based policy and practice (e.g., Bayley 2008; Bullock and Tilley 2003). In Australia, many police organisations are collaborating with universities and researchers. For example, the Tasmanian Institute of Law Enforcement Studies (TILES) situated in the University of Tasmania was formed in 2002 by the University of Tasmania and the Tasmanian Department of Police and Emergency Management. In the US, programs involving community participation, proposed and designed originally by academics such as Skolnick and Bayley (1986) and Wilson and Kelling (1982) have encouraged police organisations in the US to experiment widely and substantial progress has been made. As Goldstein points out, police receptivity to this research has gone a long way to dispelling some of the 'police resistance to change' problems associated with police organisational reform (Goldstein 1990).

Although this signifies a change for the better, patterned stereotypes and defensive positions on both 'sides' still exist as an impediment to the realisation of police–academic partnerships based on sets of shared principles, processes and outcomes (Fleming 2005). Where police and academic partners do come together, as we have done in Nexus, there are a host of tensions and challenges that still need to be resolved and deliberated.

The Australian National University (ANU) and Victoria Police are committed to establishing partnerships where academics and practitioners come together to learn from one another. The enthusiasm for this partnership in Victoria Police is largely due to the positive support of its Chief Commissioner and her commitment to developing collaborative research projects in furtherance of police professionalism and evidence-based practice. What this requires is for academics and police to identify what these challenges are and how they can be addressed. And those who know best about daily challenges are the police at the coal face (Birzer 2002). Bringing academic and practitioners together has not always been easy. Practitioners and researchers have operated on different planets for a long time with police 'hold[ing] to a central ethic of distrust of the academic' (Young 1991: 38). As Foster points out:

> Researchers see the worlds they observe in relation to how that world ought to be, or what they would like it to be. Police officers, by contrast, more rooted in the imperfections and messiness of worlds as they find them, are both perhaps less aspirational or optimistic about the possibilities of change. ... (Foster 2003: 222)

Police are often 'unsympathetically portrayed as resistive, irrational and unreceptive to the questions and ideas generated by these external researchers' (Bradley 1992: 3; Punch 1975: 8). Academics are often considered 'too theoretical and not grounded in the real world' (Perez and Shtull 2002: 169–170). Greenhill (1981: 103) points out that the lack of 'cultural fit' between police and academics is relational, with police people who were not 'at risk'. These officers became 'champions' of the model and actively participated in the pilot and promoted it strongly within the Wodonga Police.

Roundtable discussions led by members of the Nexus Team were held regularly with the local police to talk through aspects of the model and new developments in the world of policing. Some of these discussions were somewhat robust, with police members articulating more conventional ways of acting and thinking about youth safety issues. But for the most part, these discussions provided the opportunity for shifts in thinking and a real engagement, with new possibilities for youth apparent. The involvement of the agency champions. The ongoing engagement between the local police and the ANU researchers was made possible by the (sometimes sceptical) support of the senior management at Wondonga who had been directed by Victoria Police to assist in meeting the objectives of the Nexus Project and more generally, the strategic plan of the organisation (Victoria Police 2003).

The process of measuring the contributions of the Nexus pilots is a complex one and it continues to be subject to discussion on the part on ANU and Victoria Police. It involves the continuing production of knowledge about whether, and to what extent, particular process and outcome level standards are being met. The establishment of such standards is protracted, involving continued reflection, deliberation and negotiation between pilot partners. Police partners, for example, may be most interested in establishing performance measures that are easily quantifiable, such as crime or victimisation rates. Other partners may be more interested in what police might perceive as 'intangible' outcomes, such as greater satisfaction with the process of working with other agencies or groupings. Measurement is complex because it involves acknowledging the unique objectives of each partner and establishing a joint way forward which assists each partner in addressing their individual dilemmas (Fleming 2006). In carrying out this phased approach to knowledge generation and 'ideas building', Nexus entails a process of mutual capacity building, not simply between the central partners, but also between all site-level partners involved in the design and implementation of the pilots.

Turning our attention back to the police–academic partnership, although the former function as knowledge generators in the course of their everyday work, such as in the area of criminal investigations, they have not traditionally been required to build their capacities as academic researchers. As such, Nexus has undertaken to assist members of Victoria Police to play an active role in choosing research methodologies and in developing ethics research protocols. This process has occurred largely in the form of 'coaching', whereby academic members of the Nexus team work with police members in discussing research requirements, devising research strategies and preparing the necessary paperwork, such as ethics applications.

In some cases, once a choice is made to utilise a particular research method, such as focus groups or surveys, police members themselves carry out the focus groups or administer surveys on their own. As discussed earlier, police-led focus groups occurred in relation to the youth safety project, and focus groups were also conducted for a different Nexus project on inter-agency responses to family violence. In a third Nexus project related to safety on the public transportation system, approximately eighty members of the Transit Safety Division from Victoria Police administered surveys focused on public perceptions of safety from a 'whole of

wanting to uphold mystifications of their 'unique' profession: 'Police often see sociological work as ill-informed and sociologists tend not to take seriously what the police do'. The difficulties of negotiating access has also been cited as a problem for academics (Holdaway 1982). There are widely held beliefs in police organisations that 'nobody understands police work that hasn't been on the street' (Perez and Shtull 2002: 170). In this context, Birzer notes:

> The partnership between [police] practitioners and researchers will have to more fully blossom into a meaningful collaboration if evolving police strategies are to become fully effective. If this is accomplished, it will assuredly result in a much more salubrious state for both researchers and practitioners when developing theory and practical protocol. This means that practitioners will increasingly have to view research as a foundation for policy and practice. Likewise, researchers will have to increasingly realise the multiple realities that exist beyond the ivory tower and that by tapping into the rich experience base of practitioners is one avenue to more fully understand the multivariate world of policing. (Birzer 2002: 156)

Birzer (2002: 156) suggests that there is more to a successful police–university partnership than simply greater and easier *access* to the world of the other partner and to their unique forms of knowledge and capacity. Police should not simply be viewed, or view themselves, as simply enlightening researchers about the realities of policing. Rather, their knowledge and that of the researcher should provide a foundation on which to build a collaborative generation of new, actionable knowledge for policing that can be validated and diffused. It is important to support the identity of police members—regardless of rank—as agents of change and to assist them in enhancing their capacity as knowledge workers and ideas generators.

Police–academic partnerships need to be embedded through processes that entail a central role for police in the identification of research problems, the framing of research questions, as well as in the design and evaluation of intervention projects. In this vein, the aim of the Nexus project is to engage the police directly in a process for generating innovative ideas about ways to mobilise the capacities and knowledge of external groups in governing security. In the Nexus project, police are supported, for example, in developing new ideas for exploring opportunities to sit back in certain policing arrangements, so that other groups are able to play an active role in the governance of security. These explorations require radical rethinks for individual police officers and of the public police organisation. However, these rethinks are informed by the changes in the field of policing that these police officers have to acknowledge and address in their daily working lives.

In giving effect to this collaborative notion of knowledge production and praxis, PAR is a strong and relevant method from which to move forward. While there are very few cases of the use of PAR with police, Geva and Shem-Tov's (2002) work with the Israeli Police is a documented example. Geva and Shem-Tov are aware of the importance of aligning the research methodology with the outcomes of the research (i.e., more community oriented and collaborative policing practices). However, methodologies are also informed by theory. The underlying assumption that police officers are social agents demands a research approach that draws upon and expands the knowledge base of individual officers and encourages more reflective activity.

The PAR approach to research in this context is one that we have used in a variety of ways in the Nexus project.

The nexus project in Victoria

There is considerable variation across the various issues we are involved in as part of the Nexus collaboration with Victoria Police, but we apply the same phased approach to the process of gathering knowledge and generating new ideas. Wood and Marks describe these phases elsewhere (Wood and Marks 2006; Wood 2006: 230). In summary they are:

- 'mapping' forms of knowledge and capacity currently deployed in governing a security problem;
- conducting an in-depth research module on aspects of existing security governance arrangements;
- designing a new nexus arrangement to be piloted;
- implementing and reviewing the nexus pilot.

We will explore these phases in relation to one of the issue areas, youth safety in a rural town of Victoria.

Youth safety

The "mapping" process identifies various agencies and groups that play a role in the governance of a particular problem. Victoria Police identified youth safety as an area that required more innovative understandings and interventions as part of a broader safety delivery network. In this project, Nexus team members from the ANU—with the assistance of Victoria Police and local partner organisations—mapped those agencies in the relevant area that played a role in youth service delivery; say for example, youth justice, mental health, family and community services and education. The team interpreted 'safety' and 'security' very broadly, deferring to the perceptions of different agencies with respect to the needs of young people and the factors that contributed to delinquency, crime or other issues of health and well-being. We gleaned these perceptions through analyses of official documentation and through conversations with agency representatives about the project and its potential directions. As a result, the 'map' developed did not focus simply on the place and role of criminal justice agencies in the governance of youth safety.

Our 'mapping' suggested that existing networks of youth service delivery provided little opportunity for young people to exercise agency. They rarely played a role in defining issues of safety and/or devising initiatives and programs aimed at addressing those issues. The police were always the fallback agency when youth felt at risk or acted in risky ways. There were few organisational structures and processes focused on the beliefs and situated knowledge of young people themselves. Based on this assessment, we conducted in-depth research with young people aimed at exploring how they think about security, and in this context, the assistance they perceived to be available to them. An ANU academic and a youth worker representing the local government (a key project partner) conducted focus groups with a sample of school children from grades six, seven and eight over a period of

several months. Two schools, one primary and one secondary, were identified as pilot schools.

At the same time we wanted to understand the 'webs of meanings' that informed police officers' understandings of youth issues, and to place their practices in the context of such underlying beliefs. Focus groups with local police officers were facilitated by police members from the Nexus Team and the transcripts were analysed by Nexus Team members. The qualitative research with the young people and with the police supplemented our initial map of 'safety partners' by providing us with a richer perspective on how security was imagined and governed beyond the immediate realm of the police and the criminal justice system (Marks and Wood 2008).

The mapping and research phases led to a document informing the design of a new model to be piloted by police and their safety partners. Inspired by the core principles and procedures of a local capacity governance model in South Africa (see Shearing 2001), the goal of this model is to mobilise the knowledge and capacity of young people in identifying and addressing safety and well-being issues that they see as priorities in their everyday lives. The model places young people and youth agencies at the centre of a problem-solving process and offers a process and set of guidelines (see below) for structuring deliberative problem solving around safety and well-being issues that young people are experiencing in their everyday contexts of home, school and the broader community. The role of various agencies and community groups in this process is not to steer the agendas of the problem-solving groups, but rather to make themselves available—through nominated 'agency champions'—to be mobilised on a case-by-case basis when their unique knowledge and resources are relevant in addressing an issue. As stressed by one of the school principals, this model should be understood more broadly as a governance model, or perhaps more aptly, a 'microgovernance' model (see Burris 2004). The model has the potential to address a range of social and welfare issues relevant to young people and is designed to complement and supplement other governance processes in Victorian schools that are increasingly oriented towards restorative approaches to behaviour management (see generally Wood and Marks 2006; Marks and Wood 2008).

A weekend workshop was held with the young people involved, representatives of key youth service providers, Nexus members and two local police officers to discuss the model and to 'test out' model processes. One of the aims of this workshop was to explore means of aligning competing worldviews in order to identify a shared language and shared meanings so that an effective network to deal with local youth safety issues could be created. However, the main objective of this workshop was to test out the youth-directed problem-solving model that had been shaped by the discussions that took place in the focus groups.

The two police officers present had the opportunity to share their views of the role of the police within the model with the participants, where the possibility exists that they are not necessarily primary players. Concerns expressed by the police and other adult participants at the workshop around mandatory disclosure and the importance of institutional rules and laws led to the development of a set of guidelines. The guidelines are one of the core components of the model, which was then piloted in the two Wodonga schools. After the workshop, the officers spoke to participants about how they had been exposed to a completely new way of understanding youth safety issues and also had the opportunity to meet young

journey' perspective. In such cases, these research processes have provided a learning experience for police members, honing the skills required in extracting the knowledge of particular groupings and in understanding different perspectives on security and its governance.

Within Victoria Police and in many other English speaking country police agencies, there is a growing interest in police officers furthering their education (Lee and Punch 2006), including obtaining post-graduate university degrees and undertaking leadership and management training. PAR-inspired projects like Nexus—and its youth safety project—are intended to complement the capacity-building methodologies found in formal university training or other forms of learning 'in the classroom'. In practical settings, Nexus centres on police members building their capacities as field researchers and ultimately as 'coaches' of field research in their own right. The assumption is that this new cohort of police researchers will coach other police members in this and other research methodologies. A similar process has occurred in relation to the development of ethics protocols. In some cases, ethics protocols have been developed jointly with academic and police members of the Nexus team, while in the case of the transit safety project, the protocol for the public perceptions survey was developed entirely within the police organisation.

Challenges to collaborative knowledge production

The above discussion sought to illustrate key links between the methodological practices of Nexus and its underlying theory of police reform and police cultural change. In this section, we will outline several operational challenges that Nexus has encountered in relation to organisational structures, police procedures and general process and management issues. These of course can be discussed in a general context as issues associated with working with operational law enforcement agencies generally (Fleming 2005). Police organisations are pivotal institutions in our society, performing wide ranging functions in an effort to meet the increasingly high expectations of the community. Traditionally, police organisations have worked alone, reacting to crisis and public pressure and being assessed by governments and communities accordingly. Their research has traditionally been the province of their own research and policy units and primarily concerned with improving internal management with a focus on administration, surveys and the occasional special project.

The research capacities of police organisations have changed considerably in recent years. Victoria Police in particular have expressed their commitment to research through their extensive involvement in ARC-funded projects to which they contribute significant financial and in-kind resources. Extending their previous commitment to 'local priority policing' and problem-oriented solutions, they have recently devised a new set of service delivery principles that stress not only the importance of research as foundational to strategy development, but also requirement to give members of all ranks the space to be creative thinkers and innovators. Such efforts, however, exist alongside the traditional requirements of public policing agencies generally to meet objectives and desired outcomes that often have little to do with research.

Fleming reminds us that police organisations are primarily conflict-driven organisations. They are necessarily pragmatic and task-oriented and community expectations demand that this is so. There are difficulties involved for police organisations negotiating with researchers new theories, new concepts and new ways of doing business, when there is 'an ever present, urgent need to provide immediate relief from threatening problems' (Fleming 2005). Policing is an 'extraordinarily complex endeavour' (Goldstein 1990) and there is always a tension between unresolved priorities and the consequences of demands for change and reform (Fleming and Rhodes 2005).

In today's police organisations the importance of accountability, performance management and managerialist strategies generally means there is a strong emphasis on maximising performance and minimising cost. Measurement and meeting key performance indicators will directly or indirectly impact on research initiatives. Resource allocation and research activity may well be determined by what is measurable. Staff turnover in police organisations is also an issue. If a project leader or senior practitioner in the project is transferred or promoted, for example, it is not always a given that that person will be replaced with some one who shares a similar commitment to the project (Fleming 2005, 2006). These and other challenges to police partnerships of any kind are applicable to all police organisations, but it would be a mistake to assume that working with one police organisation is the same as working with another. Structural and organisational characteristics and leadership styles differ; contractual arrangements will be different and the demographics of a city shape and determine the way in which police do business in their various communities. Most importantly, in the context of research—and this is true across all police organisations—the support and overall commitment of the chief police officer is crucial if the project is to be sustained. This has certainly been true of Nexus and Victoria Police where standing governance committees such as the Organisational Development Standing Committee monitors, supports and acts as a high level 'think tank' for innovations and projects such as Nexus. New governance arrangements, enacted through bodies such as this, indicate a commitment to a move away from traditional, top-down decision making and planning processes. More participatory, outcome-based approaches to management in Victoria Police is important ground-ing for increasing the base of critical thinkers in the organisation and for engaging with a range of agencies, including academic institutions, that have an interest in making policing 'smarter'.

Notwithstanding the support of the Chief Commissioner in Victoria, however, there were many moments in the Nexus project where disagreements and issues arose between the police (particularly at the local level) and ANU researchers. In the youth safety project, for example, local police officers questioned whether time spent designing the model was worthwhile considering the organisation's limited resources and the more pressing problems of dealing with youth at risk. Others remained unconvinced about the commitment and capacity of network partners. These arguments led to renewed discussions about the objective of Nexus, how it relates to Victoria Police's strategic plans and what the benefits are likely to be for the community and for the local police. The differences were resolved and the model has been successfully introduced into the three schools (including the initial two pilot locations) and the local police have committed to their continued involvement in the pilot. Such deliberations thus proved fruitful for different members of Victoria Police involved in the project, as they prompted a rethinking of accepted business and practices within the organisation, and opened up new spaces for reflection. Efforts to diffuse and tailor the youth safety model to a different state jurisdiction are being initiated by the local police there.

Police may remain sceptical of researchers even while the project is in progress. It is therefore important that academics and police jointly negotiate appropriate styles and tools for communicating and working together. The ways in which this is done will be contingent on the organisation, the project and those involved. In running the Police focus groups with local police on youth safety issues, for example, the facilitators from Victoria Police were often asked about their own views and experiences as police officers. The shared identity of the focus group participants and the facilitators as police officers allowed for immediacy and the questioning of traditions between 'insiders'.

The nature of police work has the potential to limit officers' capacity to be proactive and innovative agents of cultural change. Police organisations are often crisis driven and time for reflection is not a priority (Fleming 2005). They remain hierarchical organisations despite attempts at more participatory management practices and the views of rank-and-file officers are often overlooked in planning and decision-making processes (Fleming 2005; Wuestewald et al. 2006). Police are also pragmatists who want to get things done in ways that are known to 'work'; experimenting is often seen as resource wasting. This, and uncertain outcomes, can be discomforting to police given their high political profile (Bayley 1994; Fleming 2004).

Building good relationships between researchers and academics invariably require some readjustment on the part of both parties. From our perspective, such partnerships are nonetheless worth pursuing and essential to building the capacity of police members—regardless of rank—to realise their potential as change agents. For change in policing to occur from the 'bottom-up', it is essential that *all* police members are seen as change agents and capable of being reflective about their beliefs and their practices.

Collaborative projects like Nexus must ensure that the police emerge from such projects with a sense of achievement and with the knowledge that they can contribute to change and innovation through partnerships and by designing and participating in new public safety institutions and networks (Marenin 2004).

Conclusion

Although appeals to culture are often made in attempts to explain reform failure (Fleming and Rhodes 2006: 193), we have explicated a view of culture that suggests the potential for *all* police members to be change agents. Although the practices of police are shaped by the 'webs of meanings' surrounding their situated lives, they are not determined by them. They do have the ability to reflect on the relationships between their situated beliefs, knowledge and practices and to adjust those in accordance with their environment. If we accept this view, then 'culture' needs to be understood at both the macro and the micro level as police officers individually interpret, respond to and act upon their external and organisational environments.

We have suggested that cultural change may take place in small steps rather than great leaps. Change occurs as individual police officers at both the top and the bottom come to see the value in new ways of thinking and acting and are willing and indeed, empowered, to challenge established practices. The possibility for this to occur is greatest when the agency of police officers is recognised and when they are actively involved in knowledge building processes. The Nexus project in Victoria has explored these possibilities through a range of initiatives and projects.

This paper has identified some conditions under which collaborative research partnerships between academics and police (regardless of rank) may be established. It has suggested a PAR orientation, with an emphasis on interaction, planning, reflection and observation that challenges existing bureaucratic traditions, and allows officers to be exposed to research in a collegial collaborative environment. It provides a strong intellectual foundation for capacity building and innovative practice. If capacity building is undertaken with sufficient numbers of police officers in different parts of the organisation, their individual contributions can be pulled together and serve as exemplars of innovation.

However, a PAR approach on its own will not automatically deliver the desired outcomes. As this paper has suggested, the police organisation's leadership and commitment to the project is crucial. The phased approach to the process of gathering knowledge and generating new ideas (i.e., mapping, researching, designing and implementation) will not proceed well if senior management is not supportive and/or prepared to provide the resources required for such a project.

Other challenges to collaborative research between researchers and academics stem from the nature of police organisations themselves. Police organisations have a high political profile, pursue multiple objectives, are primarily reactive, and constantly under pressure to meet the high expectations of various communities and performance management criteria. Traditionally, such organisations have had research units, primarily concerned with internal research reports and data collection. It is, and should be considered, a challenge for academics to adapt to this environment. For some police managers, the short-term political fix is often preferable to the often long-term requirements of research projects. The allocation of precious resources to what are often perceived as uncertain and indeterminate outcomes and the need to focus on performance measurement requirements at all levels can serve as constraints on a willingness to participate in such endeavours. Communication will be the key.

Clearly, as the paper has argued, police and academics alike will need to adapt to their relatively new environments and endeavour to create collegial and deliberative spaces within which collaborative projects can thrive.

Perhaps the greatest challenge lies in providing the opportunity and the environment that empowers *all* participants to reflect on the 'webs of meaning' and beliefs that shape and determine their behaviour and attitudes. In that reflection we would hope that participants may adjust those beliefs when confronted with innovative practice and new ideas regardless of where that innovation has come from. In doing so they are individually capable of changing their working environment and in effect, becoming a '*change agent*'.

Rhodes has suggested that academics can provide multiple narratives to policymakers and practitioners with a view to enabling them to see things differently (Rhodes 2006: 31). The Nexus project represents one attempt at establishing a new approach to collaborative research. In providing these multiple narratives, the project has endeavoured to connect the 'situated' knowledge and capacities of police officers with those of academics committed to innovation in policing, and to the governance of safety and security more generally.

Acknowledgements

The authors are grateful to David Bradley, Peter Grabosky, Tess Walsh, and an anonymous reviewer for their constructive comments. The Nexus Project was made possible through the financial support of the Australian Research Council (Project ID LP0348682). This paper was written when Jennifer served as a Fellow at the Regulatory Institutions Network, Australian National University.

References

Bayley, D., 1994. *Police for the Future*. New York: Oxford University Press.

Bayley, D., 2008. "Police reform: Who done it?". *Policing and Society*, 8 (1), 8–19.

Bevir, M. and Rhodes, R.A.W., 2006. *Governance Stories*. London: Routledge.

Birzer, M.L., 2002. "Writing partnerships between police practitioners and researchers". *Police Practice and Research: An International Journal*, 3 (2), 149–156.

Bradley, D., 1992. Universities and Policing: A Research Based View. Paper given at the Annual Conference of the Australasian Association of Criminal Justice Educators, Goulbourn, NSW: Australian Police Staff College, Charles Sturt University.

Bradley, D., Nixon, C., and Marks, M., 2006. "What works, what doesn't work and what looks promising in police research networks". *In*: J. Fleming and J. Wood, eds. *Fighting Crime Together: The Challenges of Policing and Security Networks*. Sydney: University of New South Wales Press, 170–194.

Bullock, K. and Tilley, N., 2003. *Crime Reduction and Problem-oriented Policing*. Collumpton: Willan Publishing.

Burris, S., 2004. "Governance, microgovernance and health". *Temple Law Review*, 77, 335–359.

Fleming, J., 2004. "Les liaisons dangereuses: Relations between police commissioners and their political masters", *Australian Journal of Public Administration*, 63 (3), September, pp. 60–74.

Fleming, J., 2005. Research Relationships with Operational Law Enforcement Agencies. Paper given at the Safety, Crime and Justice: Data and Policy Conference at the Australian Institute of Criminology, Canberra, June.

Fleming, J., 2006. "Working through networks: The challenges of partnership policing". *In*: J. Fleming and J. Wood, eds. *Fighting Crime Together: The Challenges of Policing and Security Networks*. Sydney: University of New South Wales Press, 87–115.

Fleming, J. & Rhodes, R.A.W., 2006. "Bureaucracy, contracts and networks: The unholy trinity and the police", *Australian and New Zealand Journal of Criminology*, 38 (2), August, pp. 192–205.

Foote Whyte, W., 1991. *Participatory Action Research*. Newbury Park: Sage.

Foote Whyte, W., Greenwood, D.J., and Lazes, P., 1991. "Participatory action research: Through practice to science in social research". *In*: W. Foote Whyte, ed. *Participatory Action Research*. Newbury Park: Sage, 19–55.

Foster, J., 2003. "Police cultures". *In*: T. Newburn, ed. *Handbook of Policing*. Collumpton: Willan, 196–227.

Geva, R. and Shem-Tov, O., 2002. "Setting up community policing centres: Participatory action research in decentralized policing services". *Police Practice and Research: An International Journal*, 3 (3), 189–200.

Goldstein, H., 1990. *Problem-oriented Policing*. New York: McGraw Hill.

Greenhill, N., 1981. "The value of sociology in policing". *In*: D. Pope and N. Weiner, eds. *Modern Policing*. London: Croom Held.

Grundy, S., 1986. "Action research and human interests", in: Emery, M. & Long, P., eds. *Symposium May 22–23, 1986*, Research Network of the Australian Association of Adult Education.

Holdaway, S., 1982. "'An inside job': A case study of covert research on police". *In*: M. Bulmer, ed. *Social Research Ethics*. Basingstoke: Macmillan.

Holter, I.M. and Schwartz-Barcott, D., 1993. "Action research: What is it? How has it been used, and how can it be used in nursing?". *Journal of Advanced Nursing*, 18, 296–304.

Jordan, S., 2003. "Who stole my methodology? Co-opting PAR". *Globalisation, Socieities and Education*, 1 (2), 185–200.

Lee, M. and Punch, M., 2006. *Policing by Degrees: Essex Police Officers' Experience of University Education*. Groningen: de Hondsrug Pers.

Marenin, O., 2004. "Guest editor's introduction". *Police Practice and Research: An International Journal*, 5 (4/5), 299–300.

Marks, M., 2004. "Researching police transformation". *British Journal of Criminology*, 44, 866–888.

Marks, M. and Wood, J., 2008. "Generating youth safety from below: Situating young people at the centre of knowledge based policing". *In*: T. Williamson, ed. *The Handbook of Knowledge Based Policing: Current Conceptions and Future Directions*. West Sussex: John Wiley and Sons.

McKernan, J., 1991. *Curriculum Action Research*. London: Kogan Page.

McTaggart, R., 1991. "Principles of participatory action research". *Adult Education Quarterly*, 41 (3), 170.

Perez, D. and Shtull, P., 2002. "Police research and practice: An American perspective". *Police Practice and Research: An International Journal*, 3 (3), 169–187.

Poole, M., Mansfield, R., and Gould Williams, J., 2006. "Public and private sector managers over 20 years: A test of the 'convergence thesis'". *Public Administration*, 84 (4), 1051–1076.

Punch, M., 1975. "Research and the police". *In*: J. Brown and G. Howes, eds. *The Police and the Community*. Boston: Lexington Press.

Reiner, R., 1992. *The Politics of the Police*. New York: Harvester Wheatsheaf.

Reuss-Ianni, E. and Ianni, F., 1983. "Street cops and management cops: The two cultures of policing". *In*: M. Punch, ed. *Control in Police Organization*. Cambridge, MA: MIT Press.

Rhodes, R.A.W., 2006. "The sour laws of network governance". *In*: J. Fleming and J. Wood, eds. *Fighting Crime Together: The Challenges of Policing and Security Networks*. Sydney: University of New South Wales Press, 15–34.

Shearing, C., 2001. "Transforming security: A South African experiment. *In*: H. Strang and J. Braithwaite, eds. *Restorative Justice and Civil Society*. Cambridge: Cambridge University Press, 14–34.

Sklansky, D., 2007. "Seeing blue: Police reform, occupational culture and cognitive burn-in", in: O'Neill, M., Marks, M. & Singh, A-M., eds. *Police Occupational Culture: New Debates and Directions,* Amsterdam, The Netherlands: Elsevier.

Skolnick, J. and Bayley, D., 1986. *The New Blue Line: Police Innovations in Six American Cities*. New York: Free Press.

Victoria Police. 2003. *The Way Ahead: Strategic Plan 2003–2008,* Victoria Police, Melbourne.

Wilson, J. & Kelling, G., 1982. "Broken windows", *The Atlantic Monthly*, March, pp. 29–38.

Wood, J., 2000. *Reinventing Governance: A Study of Transformations in the Ontario Provincial Police*. Doctoral dissertation. Centre of Criminology, University of Toronto.

Wood, J., 2006. "Research and innovation in the field of security: A nodal governance view". *In*: J. Wood and B. Dupont, eds. *Democracy, Society and the Governance of Security*. Cambridge: Cambridge University Press, 217–240.

Wood, J. & Marks, M., 2006. "Nexus governance: Building new ideas for security and justice", in: Slakmon, C., Rocha Machado, M. & Cruz Bottini, P., eds. *Novas Direções na Governança da Justiça e da Segurança,* Ministry of Justice of Brazil, United Nations Development

Programme—Brazil, and the School of Law of the Getulio Vargas Foundation—São Paulo, Brasília-D.F., pp. 719–738.

Wuestewald, T., Steinheider, B. & Bayerl, P., 2006. From the Bottom-Up: Sharing Leadership in a Police Agency'. Paper presented at the Police Reform from the Bottom-Up Conference, 12–13 September, University of California, Berkeley.

Young, M., 1991. *An Inside Job: Policing and Police Culture in Britain*. Oxford: The Clarendon Press.

Research for the front lines

David Thacher

Public Policy and Urban Planning, University of Michigan, MI, USA

It is a truism in the sociology of science that scientific knowledge bears the imprint of particular perspectives, interests, and values. In social science, it is especially common to find that research serves the needs of managers and policymakers better than it serves the needs of front-line workers. This paper analyzes the traces of that tendency in police research. By examining three features of front-line police work (the need to improve programs rather than assess them, the need to attend to an enormous number of situational details, and the need to cope with ambiguous and contradictory goals), I argue that common approaches to police research address managerial and policy concerns better than line officer concerns. To help rectify this imbalance, I discuss three variations on an alternative research strategy that deserves more emphasis in policy-oriented police research—one grounded in concrete case study description and analysis that often eschews causal generalizations.

It is a truism in the sociology of science that all knowledge bears the imprint of particular perspectives, interests, and values, so that any particular scientific program serves the priorities of some groups rather than others. From a normative viewpoint it is not even clear that this influence is always nefarious. Aristotelians once valorized a disinterested approach to scientific inquiry, but the idea that knowledge *should* strive to advance specific human interests is at least as old as Francis Bacon, who insisted that 'it is by witness of works, rather than by logic or even observation, that truth is revealed and established.' As Bacon himself went on to note: 'It follows that the improvement of man's mind and the improvement of his lot are one and the same thing' (Farrington 1948: 93). From this perspective, scientists' views about what it means to 'improve man's lot'—and about whose lot in particular they should try to improve—unavoidably influence the scientific agenda.

To claim a connection between truth and (non-cognitive) values is faintly scandalous for the obvious reasons, but at the general level I have invoked this claim it is impossible to deny. At minimum, no one doubts that the questions scientists ask are legitimately shaped by human interests, so which truths they discover (if not the very fact that those truths are true) depends on the interests to which they and those who influence their work are committed (e.g., Taylor 1985). That conclusion is so undeniable that the distinguished and decidedly non-radical philosopher of science William Newton-Smith (1984) dubbed it 'Boring Interest Thesis 1', and it is amply illustrated by agricultural and health research that serves first-world needs more effectively than third-world needs (e.g., by developing cures for diseases associated with obesity and old age, and by emphasizing research about the impact that expensive capital inputs, such as mechanization, chemical fertilizers, and pesticides, have on agricultural yields) (Tiles 1987: 295).

However obvious, the point always bears repeating in a context like this one because it raises two further issues that deserve attention. First, while the bare fact that interests shape the development of scientific knowledge is obvious, the specific ways in which they do so can be subtle, so in any particular context we should investigate those influences with care. Second, the fact that scientific research typically serves some interests better than others implies that we should evaluate any scientific research agenda partly based on whether it addresses the *right* mix of human interests. That question is a matter of ethics and political theory. It raises questions about the claim that different groups and interests ought to have on social development—specifically, on the development of relevant knowledge—or, put differently, it raises questions about the extent to which there is a social interest in satisfying the knowledge interests that each group has.

This paper examines these two issues in the context of police research in order to ask how such research can and should serve line officer priorities, and what exactly that imperative would mean. My thesis is that the dominant approach to police research in the US today embodies the interests and perspectives of police management and unduly neglects the interests and perspective of line officers. To make this case, I will describe three distinctive features of the line officer perspective, analyze the kind of research that is relevant to each, and note the limitations of dominant research models in this regard.

Research for policy or for practice?

Policing is hardly the only field where research tends to neglect the needs of front-line practitioners. David Laws and Martin Rein describe this tendency in an analysis of knowledge for policy and practice that draws its major examples from education.

Laws and Rein (1997) begin by sketching a three-part model of the relationship between knowledge and action. Many analyses of usable knowledge rely on a dyadic framework—one that distinguishes between knowledge and action and asks how the former can serve the latter—but Laws and Rein argue that in fact at least three distinct perspectives can be identified: the perspective of front-line practitioners who deliver services directly to clients; the perspective of policymakers and upper managers who define agency goals through their interactions with the political process; and the perspective of researchers who attempt to develop knowledge that is both useful and generalizable (1997: 53).

In Laws and Rein's account, the 'practice' leg of the triad is particularly susceptible to neglect. They illustrate that pattern with a case study of Michigan's initiative to reform the way reading was taught and evaluated in the mid-1980s. On their account, the reform effort ultimately had at most a modest effect on teaching practice, and they attribute that failure partly to the neglect of the front-line practitioner perspective in the research program the reform was based on. Teachers rarely met with researchers and had no opportunity to discuss their practice problems with them. Instead, they received brief handouts of research findings or listened to summaries of the findings from administrators.

Policing scholars will undoubtedly find this basic pattern familiar, inasmuch as police research seems to be developed in interaction with policymakers and upper management. Examples from many other fields might be cited. What drives this common pattern, in which the research-policy dyad crowds out the perspective of practice?

Program assessment and program improvement

Laws and Rein themselves do not answer this question directly, but they suggest one aspect of a possible answer in their discussion of evaluation research. On their view, evaluation research as currently practiced emphasizes questions that address policy concerns more readily than practice concerns:

> Evaluation research is sponsored by oversight agencies asking a different question than that of the practitioners they are evaluating. These agencies face policy concerns about how to allocate scarce resources among different strategies for dealing with a problem. This is very different from the practice question of how to make a particular strategy work. Where practice asks how to act and how best to fix a program within the limits of what you know, what you have, and what you can get agreement on, policy asks whether it is worth supporting the program at all. (Laws and Rein 1997: 53)

Thus, for an officer assigned to foot patrol, the major question is not whether foot patrol works but how best to carry it out. The same is true for an officer assigned to directed patrol, community engagement, problem solving, hot spots gun policing, order maintenance, traffic duty, or any other policing task.

This front-line interest in refining and expanding the possibilities of practice contributes an essential ingredient of intelligent policing. Where the policy interest described by Laws and Rein motivates rational choice among existing alternatives, the practice interest motivates the generation of new alternatives to evaluate in the first place. The essential role of this second task in truly rational choice is often overlooked, but Robert Nozick has described it lucidly:

> A choice of action is made among alternatives. Better choosing among the existing alternatives is one way to improve the results. Another way is to widen the range of alternatives to include promising new ones. An imaginative construction of a new alternative, heretofore not thought of, might be what makes the greatest improvement possible. ... In some situations, much more might be gained by generating new alternatives and choosing among them roughly than by choosing finely and with perfect discrimination among the existing alternatives only. The second best among the new alternatives might be far superior to the very best among the old ones. It is as important to cultivate the relevant imaginative powers as to sharpen the discriminative ones. Without the exploration and testing of other imaginative possibilities, the procedures of rationality, by focusing only upon the *given* alternatives, will be myopic. (1993: 173)

In this respect, Laws and Rein's 'practice' interest contributes an essential ingredient to rational policing. It cannot be reduced to or replaced by the policy interest in determining whether to support a strategy at all.

The 'what works' movement in police research, although it has had many worthwhile effects, tends to obscure this distinction because it emphasizes only one aspect of instrumental rationality—the evaluation of existing alternatives to determine their relative merits. In particular, the randomized field experiments that some policing scholars view as the only truly compelling source of knowledge often provide no information that can be used to improve practice, and as a result they contribute nothing to Nozick's second prong of instrumental rationality. Enthusiasts for randomized controlled trials sometimes dismiss this kind of concern as anti-scientific sentimentality, but in doing so they display their ignorance of the best scientific literature about field experiments. Economist James Heckman, who won the Nobel Prize for his contributions to econometric methodology, has repeatedly stressed the weakness of evaluation practice I am describing. For example, in joint work with economist Jeffrey Smith, he wrote:

> Policymakers often do not care solely about whether or not a particular program "works" in the sense of having benefits that exceed its costs. When programs fail, it is important to understand why they do not work. Without this information, which is not available from typical black-box experimental analyses, the only alternative open to politicians is to eliminate one program completely and start fresh with another. (Heckman and Smith 1995: 94)

Heckman and Smith conclude with a harsh assessment of field experiment practice: 'The end result of a research program based on experiments is just a list of programs that 'work' and 'don't work', but no understanding of why they succeed or fail' (1995: 108). Here I mean to emphasize that the negative consequences of this gap bear especially on front-line practitioners. In a division of labor that assigns the 'assessment' prong of instrumental rationality to policymakers and the 'invention' prong to practitioners, black-box evaluations serve policy needs but not practice needs.

It is not inevitable that evaluation research will address policy questions better than practice questions. To fill the knowledge gaps they identify, Heckman and Smith advocate for theoretically grounded experimental and non-experimental quantitative analyses that attempt to estimate invariant structural models. A complementary approach, particularly relevant for fields that lack the kind of formal theory that invariant structural models demand, relies on qualitative observation and analysis. That approach has been emphasized by the Manpower Demonstration Research Corporation—arguably the leading institutional expert on randomized social experiments in the world—which now incorporates a qualitative component in its policy evaluations as a matter of course (Sherwood and Doolittle 2003). These descriptive examinations of program operations not only make it possible to assess program components at a more fine-grained level; by providing detailed descriptions of program operations, they also contribute to the grounded use of imagination to identify new possibilities of practice (cf. Mead 2004; Laws and Rein 1997: 52). In that way, they provide information that practitioners can use to debug and improve ineffective programs.

In keeping with the points made at the outset of this paper, the problem Laws and Rein identify is not that common approaches to evaluation research generate incorrect conclusions. It is that only a subset of possible questions receives attention in the first place—the subset that addresses policy concerns rather the subset that addresses practice concerns (or more precisely the aspects of policy and practice concerns that I have just highlighted). An alternative approach to program evaluation would supplement attention to policy questions about the impact of a program in its current manifestation with attention to practice questions about how that program might be improved. Such an approach would treat programs as continually evolving, reshaping them in response to emerging assessments of program components and of specific actions taken in the program's name. An important version of this approach relies on case description and on reflection on program operations, which can not only assess the effectiveness of existing programs but also help to identify and imagine new programs. In this way evaluative questions about what works (the policy question) are supplemented by diagnostic questions about how to make programs work better (the practice question). These contrasting approaches to program evaluation might be called *evaluation-as-assessment* and *evaluation-as-debugging*.[1]

The desire to evaluate the effectiveness of existing programs does not simply ignore this second task: It may undermine it, in at least two ways. First, excessive zeal for evaluation-as-assessment can make efforts spent to use research to help generate new alternatives seem wasteful. 'It is too easy, and tempting, for rationality to become a device that views the imaginative generation and testing of new possibilities as irrational,' Nozick observes. 'The process of exploring new opportunities will be imperfect and apparently wasteful; many of the possibilities explored will turn out to be useless. Yet rationality must be tolerant of this and not demand guarantees of success in advance' (1993: 173). Second, excessive zeal for evaluation-as-assessment can stifle innovation by encouraging premature evaluations of the minor modifications made in the process of debugging a program. Because many policing scholars draw an analogy with medicine to analyze the form their research should take, it may be helpful to consider an example of this danger from surgery—arguably a better field to compare with policing than the field of pharmaceutical research (the most commonly discussed example of medical research in policing literature) because policing and surgery both rely on complex and hard-to-standardize interventions.[2] Researchers in surgery have repeatedly raised concerns that premature evaluation will stifle innovation; as one group explained:

> RCTs [randomized controlled trials] consume substantial resources and are therefore not justified for some questions about small modifications to treatments. Surgical technique typically progresses via such modifications, which individually are unlikely to produce detectable benefits, but which collectively may do so. During the historical progression through hand washing via the use of antiseptics to the aseptic surgical environment, the change in morbidity from surgical infection was huge, but the increment with each step was small enough to allow persistent scepticism. Small randomised trials of components of this progression showed no benefit. If a positive RCT were required before adopting each small improvement, most would be rejected, and progress would be slowed. RCTs are appropriate where a clear, clinically important choice exists between contrasting alternatives. For smaller changes, an industrial paradigm may be needed. (McCulloch et al. 2002: 1449, citations omitted)[3]

Similar concerns have been raised about complex policing innovations such as problem-oriented policing and community policing, as scholars have warned that premature attempts to 'evaluate' these reforms may stifle attempts to debug and further develop them (e.g., Kennedy and Moore 1995).

In these respects, the 'industrial paradigm' (McCulloch et al. 2002: 1449) embodied in evaluation-as-debugging provides a necessary complement to the 'what works' judgments offered by evaluation-as-assessment. Note that the point here is not simply Donald Campbell's injunction to 'evaluate no program until it is proud'; it is that evaluation itself can be used as a tool to help make a program more worthy of pride. However, it can only do that if it goes beyond black-box experimental designs.

This analysis suggests one important and readily recognizable way in which practice concerns differ from policy concerns, and it is clear how dominant approaches to policy research have a greater affinity for the latter than the former. At least two other differences between policy concerns and practice concerns reinforce this tendency to bring research and policy together at the expense of practice.

Situated knowledge and universal knowledge

Epistemologists (particularly feminist philosophers of science) have stressed a distinction between situated knowledge and universal knowledge. Very roughly, one aspect of the distinction involves the difference between features of the world for which knowledge is closely tied to the identity, situation, and background understandings of the knower and those that can be discerned in the same way by anyone (Diamond 1991). Another involves the difference between contextualized knowledge of particular events and universal generalizations not bound by the conditions that prevail in particular times and places (Toulmin 1990).

The second kind of knowledge dominates contemporary scientific practice. Indeed, many scientists and philosophers insist that anonymous, generalizable knowledge is the *only* type of knowledge that can truly be called scientific. This approach to scientific inquiry emphasizes abstract information gathered using standardized processes that do not depend on the identity, background abilities, or sentiments of the investigator. It is anonymous in the sense that it is accessible to, and it has the same meaning for, any observer (Nagel 1974),[4] and it is generalizable in the sense that it pursues timeless truths that hold across a wide range of contexts.

For present purposes, the important point is that the existence of such knowledge may serve the interests of some groups in society better than others. Granted the existence of impersonal, generalizable knowledge—abstract generalizations that can be stated and understood without regard to the personal characteristics or background understandings of the speaker or hearer—we should still ask: 'For what groups is it useful or desirable that there be such impersonal, anonymous, generalizable knowledge?' Cora Diamond illustrated this concern with a playful distinction between tourists and natives:

> Take what one might call tourist knowledge: the capacity to reply to the tourist who wants to know, what is in the soup? Is this handmade? What time does the tourbus leave? Where is the post office? And how much is airmail postage to the United States? In Northern European countries that knowledge is available in highly impersonal forms: the practices of impersonal knowledge there are all that "we" might want. As we tourists travel south, things change, the practices of impersonal knowledge-accumulation are less developed. (1991: 1011)

Tourist knowledge is authentically objective knowledge, but such knowledge serves the needs of some groups better than others: 'What the right answer is to 'Where is the post office?' is independent of the particular person who answers, but there being practice in handling such questions is useful to tourists rather than natives' (1991: 1011).

Compared with situated knowledge, universal knowledge typically serves policy interests better than practice interests. A full defense of this thesis would require more detailed analyses of the concept of situated knowledge and of the nature of practice than I can undertake here. Nonetheless, in the case of policing, several analyses of patrol officer expertise and the conflict between street cops and management cops suggest its plausibility.

Bittner, in particular, argued that the knowledge base that meets the demands of front-line police work must take a situational form: 'Policing is not technical in the sense in which engineering is,' he wrote. 'Instead, it makes great demands on experience and judgment. Experience is accumulated knowledge on which is based the understanding of practical necessities and possibilities. This understanding guides judgment' (1982: 11). Elsewhere he argued that the importance of detailed experience and situated judgment (as opposed to generalizable rules) results from the nature of the situations that police contend with. In those situations, interventions that fail to take account of complex situational details in favor of generalized 'by-the-book' responses often backfire (1990: 174–175).

Similarly, in *The Two Cultures of Policing* Reuss-Ianni concluded that officers' emphasis on situation-specific knowledge makes them skeptical of the decontextualized, abstract, universalistic information that Diamond associates with scientific analysis. For example: 'Routine data collected, including activity logs, arrest and crime coding sheets, and statistics on response time, provide standardized means of gathering information on the job. But field personnel frequently dismiss the data and the findings derived from them as irrelevant to their problems' (Reuss-Ianni 1983: 19). Police managers, by contrast, place great value on such information (ibid.: 18–19).[5]

We have a primitive understanding of what is involved in the kind of context-specific, situated knowledge that officers value. As a result, the very fact that it *is* knowledge is easily missed. Bittner warned about this problem four decades ago:

> What the seasoned patrolman means ... in saying that he 'plays by ear' is that he is making his decisions while being attuned to the realities of complex situations about which he has immensely detailed knowledge. This studied aspect of peacekeeping generally is not made explicit, nor is the tyro or the outsider made aware of it. Quite to the contrary, the ability to discharge the duties associated with keeping the peace is viewed as a reflection of an innate talent of 'getting along with people'. Thus, the same demands are made of barely initiated officers as are made of experienced practitioners. ... This leads to inevitable frustrations. ... The license of discretionary freedom and the expectation of success under conditions of autonomy, without any indication that the work of the successful craftsman is based on an acquired preparedness for the task, is ready-made for failure and malpractice. Moreover, it leads to slipshod practices of patrol that also infect the standards of the careful craftsman. (1967: 715)

He and others raised particular concerns about the fact that officers' experiential knowledge is often not shared (Goldstein 1977: 150; Muir 1977).

It can appear to be unshareable. Indeed, the transformation of knowledge into more abstract, propositional forms arose partly to facilitate its dissemination through education (Toulmin 1982). However, we do have models of other kinds of knowledge—knowledge that contributes to perception and judgment rather than to logical deduction—and yet can be shared.

One such model is knowledge about chess. As Adriaan de Groot and others have shown, the most striking difference between chess masters and chess novices is the large database of chess scenarios they have stored in their memories (De Groot 1965, 1966; Chase and Simon 1973). Chess masters and novices both select their next move by considering the possible moves open to them and examining what implications each possibility will have, and as they make these calculations, masters and novices consider roughly the same number of possible moves; they also look about an equal number of moves ahead in the game. Chess masters, however, draw from a much wider repertoire of scenarios that they have learned through both experience and study (e.g., through the study of sample chess games published in weekly newspapers). Evidence of this advantage is vividly illustrated in the fact that chess masters do far better than novices at remembering the placement of chess pieces on a board stopped in mid-game but equally poorly at remembering randomly placed pieces—i.e., in a configuration that might never arise in actual play.

In short, the key advantage that chess masters apparently have over novices is their familiarity with an extremely wide repertoire of real situations similar or identical to those that they may encounter in future play. This knowledge seems to provide them with an enormous advantage over chess amateurs even though it has the form of familiarity with particular situations rather than the form of universal generalizations. Herbert Simon (1979) has argued that many kinds of professional expertise (and human expertise more generally) may resemble expertise in chess in this respect: They all arise out of extensive familiarity with the particular situations that are encountered in practice as much as (or more than) they require any generalizable problem-solving skills, generalizations, or principles. Scholars in a number of specific professional fields have made similar arguments, sometimes drawing explicitly from this line of cognitive science research (e.g., Behn 1987; Benner 1984).

More needs to be said about the nature, logic, and uses of this kind of knowledge, but I hope that it is clear even from this rough sketch how this conception of expertise relates to Bittner's analysis of police work. Indeed, Bittner himself repeatedly suggested the relevance of case-oriented analogical reasoning to policing. For example, in his most extensive analysis of policing practice, he concluded: 'Although [patrol officer] interest is directed to the accumulation of factually descriptive information, as opposed to the desire to achieve a theoretically abstract understanding, the ulterior objective is to be generally knowledgeable rather than merely being factually informed. That is, patrolmen seek to be sufficiently enlightened to be able to connect the yet unknown with the known through extrapolation and analogy' (1990: 9). De Groot and Simon's research provides conceptual and empirical support for this interpretation of practical understanding.

If police expertise consists at least partly in a familiarity with a wide range of practical situations that they are likely to encounter in practice, then police research has good reason to value the development of detailed, contextualized case studies of well-chosen examples of those practical situations (Flyvbjerg 2001). Such vicarious experience apparently has benefits even when the cases are not explicitly used to identify generalizations about the consequences an action will have. This kind of knowledge is situated in the sense that its benefits, its significance, and even its meaning may only be accessible for those who have an extensive network of background understandings and powers of judgment that cannot be (or at least have not been) articulated.[6] It contributes to the development of professional expertise in the same way that real and vicarious experience of particular chess games contributes to expertise in chess. It meets an important need among front-line practitioners that the abstract and decontextualized knowledge that dominates police research today cannot fill.

The ambiguity of practical purpose

It is a common phenomenon of organizational life that formal organizational goals often provide incomplete guidance for front-line practitioners. That is particularly true for public agencies, such as police departments (Wilson 1968, 1989). At the highest levels, removed from the insistent demands that concrete situations place on service delivery, managers and political overseers may be able to develop reasonably clear statements of organizational priorities. By contrast the concrete situations we encounter when we attempt to turn purpose into action tend to confound our understanding of the priorities we thought we had (Millgram 1997). As a result, we may be able to develop a clear statement about an organization's mission when we reflect on its tasks at a relatively abstract and stylized level, but once we become concrete, ambiguity and conflict are hard to avoid. Clarity of purpose is a particularly scarce resource at the front lines of an organization.

The first wave of contemporary police research that began with the American Bar Foundation studies of policing practice can be understood in this light: Concrete reports of what front-line officers actually did flew in the face of the clear and commonsensical view that police departments are responsible for crime control and/or law enforcement. Egon Bittner (1967, 1970, 1974, 1982) recognized this insight more clearly than anyone: Arguing that abstract statements about the police mandate (he called them 'specious programmatic idealizations') could not provide sufficient guidance for policing practice, he devoted the major thrust of his work to a sophisticated attempt to develop an alternative conception of the police mandate— one formulated at a lower level of abstraction based on a concrete examination of the situations that police officers actually encountered.[7] In this case, a close look at actual police work discovered a level of complexity in the police mandate that could not easily be captured in clear and simple statements about institutional goals.[8] Since this time it has become commonplace to observe that the police mandate is complex and ambiguous. My point here is that because this complexity and ambiguity becomes most pressing at the point of action, it is particularly salient for front-line officers.

Elsewhere I have discussed the implications of this kind of complexity for the form that police research should take (Thacher 2001b, 2005). Briefly, recent police research has been dominated by efforts to develop instrumental knowledge, or knowledge about the best means to a given end. Such knowledge can be very useful in situations where we have a clear and focused sense of our priorities, since in that case all that matters is which means is most effective at promoting one clear and overriding end. By contrast when our goals are ambiguous, changing, multiple, and conflicting, the most vexing questions we face are not about which means will best realize a clear and given end but about how exactly each of many ambiguous ends is relevant in a particular situation, and which end deserves how much priority over the others. One model of scholarship that can shed light on such questions combines ethnographic description with moral analysis in order to develop something like a case ethics approach to policing practice. Such research develops detailed case studies of difficult practical dilemmas, examines our considered judgments about how police should handle those dilemmas, and compares those judgments to our convictions about other cases. That process of case description and analysis allows us to refine our normative understanding of police work. The focus on concrete cases rather than abstract analysis of ethical principles is valuable because we often have more confidence in concrete judgments about what should be done in a particular situation than in the abstract principles that purportedly justify them.[9]

I have elaborated on the types of research I have in mind elsewhere (Thacher 2001b, 2004a, 2006), and I have tried to illustrate it in analyses of order maintenance policing (2004b) and community engagement (2001a). Here I mean to extend that argument by suggesting that the case ethics approach I have outlined has special relevance to front-line policing. Insofar as police managers and elected officials are particularly concerned with the relatively clear goals that their agencies are formally committed to, instrumental knowledge may serve (what they take to be) their purposes well. But, insofar as front-line officers confront more normative ambiguity—an ambiguity pressed on them by the continually surprising situations they encounter, the concrete demands of which cannot be entirely captured in general statements of goals—it may be impossible to meet their needs without incorporating the alternative approach I have suggested.

Conclusion

Science serves human interests, and human interests are diverse, so we cannot content ourselves with a single approach to science. Divergent interests exist even within a single institution like policing (Reuss-Ianni 1983), and although some of those differences may reflect error or bad faith, there is no reason to expect that they all do. As a result, we cannot content ourselves with a single approach to police research.

I have especially suggested that the classically scientific approach to scholarship that has recently come to dominate police research may be more relevant to management concerns than officer concerns (or, more precisely, to the specific officer concerns that I have highlighted in this paper). To complement that approach, I have discussed three variations on an alternative research theme—one grounded in concrete case study description and analysis of various sorts that often eschews causal generalizations.

I have referenced more extended descriptions of these approaches throughout this paper, but two points are worth adding here. First, although the approaches I have discussed draw from ethnographic and interview-based techniques, only some varieties of ethnographic and case study research will meet the needs I have discussed. In order to develop the kind of situated knowledge that can successfully inform front-line practice, ethnographic description cannot remain at the level of generalized description, and research interviews cannot restrict their attention to generalized attitudes. Instead researchers must strive for concreteness, depicting particular people in particular places taking particular actions in response to particular situations (Flyvbjerg 2001). Second, description and value-neutral interpretation is not enough. To help resolve the normative ambiguity that stands out as a major challenge for front-line practice, police research needs to engage the normative questions posed by the situations that research subjects confront. One way to do that is to use case study material to test and refine overarching normative theories (Thacher 2001b, 2006). Another is to develop analogical comparisons with other cases in the literature (Thacher 2004a).

The research approach I have advocated draws from substantially different methodological and epistemological traditions compared with those that dominate policing scholarship today. Organizationally, however, it departs only modestly from existing research practice: In principle, the approaches I have described can be carried out by independent researchers who study police as outside experts. In practice, however, researcher-led scholarship may eventually run up against fundamental limitations, since situated knowers presumably have unique access to some kinds of situated knowledge.[10] In that respect, the participatory action model of research that has been recommended and practiced by several policing scholars (e.g., Goldstein 1990; Bradley et al. 2006; Wood et al. 2007; Wuestewald and Steinheider 2007) holds considerable promise as a model of research for the front lines.

I do not mean that the kind of research I have advocated as is all that officers need. I have identified three aspects of the practice problems that officers must solve that make this kind of knowledge valuable, but my picture is undoubtedly partial; undoubtedly there exist other characteristics of front-line practice problems that are better addressed by other kinds of knowledge. Here I have tried to focus on a few important aspects of the practice perspective that are not well served by dominant research strategies in order to suggest how police research might better support bottom-up reform. Undoubtedly these observations apply to many other policy fields as well, since the distinction between practice needs and policy needs that I have examined is hardly unique to policing.

Acknowledgements

Thanks to David Bradley, John DiNardo, Shobita Parthasarathy, David Sklansky, and an anonymous reviewer for helpful comments and discussion.

Notes

1. I have of course not spelled out the details of either conception of evaluation here. Discussions relevant to the second approach include Schön (1997), Mead (2004), and Lennon and Corbett (2003).
2. In this connection it is worth noting that the use of randomized controlled trials to evaluate new surgical innovations is controversial and began to decline over two decades ago (Pollock 1993; Panesar et al. 2006).

3. Lawrence Sherman, the leading advocate of the 'what works' paradigm in police research, has discussed this same episode in the history of surgery, but his account is potentially misleading. Sherman (1992: 58) argues the lack of RCT evidence about antiseptic surgical procedures meant that many surgeons were too slow to adopt these lifesaving techniques, but McCulloch and his coauthors explain how overuse of RCTs would also have prevented the adoption of lifesaving techniques.

4. Taken literally no knowledge qualifies under this definition: Since Kant every serious philosopher of science has recognized that we grasp propositions against a background of assumptions and concepts that may vary from person to person. Nevertheless, the notion of anonymous knowledge is clear enough as a relative matter; as Nagel notes, the scientific aspiration is to develop progressively *more* impartial knowledge. (Nagel's own point is that the aspiration cannot succeed even in principle for features of the world that have a subjective realization, such as consciousness.)

5. If it needs to be said, I do not intend to romanticize officer knowledge preferences, which have their own drawbacks (q.v. Reuss-Ianni 1983: 18). I mean to argue that those preferences emphasize a valid and important form of knowledge, not that they exhaust all such forms.

6. As a chess novice, I scratch my head when I read the chess column in the weekly paper—and not because any specialized terminology is being used.

7. Bittner apparently vacillated between normative and descriptive conceptions of his task. Compare his statement of his objectives in 'The Police on Skid Row' (which he described as an attempt to 'disclose the conception of the mandate to which police feel summoned', insisting that 'it was entirely outside the scope of the presentation to review the merits of this conception') to that of *The Functions of the Police in Modern Society* ('the task we have set ourselves it to elucidate the role of the police in modern society by reviewing the exigencies located in practical reality which give rise to police responses, *and* by attempting to relate the actual routines of response to the aspirations of a democratic polity') (Bittner 1967: 715, 1970: 5, emphasis in original). For an argument that empirical research can in fact contribute to normative understanding—notwithstanding the maxim that it is impossible (unethical?) to derive ought from is, which Bittner himself invoked—see Thacher (2006).

8. Of course Bittner's own conception (especially Bittner 1974) was nuanced and influential. Important critiques can be found in Kleinig (1996) and Ericson and Haggerty (1997), though each of these analyses presents their own difficulties.

9. As Henry Richardson put it, 'Among moral judgments that stand most firm are some quite concrete, even particular ones—about the evil of the Holocaust and of the My Lai massacre, about the admirable character of Mother Theresa's work with the poor and sick of Calcutta, about the injustice of Idi Amin's rule, and so on. ... Conversely, it is so difficult to frame satisfactory general principles for ethics or for practice that we are constantly indicating our doubts about them by hedging them in one way or another' (1997: 138; cf. Jonsen and Toulmin 1988).

10. In feminist epistemology, this idea underlies many arguments for stronger representation of women in science (Anderson 2006 provides excellent discussion of this point). A parallel argument in the present context would call for stronger representation of front-line officers.

References

Anderson, E., 2006. "Feminist epistemology and philosophy of science", *In*: Zalta, E.N., ed. *The Stanford Encyclopedia of Philosophy*, Fall 2006 edn. Available at: <http://plato.stanford-d.edu/archives/fall2006/entries/feminism-epistemology/ >

Behn, R., 1987. "Knowledge about public management: Lessons from chess and warfare". *Journal of Policy Analysis and Management*, 7, 200–212.

Benner, P., 1984. *From Novice to Expert: Excellence and Power in Clinical Nursing Practice*. California: Addison-Wesley.

Bittner, E., 1967. "The police on skid row: A study in peacekeeping". *American Sociological Review*, 32, 699–715.

Bittner, E., 1970. *The Functions of the Police in Modern Society*. Bethesda, MD: NIMH.

Bittner, E., 1974. "Florence Nightingale in pursuit of Willie Sutton: A Theory of the Police". *In*: H. Jacob, ed. *The Potential for Reform of Criminal Justice* 3. Beverly Hills: Sage.

Bittner, E., 1982. "Emerging police issues". *In*: B. Garmire, ed. *Local Government Police Management*. 2nd edn. Washington, DC: ICMA.

Chase, W. and Simon, H., 1973. "Perception in chess". *Cognitive Psychology*, 4, 55–81.

De Groot, A., 1965. *Thought and Choice in Chess*. The Hague: Mouton.

De Groot, A., 1966. "Perception and memory versus thought: Some old ideas and recent findings". *In*: B. Kleinmutz, ed. *Problem Solving: Research, Method, and Theory*. New York: Wiley.

Diamond, C., 1991. "Knowing tornadoes and other things". *New Literary History*, 22, 1001–1015.

Ericson, R. and Haggerty, K., 1997. *Policing the Risk Society*. Toronto: University of Toronto Press.

Farrington, B., 1948. *The Philosophy of Francis Bacon: An Essay on Its Development From 1603 to 1609 with New Translation of Fundamental Texts*. Liverpool: Liverpool University Press.

Flyvbjerg, B., 2001. *Making Social Science Matter*. New York: Cambridge University Press.

Goldstein, H., 1977. *Policing a Free Society*. Cambridge, MA: Ballinger.

Goldstein, H., 1990. *Problem-oriented Policing*. Philadelphia: Temple University Press.

Heckman, J. and Smith, J., 1995. "Assessing the case for social experiments". *Journal of Economic Perspectives*, 9, 85–110.

Jonsen, A. and Toulmin, S., 1988. *The Abuse of Casuistry*. Berkeley: University of California Press.

Kennedy, D.M. and Moore, M., 1995. "Underwriting the risky investment in community policing: What social science should be doing to evaluate community policing". *The Justice System Journal*, 17, 271–289.

Kleinig, J., 1996. *Ethics in Policing*. New York: Cambridge University Press.

Laws, D. and Rein, M., 1997. "Knowledge for policy and practice". *In*: D. Tucker, C. Garvin and R. Sarri, eds. *Integrating Knowledge and Practice*. Westport, CT: Praeger, 46–61.

Lennon, M. and Corbett, T., 2003. *Policy into Action: Implementation Research and Welfare Reform*. Washington, DC: Urban Institute Press, 193–229.

McCulloch, P., Taylor, I., Sasako, M., Lovett, B., and Griffin, D., 2002. "Randomised trials in surgery: Problems and possible solutions". *British Medical Journal*, 324, 1448–1451.

Mead, L., 2004. Policy Research: The Field Dimension. Paper presented to the Association for Public Policy Analysis and Management, 30 October, Atlanta, GA.

Millgram, E., 1997. *Practical Induction*. Cambridge: Harvard University Press.

Muir, W., 1977. *Police: Streetcorner Politicians*. Chicago: University of Chicago Press.

Nagel, T., 1974. "What is it like to be a bat?". *Philosophical Review*, 83, 435–450.

Newton-Smith, W., 1984. "The role of interests in science". *In*: A. Phillips Griffiths, ed. *Philosophy and Practice*. New York: Cambridge University Press.

Nozick, R., 1993. *The Nature of Rationality*. Princeton: Princeton University Press.

Panesar, S., Thakrar, R., Athanasiou, T., and Sheikh, A., 2006. "Comparison of reports of randomized controlled trials and systematic reviews in surgical journals: Literature review". *Journal of the Royal Society of Medicine*, 99, 470–472.

Pollock, A.V., 1993. "Surgical evaluation at the crossroads". *British Journal of Surgery*, 80, 964–966.

Reuss-Ianni, E., 1983. *The Two Cultures of Policing*. New York: Transaction.

Schön, D., 1997. *"Notes for a Theory-of-Action Approach to Evaluation"*. mimeo.

Sherman, L., 1992. *Policing Domestic Violence*. New York: Free Press.

Sherwood, K. and Doolittle, F., 2003. "What lies behind the impact? Implementation research in the context of net impact studies". *In*: M. Lennon and T. Corbett, eds. *Policy into Action: Implementation Research and Welfare Reform*. Washington, DC: Urban Institute Press, 193–229.

Simon, H., 1979. "Information processing models of cognition". *Annual Review of Psychology*, 30, 363–396.

Taylor, C., 1985. Neutrality in political science. *In*: *Philosophical Papers*. Cambridge: Cambridge University Press.

Thacher, D., 2001a. "Equity and community policing: A new view of community partnerships". *Criminal Justice Ethics*, 20, 1–16.

Thacher, D., 2001b. "Policing is not a treatment: Alternatives to the medical model of police research". *Journal of Research in Crime and Delinquency*, 38, 387–415.

Thacher, D., 2004a. "The casuistical turn in planning ethics: Lessons from law and medicine". *The Journal of Planning Education and Research*, 23, 269–285.

Thacher, D., 2004b. "Order maintenance reconsidered: Moving beyond strong causal reasoning". *Journal of Criminal Law and Criminology*, 94, 381–414.

Thacher, D., 2005. "Police research and the humanities". *Annals of the American Academy of Political and Social Sciences*, 593, 179–191.

Thacher, D., 2006. "The normative case study". *American Journal of Sociology*, 111, 1631–1676.

Tiles, M., 1987. "A science of Mars or of Venus?". *Philosophy*, 62, 293–306.

Toulmin, S., 1982. "Equity and principles". *Osgoode Halle Law Journal*, 20, 1–17.

Toulmin, S., 1990. *Cosmopolis*. Chicago: University of Chicago Press.

Toulmin, S., 2001. *Return to Reason*. Cambridge, MA: Harvard University Press.

Wilson, J.Q., 1968. *Varieties of Police Behavior*. Cambridge: Harvard University Press.

Wilson, J.Q., 1989. *Bureaucracy: What Government Agencies Do and Why They Do It*. New York: Basic.

Wood, J., Fleming, J., and Marks, M., 2007. "Building the capacity of police change agents: The nexus policing project". *Policing and Society*, 18, 78–94.

Wuestewald, T. & Steinheider, B., 2007. "From the bottom up: Sharing leadership in a police agency". *Police Practice and Research*, forthcoming.

The neglect of police unions: exploring one of the most important areas of American policing

Samuel Walker

School of Criminology, University of Nebraska at Omaha, Omaha, NE, USA

Police unions are widely recognized as having a major influence on American policing, with respect to day-to-day management, disciplinary procedures, and police–community relations. Despite this important influence, however, police scholars have neglected police unions. The reasons for this neglect are not clear, as scholars have investigated other highly sensitive police issues such as the use of excessive force and corruption. This paper examines the most important dimensions of the impact of unions on policing and outlines an agenda for future research.

Introduction

The nature and impact of police unions in the USA is a seriously neglected area of research in the field of police studies. There is very little published research on unions despite the wide recognition that unions have a major impact on policing in many different areas. The recent report by the National Academy of Sciences (2004), *Fairness and Effectiveness in Policing: The Evidence*, a comprehensive review of the literature on American policing, contains exactly one reference to police unions in the index.

The neglect of police unions has seriously impeded understanding of American policing, particularly with respect to basic police management, innovation and reform, police–community relations, and police accountability. Anecdotally, police chiefs routinely complain that they are unable to undertake certain innovations because of the police union and the collective bargaining agreement. These limitations affect the deployment of officers in the field, the development of innovative programs, and effective discipline of officers. Similarly, community civil rights activists frequently allege that the police union prevents the fair and thorough investigation of officer misconduct and the proper discipline of officers who have in fact engaged in improper activity. Social scientists should not take these allegations at face value, since they are made by persons with a direct interest in the issues involved. Nonetheless, these allegations are sufficiently serious and have been made so persistently over the years that they should be matters of great interest to police scholars.

Investigating the allegations regarding police unions is crucial to addressing a number of important issues in policing. Do police unions impede innovation in police organizations? Do certain provisions of collective bargaining agreements, for example, limit the ability of chief executives to redeploy officers as part of community policing programs? Do police unions impede the investigation of officer misconduct, and in that respect hinder meaningful accountability? Do police unions obstruct the development of programs designed to improve police–community relations? These are not peripheral issues in American policing. Innovation, accountability, and police–community relations are matters of urgent concern to policymakers, to community leaders, and to scholars seeking to understand American policing.

With one notable exception, virtually all of the published items that express an opinion on the impact of police unions regard them as having a negative effect, particularly on innovation, accountability, and police–community relations. The one item expressing a positive interpretation, by a police union official, regards them as 'a source of stability in the police world,' where 'police chiefs come and go.' This author also argues that union leaders and members are ready and willing 'to be consulted on regarding policy and strategic issues' (Kliesmet, 1985, p. 284). Given the paucity of independent research on police unions, however, neither the highly positive nor the highly negative interpretations of the impact of police unions can be verified.

The neglect of police unions is extremely curious and defies ready explanation. Because of their impact on matters of urgent public concern – police–community relations, discipline for use of excessive force, etc. – one would expect significant and sustained research on the subject. The police–community relations crisis of the 1960s stimulated an enormous body of research that continues today (Walker, Spohn, & DeLone, 2007). This includes an extremely valuable body of research on police use of force, including both deadly force and less lethal force (Alpert & Dunham, 2004). The best of this research, moreover, meets the highest standards of social science research. The racial profiling controversy that burst upon the nation roughly around 1999 has also stimulated a large and still-growing research effort (Fridell, 2004).

The purpose of this paper is to provide a brief overview of the literature on police unions, to review the various areas of policing where unions have some impact, to discuss the possible reasons for the neglect of this important subject, and in doing so place unions in the larger context of police studies in the USA. The paper concludes with a suggested agenda for research on police unions. For reasons of space and focus, this paper does not go into detail about the long history of police unionism in the USA (Walker, 1998).

Preliminary considerations

At the outset, it is appropriate to explain some basic considerations that guide the discussion that follows.

First, this paper proceeds on the assumption that employees have a fundamental right to join unions of their own choosing and to engage in collective bargaining over the terms and conditions of their employment (Keenan & Walker, 2005, pp. 185–243). This includes public as well as private sector employees. The precise scope of union rights vis-à-vis management rights in any particular employment setting is, of course, subject to considerations of law, policy choices, and negotiations.

As a part of the basic right to join unions, employees also have a basic legal right to due process with respect to disciplinary actions. This includes, at a minimum, the right to notice about any charges of misconduct, the right to a fair hearing over any alleged misconduct, and a right to appeal any adverse disciplinary action including termination. The precise scope of these rights is, of course, a matter of policy debate and negotiations, subject to considerations of law, policy choices, and negotiations (Keenan & Walker, 2005).

Second, this paper proceeds on the basis of several social science perspectives. The most important involves how the subject of police unionism is framed, and how such frames shape thinking and research. Among most community activists and many if not most police scholars, police unions are generally framed in negative terms. Specifically, unions are viewed as having an extremely adverse effect on discipline, accountability, and police–community relations. This paper approaches police unions from a neutral perspective, regarding them as capable of potentially positive and negative effects. Whatever their negative effects on certain areas, the record indicates positive contributions in some other areas. (Prior to unionization in the late 1960s, for example, police officers were often subject to arbitrary and punitive discipline. Unionization also contributed to professionalization by securing adequate salaries and benefits (Juris & Feuille, 1973).)

Additionally, this paper views police unions as a complex and changing phenomenon. There is a tendency among many observers, particularly critics, to stereotype them as an undifferentiated and unchanging phenomenon. As several sections in the discussion that follows indicate, this paper holds that police unions vary from department to department and also change over time.

The neglect of police unions

The literature on police unions is extremely limited and unbalanced. A substantial portion of the extant literature, moreover, is published by labor economists and/or in labor economics journals, rather than in the social science journals where the bulk of the police studies literature is published.

In the past 33 years there have been only about 19 published items – scholarly articles, books, book chapters, or reports by government agencies or private non-profit groups – on police unions in the USA. (This does not include published articles or reports on police unions in Canada, UK, Australia, or other countries.) The 19 items include nine articles in refereed journals, three books, one book chapter, and six reports by government agencies or private organizations. Interestingly, over half of the items (10 out of 19) were published between 1973 and 1979, suggesting a declining interest in the subject over the years. Only one item (a book chapter) was published between 1981 and 1996. There was a flurry of research in the early to mid-1970s when police unionism was first establishing itself. These items were clearly immediate responses to a new phenomenon in policing. Of the six articles in refereed journals published since 1996, two are in labor economics rather than standard criminal justice journals. (The net result of this is that, given the traditional specialization on the part of academics, many social scientists do not read the labor economics articles.) A search of law journals, meanwhile, yielded five additional articles dealing with police unions. Only one very short (5 pp.) book chapter discussed issues for research on police unions (Jacobs, 1985). Finally, only one recent social science article could be considered a general study of police unions as an institution (Kadleck, 2003).

In October 2006, almost coincident with the Berkeley Conference on police unions, the COPS Office of the US Justice Department published a two-part report on unions. Designed as a 'how to' manual to help management and police unions collaborate to facilitate innovation, the various chapters in the report do not meet the standards of refereed scholarly publications. Nonetheless, the report represents the most comprehensive information on police unions in over 30 years. In addition to a national survey of 181 police chief executives and police union presidents, it contains several chapters with narrative descriptions of labor–management issues related to police reforms (Office of Community Oriented Policing Services, 2006).

The prevalence of police unions

Police unions are a prevalent feature of American policing, although that prevalence varies substantially by region and size of department. The 2003 LEMAS report on *Local Police Departments* indicates that only 41% of all local departments have collective bargaining. This is very misleading, however. Collective bargaining exists in over 80% of all the agencies in communities with 500,000 or more people. This represents the overwhelming majority of sworn police officers in the USA. The largest 189 (out of almost 13,000) departments employ 52% of all officers. Collective bargaining exists in only 13% of the agencies in communities with populations under 2500 people. Since 47% of all police departments have nine or fewer sworn officers, this represents a huge percentage of all agencies but a small percentage of all the sworn officers in the USA (Bureau of Justice Statistics, 2006).

The LEMAS data are supported by data in the 2006 report on *Police Labor–Management Relations*. Three-quarters (74%) of the 100 largest municipal police departments had unions with collective bargaining agreements. Size and region were the most important variables. Only one of the 25 largest departments had no collective bargaining agreement, while half of the smallest 20 in the sample (Nos. 81 through 100) had no contract. Only five of the 26 without contracts involved cities outside the southeastern region (Office of Community Oriented Policing Services, 2006, pp. 185–189).

Police unions are also relatively rare in the southeastern region of the USA where unionism has traditionally been very weak even in the private sector. There are no police unions in North Carolina, South Carolina, Georgia, or Mississippi. (There are reasons for questioning the accuracy of some items in the annual LEMAS survey, largely as a consequence of the methodology used, and we should not accept its data at face value (Walker & Katz, 1995).) In cities outside of the southeast, however, police unionism is the norm and has been for many decades. The prevalence of unionism in big cities further distorts public perception of police unionism, since activities by unions in response to controversies in New York City, Chicago, and Los Angeles, for example, often gain national publicity.

Unlike the general pattern in the private sector and even most of the public sector, there is no national police union. Just as policing itself is highly fragmented in the USA, so police unionism is fragmented into highly autonomous local unions. Many belong to different national federations (e.g., the Fraternal Order of Police), but the police unionism is not centralized as is the case with public school teachers (Juris & Feuille, 1973, pp. 26–32). The 2006 COPS report characterized police unionism as 'disorganized labor for police officers,' with a 'maze of different union affiliations' (DeLord, 2006, p. 39).

The importance of police unions

Virtually everyone with an interest in American policing – police managers, public officials, community activists, and police scholars – recognize the importance of police unions – at least in conversation. Community activists have been particularly concerned about what they see as the negative impact of unions on discipline, accountability, and community relations. Because there has been no overall assessment of the nature and impact of unionism on policing, the full impact on policing is probably not recognized by most people.

The following section attempts to identify the major areas of impact and the nature of the known or potential impact in each one. As the discussion below indicates, there is considerable overlap with many of these areas. Police discipline and accountability issues, for example, have direct impact on police–community relations.

Impact on police management

Police unions have a direct and significant impact on the management of law enforcement agencies. Unionism, in both the private and public spheres, represents a form of *shared governance*, with employees, acting through their union, having some voice in some but not all areas of management. As one contributor to the 2006 COPS report on police unions put it, 'Gone are the days of the traditional, stand-alone police chief show style of leadership was to hand down directives for change ...' (Wilkinson, 2006, p. 59).

The significance of shared governance in policing must be seen in the context of the history of American police management and in particular the history of police reform in the twentieth century. The police professionalism movement appeared early in the twentieth century as a self-conscious effort to replace the tradition of political influence over policing and to institute both a mission of non-partisan public service and modern notions of management (Walker, 1977).

As it developed, the new tradition of professional police management was highly authoritarian. The history of police reform is largely the story of strong chiefs who unilaterally imposed professional standards in their respective departments. The leading examples include August Vollmer in Berkeley, O.W. Wilson in Wichita and later Chicago, William Parker in Los Angeles, and Clarence Kelley in Kansas City (Sherman, 1978; Walker, 1977). Reformers both inside and outside of policing developed the strong belief that reform could only be accomplished through authoritarian, top-down management. Reformers regarded rank-and-file officers as uneducated and incompetent individuals who, as a group, needed to be uplifted through the imposition of higher recruitment standards, better training, and of course expert leadership.

The advent of police unionism in the late 1960s and early 1970s was a rude shock to police reformers. Many despaired that reform would be stopped in its tracks with the rank and file having a formal, legally required voice in management decisions (Ayres, 1975; International Association of Chiefs of Police [IACP], 1974). These fears were fueled in part by many of the early conflicts over police unionism where unions opposed reforms designed to improve relations with the African American community (Halpern, 1974; Juris & Feuille, 1973; Levi, 1977).

Quite apart from specific issues in collective bargaining agreements that limit the power of police chiefs (discussed below), unions periodically conduct votes of no confidence in a chief. Although such votes are purely rhetorical gestures with no actual power, they undoubtedly have a disruptive effect on day-to-day management (News Channel 8, 2006).

The neglect of police unions even in management circles is indicated by the most respected textbooks on the subject. The most recent edition of O.W. Wilson's classic *Police Administration*, for decades regarded as the 'Bible' on the subject, devotes exactly 16 of 600 pages to police unions (Fyfe et al., 1997).

Union contracts today typically give unions a voice in a number of important issues related to the management of police departments. These issues include the following.

Personnel standards

Recruitment and promotion standards are generally the responsibility of civil service systems that are independent of law enforcement agencies. Nonetheless, unions have been successful in gaining the right to negotiate over some personnel issues (Burpo, 1979; Griesinger, Slovak, & Molkup, 1979).

One of the most important involves mandatory drug testing for current employees. In another recent case, the union has challenged physical fitness standards that involve penalties for officers who do not maintain minimum height and weight standards (*Stamford Advocate*, 2006).

Assignment of officers

The power of police managers to assign and deploy police officers is directly and indirectly affected by collective bargaining. While this is basically a management right, certain collateral issues limit management's actual power. In the 2006 national survey, 63% of the police chiefs and 70% of the union presidents perceive the 'scheduling of personnel' involving 'some problem' or a 'serious problem.' Roughly similar percentages of both groups perceive the assignment of personnel and the rotation of personnel to be problematic (Office of Community Oriented Policing Services, 2006, p. xxvii).

Union contracts typically require that officers be assigned on the basis of seniority. Thus, a police chief does not have free hand to assign particular officers to (or away from) high crime areas or areas where community relations are volatile. The seniority rule applies to the assignment of patrol officers and to sergeants (Rynecki, Cairns, & Cairns, 1978). The major result is that, typically, the youngest and least experienced officers (and sergeants) are assigned to the most volatile patrol areas: the highest crime neighborhoods during the high crime periods of the day (roughly 4 p.m. to midnight). Some departments have developed a fourth shift, operating during the high crime period from roughly 6 p.m. to 2 a.m. and overlapping the traditional shifts, in order to deploy more officers during that critical period. In some instances this innovation has been challenged by police unions as a change in working conditions (Juris & Feuille, 1973, pp. 125–126). To the extent that a proposed innovation would involve required overtime pay, the contract requirement might discourage implementation of that particular program.

Some union contracts limit the ability of police chiefs to deploy one-officer patrol units. Since at least the 1950s it has been recognized that one-officer patrols are both more efficient and no less safe than two-officer units. Under some contracts, however, police chiefs are not free to disband two-officer units and deploy one-officer units (Juris & Feuille, 1973, pp. 133–134).

The implementation of community policing in Chicago (the CAPS program) illustrates the potential impact of union contracts on the assignment of officers. Under the contract, 'it was impossible for downtown [District] managers to do any detailed tinkering with the matching of officer's skills to varying district conditions.' The contract also required overtime pay for officers assigned to 'important components of the program.' The FOP, the local union, 'remained tolerant' of CAPS, however, and community policing was successfully implemented. Eventually, it even endorsed the program (Skogan & Hartnett, 1997, pp. 94–95; see also Polzin, 2006).

While the union contract did not impede community policing in Chicago, research is needed on the experience of other departments on the question of the extent to which the union contract limited or perhaps even prevented changes in assignment related to innovative programs or other routine changes in a department's mission.

Impact on innovation

Union contract restrictions on the assignment of officers may also have an effect on innovation. The impact of unions on innovation and change in police organizations is the principal focus of the 2006 COPS report on police unions (Office of Community Oriented Policing Services, 2006). The case of community policing in Chicago discussed above illustrates the potential impact on one major innovation.

In a more general sense, it is widely believed – but not investigated or proven – that police unions stifle good management in general, innovation in particular, and limit productivity in police departments (Byrne, Dezhbakhsh, & King, 1996, pp. 566–584; IACP, 1974, pp. 8–9, 51–59). This view holds that, regardless of whether a particular issue is subject to negotiations under the local contract, a police chief is ever-mindful of the possibility of a challenge to any new measure – either in the form of a threatened or actual grievance or simply passive resistance. Even a blatantly ludicrous claim by the union that a certain change is subject to negotiations can stall implementation until the matter is resolved. In one recent case, for example, the police union opposed a plan to transfer the dispatching function to another agency (*Berkshire Eagle*, 2006).

Unions, of course, are not the only source of opposition to innovation in policing. The 2006 survey conducted for the 2006 COPS report on police unions found both police chiefs and union presidents ranking supervisors and middle managers as slightly more resistant to innovation than the union. Both groups ranked non-cooperation by rank-and-file officers as the greatest obstacle (Office of Community Oriented Policing Services, 2006).

As David Bayley argues, the last quarter century has been a time of enormous innovation in American policing (Bayley, 1994). Since most of this innovation has occurred in large police departments, it has occurred within a context of collective bargaining. We can assume, therefore, that some departments have been able to manage innovation better than others: instituting organizational reforms more quickly and maintaining innovations over time. An important but as yet unanswered question is the extent to which successful innovation is the result of different management strategies for relating to the local union and the terms of the collective bargaining contract.

The example of the Chicago community policing case illustrates a point, discussed in more detail below, that unions cannot be stereotyped as an undifferentiated or unchanging phenomenon. In that case the union did not oppose an innovation, even though the contract gave it the opportunity to obstruct it, and eventually became a supporter of it.

Unit determination

Determining which employees are a part of the collective bargaining unit ('unit determination') is a threshold issue in all labor relations. In policing, the relevant issue is whether the unit consists only of rank-and-file officers or also contains officers at the rank of sergeant, lieutenant, captain, or even deputy chief. Practices across the country vary considerably. In some departments, the union represents only the rank and file. In some large departments there are separate unions representing different ranks. This further complicates the task of police chiefs who must secure agreements with more than one union. In some other departments the collective bargaining unit includes supervisors up to and including deputy chiefs (IACP, 1974, p. 3; *Oakland Tribune*, 2006).

The composition of the unit has a significant impact on police management. When first-line supervisors or middle managers are part of the collective bargaining unit, the relationship to rank-and-file officers is complicated, and some would argue compromised. Common sense suggests that it is difficult for a supervisor to review the performance of a subordinate when they are both members of a labor organization that may file a grievance against the supervisor and the department.

Impact on discipline and accountability

The impact of police unions on discipline and accountability is arguably the issue that causes the greatest concern among community activists, public officials, and many police executives. The impact is felt in several different ways.

First, police unions play a role in reinforcing the norms of the police subculture (see the discussion below). One of the most important aspects of this involves the 'code of silence,' the refusal of officers to testify against other officers who are accused of misconduct. The code has been widely cited as perhaps the major obstacle to the effective investigation of misconduct and the discipline of guilty officers (Christopher Commission, 1991, p. 120; Human Rights Watch, 1998; Mollen Commission, 1994, p. 53; Skolnick & Fyfe, 1993, pp. 108–112). Missing from these discussions, however, is any analysis of the extent to which the police union sustains the code of silence by (1) negotiating a contract that inhibits thorough investigations of misconduct; (2) providing tangible support for accused officers in the form of experienced legal representation; (3) providing moral support for accused officers through organized group solidarity.

Second, there are specific provisions in many collective bargaining agreements that inhibit investigations. Police union contract provisions typically specify detailed procedures for the investigation of alleged misconduct, including the time, place, and manner of interviews or interrogations, etc. Many, if not most of these provisions represent legitimate due process protections for employees. These include the right to notice of charges, the right to legal representation, the right to a hearing, and the right to an appeal, among others (Juris & Feuille, 1973, pp. 142–145).

About 14 states also have state Police Officers Bills of Rights (POBR) which contain provisions similar to those in police union contracts. In their content analysis of these statutes, Keenan and Walker found a few provisions that inhibit accountability. The Maryland POBR prohibits questioning of officers by investigators who are not sworn officers. Such a prohibition precludes the investigation of complaints by an independent citizen oversight agency (Keenan & Walker, 2005, pp. 181–243).

All of these impacts on discipline and accountability have a consequent impact on police–community relations, a separate and important area of impact that is discussed below.

Police unions have had a major impact on the development of citizen oversight of the police. They have been and continue to be the major force opposing the creation of independent citizen oversight agencies, whether in the form of civilian review board or police auditors, or some other arrangement. Most famously, pressure by the local police unions were responsible for the demise of the two major civilian review boards in the 1960s, in New York City and Philadelphia (Walker, 2001). To the extent that an effective citizen oversight agency contributes to accountability, police unions can be said to play a very negative role in improving the quality of policing.

One of the most important changes since the 1960s has been the decline of opposition to citizen oversight on the part of police chiefs, leaving the field almost entirely to the unions. Most big city chiefs today realize that to maintain good relations with the African American community they cannot appear to be strongly opposed to citizen oversight (Walker, 2001).

Unions have fought the creation of citizen oversight agencies on several grounds. They include opposing the concept per se, arguing that it violates provisions of the local city charter, arguing that it violates either the existing collective bargaining contract regarding discipline and/or the state police officers bill of rights law (Kramer & Gold, 2006). In one recent instance, the police union was actively involved in the creation of a new form of citizen oversight, but some community activists argued that subsequent contract negotiations with the union effectively 'gutted' an agreed-upon form of oversight (Office of Community Oriented Policing Services, 2006, pp. 95–104). Once a citizen oversight agency has been created, police unions have often waged a guerilla war against them. Tactics have included discouraging officer cooperation with investigations, challenging certain provisions in court, and seeking legislative repeal of the enabling ordinance. Unions have been particularly aggressive in legal challenges to subpoena power for citizen oversight agencies and the requirement that officers be compelled to participate in investigations of alleged misconduct.

One aspect of the neglect of police unions has been the failure of accountability advocates to involve union leaders in discussions of reform measures. In one of the first (and still few) efforts to involve unions in the dialogue, the 1996 National Symposium on Police Integrity not only invited several union leaders to speak, but included among its final recommendations one calling for 'research on the perspective of labor organizations on integrity and ethics ...' Involving unions was also included in several other Symposium recommendations (US Department of Justice, 1997, p. 55).

Impact on the police subculture

Another important area of policing that has not been studied sufficiently is the so-called police subculture. The Christopher Commission report on the Los Angeles Police Department, for example, contains a chapter with 'LAPD Culture' in the title. The chapter does not, however, contain any substantive discussion of that culture or the role of the local union in maintaining it (Christopher Commission, 1991, pp. 97–106). The related issues of the police subculture and of organizational cultures within police departments have not received sufficient scholarly attention (Armacost, 2004). The 2006 COPS report, for example, argues that 'failing to understand and respect the culture of the agency' is one of the major factors explaining the failure of police chiefs to be effective and retain their jobs. This conclusion represents a recognition of the importance of the police culture and the fact that local police cultures vary, but like other references to this phenomenon is based on anecdotal evidence (Greenberg, 2006, p. 51).

There has been very little research on the concept of the police subculture, and apart from Steve Herbert's recent work most of the discussions are based on dated and unexamined assumptions (Herbert, 1998). We can formulate three tentative hypotheses regarding the relationship of police unions to the police subculture. First, following Herbert's discussion, the police subculture is a multi-dimensional phenomenon, of which the police union is only one aspect or influence. Second, there are great differences in the informal cultures among police departments, and the relative influence of the police union varies from department to department. Third, the differences in local police subcultures have some significant and measurable difference in all aspects of policing, including overall management practices, accountability and discipline, police officer interactions with citizens, and local politics.

The idea of a distinct police subculture originated in the 1950s and early 1960s, emphasizing group solidarity, hostility to the public, secrecy and toleration of misconduct, and even violence against citizens (Skolnick, 1994; Westley, 1970). Much has changed in policing since publication of the works that defined the police subculture. At that time, African Americans and Hispanics were grossly under-represented among sworn officers, and women were not employed on an equal basis as men. In the last 30 years the composition of the rank and file has changed dramatically as a result of both equal employment opportunity considerations and a significant rise in educational levels of officers (Walker, 1985). One index of the growing diversity of the rank and file is the prevalence of non-union employee associations based on race, ethnicity, and gender.

As a result, the entire concept of a distinct police subculture needs reconsideration. Steve Herbert has described a complex, multi-dimensional view of the police subculture that is far more sophisticated than the original concept (Herbert, 1998). There is evidence of very different attitudes on the part of African American officers compared with whites, particularly on the issue of use of force (Weisburd et al., 2000). In some departments, the African American association has been publicly critical of positions taken by both management and the white-dominated police union (www.officer.com). A significant body of research, however, has found no meaningful differences in on-the-street behavior among white, African American, Hispanic, and female officers. The exception to this rule is that female officers do appear to be far less involved in serious misconduct, repeated misconduct, and as recipients of citizen complaints (National Academy of Sciences, 2004, chap. 4; Walker & Katz, 2008; Walker et al., 2007, chap. 4).

With respect to the impact of unions on the police subculture, 'code of silence' is an issue of special concern. Numerous reports (as opposed to social science research) label the code of silence as the major obstacle to accountability, because officers refuse to testify against other officers who are accused of misconduct (Christopher Commission, 1991, p. 120; Human Rights Watch, 1998, pp. 68–71; Mollen Commission, 1994, p. 53; Skolnick & Fyfe, 1993, pp. 108–112). A report on the Rampart scandal in the Los Angeles Police Department (sponsored, ironically, by the Police Protective League (PPL), the rank and file's union) concluded that the 'central problem' underlying the scandal 'is the culture of the Los Angeles Police Department.' Moreover, 'a code of silence is deeply embedded' in the department. To be sure, the PPL had certain motives in commissioning this report. Nonetheless, it is remarkable that a major police union would retain a civil liberties attorney and issue a report that candidly discusses the pathological aspects of the police subculture (Chemerinsky, 2000; Hunt, 2006). Since other officers are often witnesses to the events in question, their failure to testify, or testify truthfully, obstructs investigations. To the extent that a police union provides both a sense of group solidarity and tangible resources in the form of legal representation, it is likely that unions reinforce the code of silence. It should be noted, however, that the first publications discussing the police subculture and the code of silence appeared in an era before police officer associations had become legally recognized collective bargaining agents. Thus, it is possible that the code of silence is an inherent aspect of policing and that unions simply support it to some unknown degree.

Local police unions also play some role in shaping the public posture of the rank and file. In some departments union leaders present an often belligerent face to the public, either in opposition to management initiatives or reform demands voiced by community groups. To the extent that a union is a formal organization representing the rank and file, public postures of this sort may well reinforce solidarity among officers and by discouraging alternative points of view suppress receptivity to innovation.

Impact on city or county finances

Police unions have been generally successful in negotiating good salary and fringe benefit packages for their members. The resulting contract provisions undoubtedly have some significant impact on the finances of cities and counties. The nature of this impact is not known, however. It is believed that police (and sometimes firefighters) negotiations set the standard for negotiations by other municipal employees, although this proposition has not been researched. It is not known to what extent negotiated police salaries and benefits force cities and counties to reduce expenditures for other services such as streets, parks, and libraries (Juris & Feuille, 1973, pp. 53–55).

On the positive side, it is generally believed that the advent of police unionism in the late 1960s and early 1970s resulted in significant improvements in police salaries and fringe benefits. This helped to improve the relative attractiveness of law enforcement as a career. It should be noted that the President's Crime Commission in 1967 reported both lagging salaries and benefits and an inability of some agencies to attract qualified recruits (President's Commission on Law Enforcement and Administration of Justice, 1967, pp. 163–178). It might also be noted that nearly 20 years later, a report on police education found that the educational levels of police recruits had risen dramatically in the two previous decades (Carter, 1989).

Although the subject has not been studied thoroughly, there is widespread concern that police union contracts provide excessively generous fringe benefits and pensions. In a recent controversy, officials in Hollywood, Florida, 'pointed the finger at police officer pensions as one of the main reasons property taxes are so high' (*Miami Herald*, 2006, p. 1). Some commentators have pointed out that local officials find it easy to grant generous pension provisions because the cost will not come due until they are long out of office (Schachter, 1981; Zhao & Lovrich, 1997).

Impact on police–community relations

Police experts (apart from union members and union advocates, that is) generally believe that police unions have had and continue to have a serious negative impact on police–community relations. This refers primarily to relations between the police and local African American communities (Juris & Feuille, 1973, pp. 160–161).

The modern police union movement, in fact, originated largely in reaction to the civil rights movement and its criticisms of police conduct during the 1960s. Some commentators have noted the irony of police officers mimicking the thinking and tactics of the very civil rights groups they were reacting against. Both groups asserted their rights in the face of what they perceived as discriminatory or at least demeaning treatment by the majority of society. The tactics included organizing private interest groups, picketing, lobbying, and litigation on behalf of their interests (Juris & Feuille, 1973, pp. 18–26).

Any local unions originated or at least became more militant in response to specific police–community relations initiatives in the 1960s. Examples include opposition to the requirement that officers display names or badge numbers (so that aggrieved citizens could identify them in complaints) (Juris & Feuille, 1973, pp. 156–157). The most famous episode involved the successful campaign against the newly independent Citizen Complaint Review Board (CCRB) in New York City by the PBA (Black, 1968).

Today, on a regular basis, the actions of police unions are perceived to be hostile to improved police–community relations in several different ways.

First, police unions publicly and aggressively defend police officers accused of misconduct, particularly of using excessive force. The union in this regard represents the public face of the rank and file in ways that offend racial and ethnic minority communities.

Second, as already mentioned, unions aggressively oppose the creation of independent citizen oversight agencies, both in the political arena and in the courts (Harrell, 2006). Given the fact that the creation of citizen oversight has been a principal demand of civil rights leaders since the 1960s, this posture aggravates police–community relations.

Third, unions have fought the public release of officer disciplinary records. Keeping information about discipline secret is contrary to the principle of transparency, which police experts increasingly recognize as important, and fosters the reputation of police departments as being closed, secretive bureaucracies (*Los Angeles Times*, 2006).

In passing, it should be noted that the entire issue of secrecy in police discipline is one that demands attention. In this author's home town, the union contract forbids the public release of information about disciplinary actions. This is contrary to the practice in other professions where disciplinary actions are matters of public record. In this author's home state, for example, disciplinary actions involving lawyers and licensed medical professionals are matters of public record and are routinely reported in the local press. One consequence of this secrecy is that we have no idea what the 'going rate' is, for example, for a proven case of excessive force or for a racial slur. And as a result we have no idea how the 'going rates' in various police departments compare. Such information is essential for any meaningful analyses of police accountability (Walker, 2004b).

Fourth, unions have opposed policy changes designed to foster better police–community relations, particularly the current issue of racial profiling (Office of Community Oriented Policing Services, 2006, pp. 115–126). In one recent case, a police union argued that a departmental study of racial profiling was subject to collective bargaining. The California Supreme Court rejected this argument, but the challenge not only delayed the study but obviously projected an image of the police union being insensitive to the racial justice issues (*Metropolitan News Enterprise*, 2006).

And as discussed above, there are certain provisions of the police union contract that inhibit effective discipline and accountability.

Fifth, white-dominated police unions have played the lead role in filing reverse discrimination suits in opposition to affirmative action hiring plans. The underrepresentation of African Americans in police departments has been a major issue for civil rights activists for many decades (National Advisory Commission on Civil Disorders, 1968; Sass & Troyer, 1999).

The impact on politics

Police unions are generally a well-organized interest group, with significant financial resources and political clout. Police unions regularly endorse political candidates for office, support or oppose proposed ordinances or referenda, and influence city or county budget issues (*Sacramento Bee*, 2006). Margaret Levi argues that unionization of public employees, including all services and not just the police, 'has far-reaching political consequences' (Levi, 1977, p. 149). The 2006 COPS report on police unions contains a brief but useful analysis of the six major special interest groups that affect police departments in the local community context, with police unions being one of the six (Office of Community Oriented Policing Services, 2006, pp. 7–12).

A Google News search for just the last few months yields several examples of these activities. In perhaps the most controversial, the Houston, Texas, police union sponsored public advertisements warning about the crime rate (*Houston Chronicle*, 2006). This campaign was designed to obtain authorization for more police officers. The police union in St Paul, Minnesota, sponsored a similar campaign. Such activities can have a major impact on public perceptions about the community, including dissuading businesses or people from relocating there.

Well organized to support and provide financial assistance to candidates for local office, particularly mayor and city council. Unions have been very effective in playing the 'law and order card,' and candidates are extremely reluctant to appear to be 'soft' on crime. Union activities also affect such issues as police budgets and salaries, citizen oversight agencies, and so on. Since union-supported candidates are generally very conservative, it has contributed to the drift to the right in American politics since the 1970s (O'Brien, 1996).

In some cases, former police officers have been elected to office themselves. Two major cities today, San Diego and Portland, the current mayors are former police chiefs. The impact is complex, however, because former police chiefs do not always share the same perspective as police unions, and in fact may see some issues quite differently. (In one odd twist, in Portland, Oregon, the former police chief was the liberal candidate for mayor.)

As discussed above, police union activism in opposing citizen oversight, whether through a proposed ordinance or referendum, has had an impact on both discipline and accountability and on police community relations. Police unions have been active and often successful in lobbying for such issues as state statutes on police officers bills of rights, arbitration, or other grievance resolution mechanisms, and other issues (Keenan & Walker, 2005, pp. 185–243).

Explaining the neglect

The reasons for the neglect of police unions in American police studies is not clear. Undoubtedly, many different factors have contributed to it over the years.

One possible explanation can be dismissed rather readily. It is not the case of scholars avoiding controversial issues. There is, for example, a large body of research on police use of force, including both deadly force and less lethal forms of force. This author would go further and say that the study of police use of force is one of the highest achievements of American police studies.

It should be noted that the existing literature on police use of force is based largely on research utilizing internal use of force reports. Access to these reports requires the permission of the department itself. While scholars are still denied access in some departments today, reputable scholars undertaking a major project have no trouble finding departments willing to grant access to the necessary files. This openness, it should be said, represents a sea change in the culture of police departments and attitudes toward the value of research. By the same token, in just the last few years a large body of literature has emerged on the controversial issue of racial profiling.

If anything, one would expect that scholars with concerns about police–community relations and police accountability (and it is fair to say that these concerns have been a deep tradition in police scholarship) would have taken up the issue of police unions. This has not been the case, however.

There is no ready explanation for the neglect of police unions by police scholars. One possible explanation is simply the eccentric traditions of academic research in which research is based on previously published research, with new lines of research developing only as a result of dramatic events that upset the existing paradigm (Kuhn, 1970).

On the one hand, certain lines of research continue to be pursued. The best example of this involves routine police–citizen interaction on the part of patrol officers. Some of the most important research findings in the entire field of police studies. Closely related is the line of research on police use of force, which in turn, is closely related to research on police use of deadly force.

The case of racial profiling offers a good example of this point. Police scholars had almost completely neglected traffic enforcement by police – apart from the special case of drunk driving – for about 30 years. Yet, traffic stops are the most common form of police–citizen interaction, representing about half of all contacts. Roughly around 1999 the racial profiling controversy erupted and that stimulated a wave of research on general traffic enforcement patterns. By the same token, scholarly interest in domestic violence was also largely a function of the women's movement. In the 1980s attention focused on the deterrent effect of arrest, largely because of the spread of mandatory arrest laws and policies (Walker, 2004a).

In short, police research has a quirky and unpredictable history, with some issues pursued consistently and thoroughly, while others have been neglected until some external event disrupts the prevailing paradigm. For whatever reasons, no event has sufficiently jolted the world of police studies to put police unions on the research agenda.

A research agenda

As this paper has indicated, there are many unanswered questions related to the nature and impact of police unions. The purpose of this section is to outline a comprehensive research agenda. Some of these points have already been discussed in this paper.

Impact on police management

(A) *Routine management.* To what extent does a union constrain decision-making by a police chief on a day-to-day basis? How is this constraint exercised? Is it felt more strongly in certain areas than others?

(B) *Innovation.* To what extent does a police union inhibit innovation in police management? Are there documented cases of blocked, delayed, or altered innovative programs? Have the chiefs in some departments been more successful than others in gaining union support for innovation? If so, what strategies have proven successful?

(C) *Variations in union–management relations.* Are there measurable differences in the impact of unions on different departments? What are factors associated with relatively harmonious relations in certain departments compared with acrimonious relations in others? Are there measurable differences in the areas of day-to-day management, innovation, discipline that are associated with these different styles of management?

(D) *Indirect vs. direct effects of unions.* Does the threat, either explicit or implied, of a grievance or law suit affect the day-to-day actions of chiefs and other commanders? To what extent are such threats used in different departments? Have police chiefs developed different strategies for dealing with such threats?

Impact on discipline and accountability

(A) *Patterns of discipline.* Are there measurable differences in disciplinary patterns in unionized departments compared with non-unionized? Are officers accused of use of excessive force, for example, more likely to be disciplined or to receive more serious discipline in non-unionized departments compared with unionized ones?

(B) *Police conduct.* Are there measurable differences in patterns of officer misconduct – use of force, use of excessive force, citizen complaints, corruption, sexual abuse of citizens – that can be attributed to the presence of a union or specific union contract provisions?

(C) *The investigation of alleged misconduct.* Are there particular provisions of police union contracts that inhibit the thorough and fair investigation of officer misconduct?

Impact on the police subculture

(A) *Subculture norms.* Assuming the development of a sophisticated concept of the police officer subculture, is there a measurable difference in the norms of that subculture in unionized vs. non-unionized departments? Are there measurable differences among unionized departments? If so, what factors are associated with those variations?

(B) *Attitudes toward the community/use of force.* Are there measurable differences in officer attitudes toward the public or specific issues such as the use of force in unionized vs. non-unionized departments?

(C) *Internal racial and ethnic relations.* To what extent does the presence of a union, or specific union activities, affect relations between white, African American, and Hispanic officers?

Impact on police–community relations

(A) *Quality of police–community relations.* Are there measurable differences in the quality of police–community relations (measured, for example, through public opinion surveys) in unionized vs. non-unionized cities?

(B) *Impact of union activities.* Is it possible to determine the extent to which specific actions by the police union are, independent of other local factors, aggravate police–community relations?

Impact of city or county finances

(A) *City or county finances.* Are there measurable differences in the city or county finances in jurisdictions that can be attributed to the presence of collective bargaining? Does the presence of a union affect the relative proportion of local spending dedicated to public safety?

(B) *Pensions.* Is there any truth to the suggestion that police pensions are relatively more generous than pensions for other city or county employees? If so, is it possible to conclude that such provisions are unreasonably generous?

(C) *Local fiscal crises.* Is it possible to measure the impact of police unions on local fiscal crises? Are there any documented instances where local police unions have helped to relieve fiscal crises?

Impact on politics

(A) *Overall impact.* Is it possible to measure the impact of police union activity on local or state politics. If so, what are the areas of greatest impact? What have been the indirect effects of that impact?

(B) *Cross-jurisdictional variations.* Are there measurable differences in the impact of police unions in different communities. If so, what factors are associated with those differences?

Conclusion

Police unions are an extremely important part of American policing. They undoubtedly have a major impact on routine management, the process of innovation, accountability, and police–community relations. Unfortunately, we do not know the precise nature of that impact. Police scholars have seriously neglected the subject of police unions. Consequently, much needs to be learned about unions and their impact on policing.

References

Alpert, G.P., & Dunham, R. (2004). *Understanding police use of force.* New York: Cambridge University Press.

Armacost, B. (2004, March). Organizational culture and police misconduct. *George Washington Law Review, 72,* 515–547.

Ayres, R.M. (1975). Police unions: A step toward professionalism? *Journal of Police Science and Administration, 3*(4), 400–404.

Bayley, D. (1994). *Police for the future.* New York: Oxford University Press.

Berkshire Eagle [MA]. (2006, August 29). The union representing the town's 11 police officers plans legal action to contest the transfer of the dispatching function to Pittsfield.

Black, A. (1968). *The people and the police.* New York: McGraw-Hill.

Bureau of Justice Statistics. (2006). *Local police departments, 2003* (NCJ 210118). Washington, DC: Department of Justice. Retrieved from www.ncjrs.gov

Burpo, J.H. (1979). *Police unions in the civil service setting.* Washington, DC: Department of Justice.

Byrne, D., Dezhbakhsh, H., & King, R. (1996). Unions and police productivity: An econometric investigation. *Industrial Relations, 35*(4), 566–584.

Carter, D.L. (1989). *The state of police education.* Washington, DC: Police Executive Research Forum.

Chemerinsky, E. (2000). *An independent analysis of the Los Angeles Police Department's Board of Inquiry Report on the Rampart scandal.* Los Angeles: Police Protective League.

Christopher Commission. (1991). *Report of the independent commission to investigate the Los Angeles Police Department.* Los Angeles: City of Los Angeles. Retrieved from www.parc.info

DeLord, R.G. (2006). Disorganized labor: The mutinous side of police unions. In *Police labor–management relations (Vol. 1,* pp. 39–41). Washington, DC: Office of Community Oriented Policing Services, Department of Justice.

Fridell, L.A. (2004). *By the numbers: A guide for analyzing race data from vehicle stops.* Washington, DC: Police Executive Research Forum.

Fyfe, J.J., Greene, J.R., Walsh, W.F., Wilson, O.W., & McLaren, R.C. (1997). *Police administration* (5th ed.). New York: McGraw-Hill.

Greenberg, S. (2006). Police chief selection and survival: Looming crisis in America's major police departments. In *Police labor–management relations (Vol. 1,* pp. 47–57). Washington, DC: Office of Community Oriented Policing Services, Department of Justice.

Griesinger, G.W., Slovak, J.S., & Molkup, J.J. (1979). *Civil service systems: Their impact on police administration.* Washington, DC: Department of Justice.

Halpern, S.C. (1974). *Police-association and department leaders.* Lexington: Lexington Books.

Harrell, W. (2006). ACLU of Texas perspective on the Austin police case study. In *Police labor–management relations (Vol. 1,* pp. 102–104). Washington, DC: Office of Community Oriented Policing Services, Department of Justice.

Herbert, S. (1998). Police subculture reconsidered. *Criminology, 36*(2), 343–368.

Houston Chronicle. (2006, September 11). Billboard bombast. Scare tactics used by the Houston Police Patrolman's Union misstate facts while damaging the city's image.

Human Rights Watch. (1998). *Shielded from justice.* New York: Human Rights Watch.

Hunt, T. (2006). Systemic failures: What was wrong with the LAPD? In *Police labor–management relations (Vol. 1,* pp. 73–78). Washington, DC: Office of Community Oriented Policing Services, Department of Justice.

International Association of Chiefs of Police (IACP). (1974). *Guidelines and papers from the National Symposium on Police Labor Relations.* Gaithersburg, MD: International Association of Chiefs of Police.

Jacobs, J.B. (1985). Police unions: How they look from the academic side. In W.A. Geller (Ed.), *Police leadership in America: Crisis and opportunity.* New York: Praeger.

Juris, H.A., & Feuille, P. (1973). *Police unionism.* Lexington: Lexington Books.

Kadleck, C. (2003). Police employee organizations. *Policing: An International Journal of Police Strategies & Management, 26*(2), 341–351.

Keenan, K., & Walker, S. (2005). An impediment of police accountability? An analysis of statutory law enforcement officers' Bills of Rights. *Boston University Public Interest Law Journal, 14,* 185–243.

Kliesmet, R.B. (1985). The chief and the union: May the force be with you. In W.A. Geller (Ed.), *Police leadership in America: Crisis and opportunity.* New York: Praeger.

Kramer, R., & Gold, E.G. (2006). Collective bargaining and labor agreements: Challenges to citizen oversight. In J.C. Perino (Ed.), *Citizen oversight of law enforcement.* Chicago: American Bar Association.

Kuhn, T.S. (1970). *The structure of scientific revolutions.* Chicago: University of Chicago Press.

Levi, M. (1977). *Bureaucratic insurgency.* Lexington: Lexington Books.

Los Angeles Times. (2006, September 12). Editorial. Police business is public business: The State Supreme Court was wrong to rule that officer privacy trumps the public's right to know.

Metropolitan News Enterprise. (2006, August 15). Supreme Court rules: City need not negotiate racial profiling study with police union.

Miami Herald. (2006, September 14). Police union to defend turf in budget battle.

Mollen Commission. (1994). *Report.* New York: Mollen Commission. Retrieved from www.parc. info

National Academy of Sciences. (2004). *Fairness and effectiveness in policing: The evidence.* Washington, DC: National Academy Press.

National Advisory Commission on Civil Disorders. (1968). *Report.* New York: Bantam Books.

News Channel 8 [East Haven, CT]. (2006). East Haven Police Union holds 'no confidence' vote.

Oakland Tribune. (2006, September 5). Do deputy chiefs toe the blue line? Union, city go to court in a battle over power, public trust.

O'Brien, K.M. (1996). The effect of political activity by police unions on nonwage bargaining outcomes. *Journal of Collective Negotiations in the Public Sector, 25*(2), 99–116.

Office of Community Oriented Policing Services. (2006). *Police labor–management relations: Perspectives and practical solutions for implementing change, making reforms, and handling crises for managers and union leaders (2 vols.).* Washington, DC: Department of Justice. Retrieved from www.cops.usdoj.gov

Polzin, M.P. (2006). Joint labor–management cooperation to implement community policing: Taking police union–management relations and community policing practices to the next level. In *Police labor–management relations (Vol. 1,* pp. 133–142). Washington, DC: Office of Community Oriented Policing Services, Department of Justice.

President's Commission on Law Enforcement and Administration of Justice. (1967). *Task force report: The police.* Washington, DC: Government Printing Office.

Rynecki, S., Cairns, D.A., & Cairns, D.J. (1978). *Police collective bargaining agreements: A national management survey.* Washington, DC: Police Executive Research Forum.

Sacramento Bee. (2006, August 30). Police union opposes arena ballot measures.

Sass, T.R., & Troyer, J.L. (1999). Affirmative action, political representation, unions, and female police employment. *Journal of Labor Research, 20*(4), 572–587.

Schachter, H.L. (1981). Fiscal crisis and police union bargaining: The case of New York. *Criminal Justice Review, 6*(2), 23–30.

Sherman, L.W. (1978). *Scandal and reform.* Berkeley: University of California Press.

Skogan, W.G., & Hartnett, S.T. (1997). *Community policing, Chicago style.* New York: Oxford University Press.

Skolnick, J.H. (1994). *Justice without trial* (3rd ed.). New York: Macmillan.

Skolnick, J.H., & Fyfe, J.J. (1993). *Above the law.* New York: Free Press.

Stamford Advocate. (2006, September 11). Police union fights fitness proposal.

US Department of Justice. (1997). *Police integrity: Public service with honor* (NCJ 163811). Washington, DC: Department of Justice. Retrieved from www.ncjrs.gov

Walker, S. (1977). *A critical history of police reform.* Lexington: Lexington Books.

Walker, S. (1985). Racial minority and female employment in policing: The implications of 'glacial' change. *Crime and Delinquency, 31*(4), 555–572.

Walker, S. (1995). Less than meets the eye: Police department bias crimes units. *American Journal of Police, XIV*(1), 29–48.

Walker, S. (1998). *Popular justice: A history of American criminal justice* (2nd ed.). New York: Oxford University Press.

Walker, S. (2001). *Police accountability: The role of citizen oversight.* Belmont, CA: Wadsworth.

Walker, S. (2004a, May). Science and politics in police research: Reflections on their tangled relationship. *Annals of the American Academy of Social and Political Science, 593,* 137–156.

Walker, S. (2004b). *The discipline matrix: An effective police accountability tool?* Omaha: Police Professionalism Initiative. Retrieved from www.policeaccountability.org

Walker, S., & Katz, C.M. (2008). *The police in America: An introduction* (6th ed.). New York: McGraw-Hill.

Walker, S., Spohn, C., & DeLone, M. (2007). *The color of justice: Race, ethnicity, and crime in America* (4th ed.). Belmont, CA: Wadsworth.

Weisburd, D., Greenspan, R., Hamilton, E.E., Williams, H., & Bryant, K.A. (2000). *Police attitudes toward abuse of authority: Findings from a national study* (NCJ 181312). Washington, DC: Department of Justice. Retrieved from www.ncjrs.gov

Westley, W. (1970). *Violence and the police.* Cambridge, MA: MIT Press.

Wilkinson, S. (2006). A chief's willingness to share power has been the secret to success. In *Police labor–management relations (Vol. 1,* p. 59). Washington, DC: Office of Community Oriented Policing Services, Department of Justice.

Zhao, J., & Lovrich, N. (1997). Collective bargaining and the police: The consequences for supplemental compensation policies in large agencies. *Policing, 20*(3), 508–518.

Strange union: changing patterns of reform, representation, and unionization in policing

Jan Berry[a], Greg O'Connor[b], Maurice Punch[c] and Paul Wilson[d]

[a]Police Federation of England and Wales, UK; [b]Police Association, New Zealand; [c]Mannheim Centre for Criminology, London School of Economics, London, UK; [d] Metropolitan Police, London, UK

Unions and policing are a relatively under-researched area. But this paper, adopting a comparative approach, argues that police unions have been and still are influential, that they differ across cultures, and are involved in a variety of ways in police reform. They can be supportive of change, hostile to it, or closely involved in the reform process. Some are representative bodies where the police may not unionize while there are increasingly special interest groups based on faith, gender, and ethnicity. This paper focuses on representation and voice for ordinary officers in relation to reform in policing.

Introduction

Policing and trade unions are strange bedfellows. Firstly, modern policing in many countries was historically a centrally led enterprise of state control. This has at times led to police forces being used against the collective actions of organized labour, sometimes in bitter confrontations. Secondly, the police organization typically recruited its rank-and-file personnel from the lower strata of society – and that meant predominantly 'working class' men – yet it was precisely people from this artisan background that unions represented (Punch, 2006). Trade unions emerged during the Industrial Revolution from the socialist movements of the nineteenth century, drew their strength largely from industrial workers, often had an adversarial stance towards owners, employers, and governments, and espoused a radical alteration in the balance of power in society. They could be highly militant, could employ the powerful weapon of the strike, and often elicited strong opposition as the forebears of instability, if not 'revolution.' But, as Reiner (1978) points out, the class position of ordinary police officers, whose siblings and peers may well have been unionized, was not reflected in their social–political views which were predominantly 'conservative.' In general, then, we do not associate police organizations and the policing profession with socialist values, with animosity to the (capitalist) state, and with political militancy.

It is of some interest, however, that these two intriguing juxtapositions have not elicited a great deal of research. There was a flurry of attention in the 1970s, with Reiner (1978) in the UK and Juris and Feuille (1973) in the USA, but since then the number of publications have been meagre; an exception is Australia (Finnane, 2008). The Berkeley Conference in 2006 aimed to rectify this deficit by focusing on the role of police unions and on police reform from the 'bottom up.' In fact, not all of the agencies represented at the meeting were 'unions' in the legal sense of being the representatives of employees with the right to bargain with management on pay, benefits, and working conditions (Adams, 2006). In fact, in some countries police unions are forbidden but representative bodies or 'associations' may be allowed; there may also be a range of agencies representing higher ranks and more recently there has been a proliferation of faith and identity-based groups which distance themselves from the mainstream union(s) to plead the special interests of their members.

Here, then, we use 'unions' to include police employee representative groupings which negotiate and/or agitate for improved working conditions and enhancing the special interests of members. And in addressing the wide-ranging themes of the conference – reform, unions, governance, and the idea of 'democratic' policing with respect for the rank and file as in a participative enterprise – we will draw on our respective experiences as an academic (Punch) and as practitioner representatives (Berry, Wilson, O'Connor) from three different societies (the Netherlands, UK, and New Zealand, respectively).

The meeting opened a vast area as everything touching on criminal justice and policing is in flux. Western societies are rapidly changing to a postmodern or 'post-Fordist' mode; many trade unions are altering drastically to adjust to new-style economies, and the police organization itself has been exposed to sustained pressure for several decades to undergo reform. Not only are the drivers of this change multiple and complex, but they also differ from society to society. This comparative, cross-cultural kaleidoscope should foster detailed case studies of unions and reform. What we wish to propose is a rudimentary typology of unions; at this stage it is merely designed to draw attention to variety in order to avoid over-generalizing on the issue.

Typology of police unions

If policing has been subject to continual, if vacillating, pressure to change then this has doubtless also impacted on police unions. Indeed, trade unions in general have altered substantially in recent decades. In a nutshell, old-style industrial unionization has decreased in many countries and has tended to lose its ideological bite. And with the globalization of the economy, a number of Western societies (notably the USA and UK) have followed policies that espouse flexible labour markets and restrictions in union power. In the USA very few firms are now unionized – only 8% of the workforce in the private sector (but 36% in the public sector) – and many southern states are constitutionally opposed to the 'closed shop.' Where does this leave police unions?

The work of unions generally revolves around bargaining for pay and benefits and conditions of employment. They may also sponsor politicians, lobby interest groups and the media, and mount court cases against employers. Police unions also have two functions of specific significance, on working conditions and on discipline cases. It is the second function that places the police unions apart from conventional unions. Given the potential dangers of police work, a police union is expected to push powerfully for improved training, equipment, and personal protection. This is particularly the case in South Africa where policing is highly dangerous but where resources and infrastructure remain wanting (Marks, 2005). Given that officers may face internal disciplinary or external legal charges as a result of their work, many officers view the union as a crucial safety net that will defend them before internal tribunals and/or the courts.

There is a real ambivalence here as unions wish to foster an image of supporting a professional and ethical workforce yet feel obliged to support individual officers who have clearly been deviant. Yet when reform involves higher standards of internal control and of ethical conduct, some unions have been supportive. In England and Wales, the Police Federation (a union in all but name) agreed to assertive measures within the Professional Standards Unit of the Metropolitan Police; and the New South Wales Police Association in Australia stood behind reforms resulting from a corruption scandal (Finnane, 2008). In some cases in the USA, in contrast, police unions have been an impediment to reform and have virulently opposed oversight.

Drawing on the conference papers and other sources we argue there are a variety of models that police unions could 'fit into':

- Firstly, there is the **liberal or progressive** Dutch model which would also hold for the Scandinavian countries.
- Secondly, there is what might be called the **reactionary** model based on traditional police culture, on conservative views on criminal justice issues, on battling civilian review, and opposing special commissions to investigate police deviance. This is typical of much unionism in the USA but probably also in a number of European countries including Eastern Europe.
- Thirdly, there is the censorious, **watchdog** model of unions in transient, developing societies such as South Africa. Here the union's role is largely to ensure that the promises of change, emancipation, and equity are being implemented following a major political and institutional shift (Marks, 2007).
- Fourthly, there are **reformed** or modernized associations which have managed to change their spots. For instance, although police unions in the UK are not permitted there is the Police Federation which is close to being one (there are three separate federations for England and Wales, Scotland, and Northern Ireland). It tended to reflect the conservative views of the rank and file, had a single issue focus on law and order, and was something of a male bastion. In recent decades it has moved to be far more representative of its gender and faith composition, fostering diversity and combating discrimination. Indeed, it is now chaired by a woman.
- Fifthly, and finally, although many unions have become more open to diversity, as in the reformed category above, they have been unable to prevent the rise of gender and faith-based associations which clearly feel that the main union does not adequately represent their particular views and needs. The Black Police Officers Association in the USA was one of the pioneers; and now in the UK there are 17 of these special interest groups which are posited on the view that the majority of union members are still male and Christian 'WASPs' (White Anglo-Saxon Protestants).

In effect, we are arguing that there are a range of styles and a variety of functions in police unions across and even within cultures. To illustrate this variety in the light of the themes and analysis above we wish to present portraits of three societies – the Netherlands, UK, and New Zealand. What we show is that these unions or associations are profoundly concerned with responding to external reform, are a force to be reckoned with, give voice to the rank and file, and have adapted to wider social change.

Reform

It is debatable as to what extent reform has been stimulated from the 'bottom up.' Bayley (2006), for instance, makes a convincing case in his paper that reform of the police has typically been both externally generated and explicitly **top-down**. Yet it may be that reform campaigns have a symbiotic relation with internal pressure for, or resistance to, change and can be a reaction to internal dissatisfaction or powerful police lobbying; the movers and shakers behind reform have to seriously take into account the views of the rank and file and the political and financial clout of their representatives (Marks, 2007).

The external, top-down mode has certainly been, and still is, true of the UK where successive governments have launched a 'maelstrom' of reform from the political centre which has swept relentlessly over the police for some 20 years (Leishman, Savage, & Loveday, 1996; Neyroud, 2007). This, in turn, raises a profound issue about the varying focus of police research between societies. Scholars from the USA, for example, have been the prime initiators of police research since the 1960s and have tended to dominate publications and the academic journals. In recent years, however, there have been a growing number of significant contributions to the policing field from researchers in Britain, elsewhere in Europe, Australia, and South Africa (Newburn, 2003, 2005). But as we get to know a great deal more cross-nationally about policing from this increasing volume of work, there remains a fundamental split in the discourse about policing between mainstream American scholars and many other academics from diverse cultures.

This split is founded on the simple fact that policing in the USA is overwhelmingly local. There are myriad agencies, many of them tiny, and the central government plays a relatively modest role in driving change; it may legislate, and pump in federal funding for programs, but it cannot demand uniformity across the country. With some 18,000 agencies, police practitioners and researchers function within a paradigm of extreme fragmentation, high decentralization and diversity, wide variety in standards, weak transfer of practices, and low central control. This is diametrically opposed to many European and other countries where the dominant player in policing, and police reform, is the central state.

This was noticeable in the conference dialogue where the American scholars tended to refer to local, city-based initiatives in reform; indeed, American police unions are predominantly local. Then, given that American social scientists have, with some exceptions, a tendency to be academically and culturally ethnocentric, it must be difficult for them to transpose themselves mentally to a society where successive governments have launched a battery of reforms to modernize and centralize the nation's entire police force, as has happened in the UK (Henry & Smith, 2007).

It must be even more confusing, moreover, to contemplate a society where trade unions are still influential in shaping national policies and where the police unions are enthusiastic supporters of institutional change, as is the case in the Netherlands. But before we look at the three countries we wish to touch briefly on the broader context of change in policing in order to sketch a backcloth to the three country studies.

Structural and cultural change

The key point made above is that we have to be cautious in generalizing about police unions and police reform. Furthermore, there have also been significant changes within police organizations in recent times (Bayley & Shearing, 2001). But until quite recently, and sometimes even within the memories of serving officers, the police organization was institutionally rigid with little attention to the operational opinions and occupational interests of ordinary officers. What we are sketching is a traditional institutional climate that was 'conservative' (normatively and occupationally), hierarchical, punishment-centred, and authoritarian. There was little formal appreciation of diversity of opinion, of innovation, and of initiative.

Then in many Western societies the police were faced in the 1960s with a period of turbulence and abrasive confrontation with new developments, issues, and groups which ushered in the beginnings of organizational change (Waddington, 1999). In a sense, that initial change movement can be partly interpreted as a form of internal emancipation and institutional loosening-up. One of the key concepts which began to emerge at that time was community-oriented policing or 'COP' (Peak & Glensor, 1996). It had its roots in a wish to fundamentally transform that traditional, rigid, overtly centralized, machine bureaucracy into a flexible institution. It proposed decentralization, involvement with citizens in the communities, more autonomy for local commanders, and a less hierarchical style of work for the front-line workers. These were to be perceived more as members of a team than in the atomistic structure of traditional patrolling. To a degree, the highly participative management style at Broken Arrow which is discussed by Steinheider and Wuestewald in this special issue exudes this philosophy.

Implicit in COP was a paradigm shift that attempted to fundamentally alter the structure and culture of policing. To what extent did this ostensible structural and cultural shift also encourage diversity of opinion and enhance participation and consultation in the police world? We wish to briefly touch on three key factors that have affected reform and the unions with the emphasis on change processes which are not linear and cumulative but are often ambivalent, if not contradictory, and even unpredictably cyclical.

- Firstly, if the COP movement is viewed as a major effort to 'unfreeze' the traditional organizational style through decentralization and the granting of local autonomy to community-oriented officers, then it could be maintained that this frequently only impacted on just one segment of the organization. There are many reports that COP was something of a marginal element, even within the Uniformed Patrol Branch, while it was disparaged not only by other patrol officers but especially by other departments, especially the Detective Branch. One reason for this is that many officers, chiefs, and politicians continue to view crime control as the 'core business' of policing. Reforming chiefs are often stymied by reports of poor performance on law enforcement, by a sudden, media-led moral panic on crime, or by the replacement of a supportive political boss by a crime-oriented successor (Skogan, 2006). Police organizations tend, then, to be subject to oscillation between competing paradigms and to periodic returns to the predominant, underlying crime control mode which is seen as getting back to 'business as usual.' Another reason has been a move in the USA and elsewhere towards increased militarization, to a greater emphasis on 'command and control,' and of course, to an enhanced orientation to combating international and domestic terrorism. The latter has led to more cooperation and joint units between the police and the military. Operationally this has fostered a shift towards large-scale, military-style interventions where autonomy and discretion are limited and the individual officer is subsumed in a unit with considerable fire-power and a rigid command structure. In short, reform, in the sense of loosening the traditional organization, is patchy, often marginal and subject to both periodic reversal and revival, depending usually on external political and societal developments.
- Secondly, there has been a major institutional move to what might be called forms of 'no-nonsense' policing (sometimes referred to as 'zero tolerance'). The widespread introduction of 'New Public Management,' or NPM, and a performance culture has brought with it both a restriction in the role of the ordinary officer, now seen as a production worker with set targets, and pressure from above for management to hit the figures. And proponents of zero tolerance policing in the USA brought in top-down, assertive and even intimidating modes of management, as in Compstat-style meetings in New York (Punch, 2007). This was not consultation and participation but

'kicking butts' with sanctions for non-performance, including public humiliation and even dismissal for senior officers. Yet at the same time NPM could also usher in a broader body of managerial knowledge, drawing more on 'Human Relations,' which adopted innovative management practices from outside the public services, participative leadership, the significance of the working group, investing in human resources, orientation to the customer, competency-based learning, and so on. In this mode, the views of front-line officers are taken seriously (Hoogenboom, 2006).

- Thirdly and finally, there has been the raft of changes in policing – including civilianization, gender and ethnic diversification – that have not only challenged traditional police culture but perhaps also questioned authoritarian styles of leadership. For instance, in the Netherlands gay police officers take part in uniform in the annual Gay Parade; and police staff members have walked in Britain in a Pride Parade under the banner 'Police with Pride' (*Police Review*, 1 September 2006). These examples reveal how what was largely a male-dominated organization with an often rigid, semi-military structure has become more of a complex, matrix organization geared to diversity of personnel and the freedom to express minority lifestyle and faith-based views and conduct. Nevertheless, there is still a constant refrain that the police organization and culture remain, informally if not formally, prejudiced against gays, females, and those from ethnic minorities. This continuing tension and constant battle for voice, rights, and recognition draws on the substantial changes in the wider society which emphasize individual and group rights and which have, in turn, impacted on the working environment of policing.

Police unions and associations in three societies

Unionized and progressive policing: the Netherlands

In turning to the Netherlands we wish to make the point that in some way a police union will reflect the national or regional culture within which policing is imbedded. There may well be a variety of competing unions within one society; in South Africa, for instance, there is rivalry between the more radical and militant Police and Prisons Civil Rights Union which is politically affiliated to the ANC and has led strikes, and the moderate and apolitical South African Police Union (Kwinika, 2006). In Canada, as Roy Adams discusses in this special issue, in some provinces police have the right to strike (but the Royal Canadian Mounted Police may not strike). Next to this variety there is also often a range of bodies representing diverse segments of the institutional hierarchy and rank structure. In England and Wales, for instance, these are the Superintendents' Association and Association of Chief Police Officers (ACPO), respectively (Savage, Charman, & Cope, 2000).

Amid this diversity there is a style of policing that might be called social democratic, liberal, or even progressive policing. Policing in the Netherlands changed considerably in the late 1960s and early 1970s from being traditional and conservative to more liberal. The internal catalyst was provided by three young officers who took the opportunity, when asked to work on an official report on calculating force strengths, to write a radical document arguing for major changes in policing. 'A Changing Police' (POS, 1977) ushered in a genuine paradigm shift and it became the blueprint for reform for the next 20 years. In a nutshell, it argued that legitimacy was essential to policing in a democratic society and that the police had to win back that legitimacy. The path to do so was to reorganize the police to be closer and more responsive to the public through a strongly Dutch form of COP. But of particular importance here is that it stated that, for the police to be a truly responsive institution within a democratic society, it also had to be based on internal democracy. In that sense it was a plea for internal emancipation to give all officers a voice in change (Nordholt & Straver, 1983).

The context was that Dutch society, which since the war was characterized by social conformity and institutional rigidity, faced a major upheaval in the second half of the 1960s with demands for more openness, democracy, and the end to old-style authoritarian leadership. This ushered in major reform in terms of 'industrial democracy,' with employing organizations being legally bound to set up a works council (Albeda, 1977). This had to be consulted by senior management on all major decisions. The structure and culture of most Dutch companies and institutions with employees became characterized by consultation, negotiations, consensus, and compromise. This typical Dutch model of governance is close to the 'Rhineland' model of close involvement of employees and management (Punch & van Dijk, 1993). In the Netherlands the trade unions were routinely involved, and still are, in tri-partite negotiations with government and employers as a legitimate and respected third partner.

'A Changing Police' supplied the Dutch Police, then, with an ideology and an organizational model that also spoke of internal democracy, while legislation meant that every force had to establish a works council. Of importance here, moreover, is that the Dutch police unions were believers in change. Dutch society had shifted strongly to a progressive approach to many issues and these included a liberal approach to criminal justice, punishment, incarceration, pornography, prostitution, abortion, and drugs (Downes, 1988). In general the police unions also became 'progressive' and, in particular, welcomed change. The unions have remained highly supportive of change (Punch, 2006).

There are nine representative bodies in the Netherlands, national and regional, and nearly every police officer is a member of one of the bodies, giving a membership density of well over 90%. The main union, the Dutch Police Union (NPB), is affiliated to the major federation of trade unions (FNV). The unions negotiate directly with the Minister and his officials on pay and conditions although as civil servants any agreements will be coloured by settlements with other categories of government employees. There is no right to strike but officers have on occasion demonstrated openly. Recently some 13,000 officers in relays kept up a constant, noisy 'siege' of the Ministry of the Interior for several days to express their dissatisfaction with proposals for pay and conditions.

Generally the cohort of union leaders of the last two decades was seen both as good police officers and as skilled unionists. They earned wide respect, were liberal in their views, were frequently highly vocal in the media, and were supportive of change. This state of affairs has started to alter as new professional union leaders take over with no police past; also there is legislation that is weakening the powers of unions in general. But participation and consultation are part and parcel of the culture and practice of Dutch management and labour relations.

In short, the Netherlands is a society where, unlike the USA, trade unions are still taken seriously and where police unions are viewed as legitimate, sophisticated, liberal, and influential. And, of importance, is the fact that reform may not have come from below – it was initiated by middle-ranking officers on the periphery of the establishment – but it was a direct response to manifest dissatisfaction from below. And the unions, again unlike the case in much of the USA, favoured that reform.

Britain and the Police Federation of England and Wales

The Police Federation of England and Wales is the official representative organization to which all police officers from the rank of constable to chief inspector belong. The Federation was established in 1919, following a sudden strike by the majority of constables and sergeants in the London Metropolitan Police (Critchley, 1978). The Police Act of 1919 established the Police Federation as the representative body for all police officers from constable to chief inspector, its purpose was to consider and bring to the notice of the authorities 'all matters affecting their welfare and efficiency'; the Act prohibited police from joining a trade union and made it a criminal offence to induce a police officer to strike. These restrictions remain in force today.

Nevertheless, the Federation has functioned almost as a union to the extent that it has been able to secure substantial improvements in pay and conditions of service and it is able to negotiate on a range of collective matters (Mawby & Wright, 2003). Furthermore, major reforms in the police organization have been due in part to initiatives launched by the Federation. Some academics have taken a sceptical view of the Federation; Reiner (2000), for instance, traced its development from 'humble professional association' to 'media opinion leader.' He attributed this to a period in the early 1970s when the Federation came to prominence by campaigning to reverse the liberalizing trend in penal and social policy. At that time the Federation was able to sponsor two members of Parliament (the Labour Party was highly dependent on union support both financially and in Parliament). That association with a narrow, single-issue, 'law and order' agenda has significantly diminished (McLaughlin & Murji, 1998). In a number of respects the Federation has modernized itself and this can be seen especially in the crucial field of promoting greater diversity (Neyroud, 2003).

The Police Federation has fully entered the debate about police reform and has participated in all the discussions at various levels that are part of the process. As the representative of around 138,000 police personnel, it participates in the process of reform from the bottom up. For since the early 1990s, the British police service has been enmeshed in a constant, relentless process of police reform. This is driven largely by the objectives of central government which were geared to reforming the public services in general and in cutting public spending. The Conservative administration of 1992–97 took two significant initiatives towards police reform. The first was the setting up of the Sheehy Inquiry (1993) into police pay. The Committee's proposals for major reductions in pay were met with immediate and virulent opposition from all of the police staff associations, including chief officers. The Minister concerned and his successor decided not to pick a fight with the entire police service. The main recommendations of the report were not implemented.

But the Conservative governments of that time were not that easily deflected and, having been stymied on Sheehy, the Government turned to its second initiative. It proposed that the democratically elected police authorities in charge of the forces outside of London should be abolished and replaced by new bodies, most of whose members would be nominated by the Secretary of State. Their task would be to set local policing priorities and ensure that their forces met both local and national requirements. The plan ran into immediate opposition from a wide spectrum of public opinion. It was seen as a centralizing measure that would put too much power into the hands of central government. Furthermore, whereas the Government insisted that the primary purpose of the police was fighting crime, the Federation's response was that protecting life was the first responsibility of policing, and preventing crime was better than detecting it. Indeed, when the Government's Bill came before Parliament it encountered fierce opposition from all sides. On two occasions, then, police representatives were able to blunt and deflect government proposals which were seen as not being in the best interest of the service. In a way these were not just defensive tactics as cutting pay would have consequences for recruitment and the quality and standing of the profession. Central control over the police has been a bone of contention since the first day of policing in Britain.

Then when the New Labour Government was first elected in 1997 it launched if anything a much wider policy of reforming all Britain's public services. It paid particular attention to the police, because law and order had become a political hot potato which strongly affected the electorate. Like the Conservatives the Government set out to strengthen central control of police forces through the National Policing Plan. The Police Reform Act 2002 purported to set the agenda for the police service for the next 10 years. The emphasis was upon increasing the number of 'civilians' who perform a wide variety of tasks which previously had been carried out by police officers. This has meant that the dividing line between police and non-police tasks has become increasingly blurred. The Federation has expressed concern about a barely hidden agenda where cheaper person power, rather than concerns with effectiveness, is the motive force.

Although the Government has financed a dramatic increase in police officer numbers there has also been a similar growth in the numbers of support staff who have taken on roles designed to release police officers for operational tasks. There has been a rapid expansion in the number of Police Community Support Officers (PCSOs). These are not sworn officers, have no powers of arrest, but may detain suspects until police arrive. They wear uniforms almost identical to those of police constables and their presence on the streets has been welcomed by the general public. The Federation has strong reservations about PCSOs. In their view, there are the positive aspects, such as reassurance for the public, but there is concern that lower-grade employees will be more attractive to cash-strapped police authorities than fully trained and fully empowered police constables.

In addition, the Government, and some chief officers, have advanced the argument for direct, 'lateral' recruitment into higher ranks of specially qualified persons (Blair, 2003). This would entail a break from the long-standing tradition which has always applied to the British Police that all officers start off as constables. So far, very few such appointments have been made but the Federation argues that they should be employed as non-sworn staff. Recently, as a further stage of the reform project, a report by HM Inspectorate concluded that a significant number of smaller police forces were no longer 'fit for purpose' because they lacked the personnel and financial resources to cope with burgeoning problems of crime and disorder. There were proposals to reduce the number of police forces from 43 to about 15 'strategic forces' in England and Wales. Although majority opinion in the police service supported the broad drift of this plan, it ran into strong opposition from local government, and a new Home Secretary shelved the scheme. Again there are fundamental differences of opinion at play about the structure, culture, composition, functions, and future of British policing.

The Federation and the other representative bodies have, then, been embroiled in continuous debate and prolonged campaigns with government and other stakeholders about the essence of policing in relation to domestic politics, changing crime patterns, and societal shifts in British society. The Federation now asserts that it put its full backing into efforts to make the police service embrace full diversity. Earlier the Federation was long seen as a male preserve and for many years it was even fervently opposed to the employment of women police officers. This attitude has changed and the Federation is now in equal partnership with the British Association of Women Police. It welcomed the Sex Discrimination Act 1976 and has provided strong moral and financial backing to women officers who have suffered sexual discrimination in any form. The Federation has, moreover, declared its resolute opposition to any form of racial discrimination.

Today, it could be maintained the Federation, and policing in Britain, is facing the largest single challenge it has ever encountered. The police reform project now touches every facet of policing. It challenges some of the basic tenets of policing philosophy, such as the retention of the unique status of the constable in law, and how this is affected by the extension of policing tasks to civilian un-sworn staff. It has thrown up deep differences of opinion between various sections of the service, with some at the top pressing for headlong reforms without, in the Federation's view, sufficient regard for the drawbacks to some of the proposals. For during the past 10 years or more, the service has been subjected to successive governmental initiatives aimed at securing improvements in overall police performance. All forces must conform to the requirements of national policing plans, drawn up by central government. The concern is that, by giving total priority to the achievement of specific targets, the police are only concentrating on what can be quantified and measured. This leaves individual officers with no time to deal with other problems that confront ordinary citizens and that often do not figure in the order of priorities. Yet this is the kind of 'reassurance' policing, based on personal contact between police officers and citizens, which has been the bedrock of British policing for generations. If this is lost, the Federation believes that the police become a uniformed coercive force rather than a service.

Police reform is a worthy objective; but, as the representative of the rank and file, the Federation clearly feels that it is protecting the traditional basis of 'policing by consent' which has typified British policing. The Federation and other bodies state that they recognize that change and reform are inevitable; and the police service must continually respond to new challenges. Indeed, the Police Federation accepted this some 10 years ago and called for a Royal Commission on Policing. This would have meant a thorough, politically independent review of the structure and purpose of policing. At the time there was little support for such a review. Instead the service has experienced a relentless, piecemeal reform process that has been riddled with unforeseen consequences. The need for a holistic review of policing remains and the Chief Officers of ACPO now agree with this standpoint. At times there has been a positive response to reform with shifting coalitions between the police representative bodies. At other times the response to continual external pressure has been to elicit unanimity between all representative levels, and not just the rank and file. For the issues at stake are not simply on pay, conditions, and welfare but on fundamental decisions relating to the structure, culture, composition, control, and essential philosophy of policing in Britain. The Federation is a major voice in all this and exerts considerable influence on the reform process.

The development of a Black Police Association

While the Police Federation claims to fully embrace diversity this is not sufficient for some interest groups based on faith, gender, or identity which seek separate representation outside its domain. This raises the question as to why a group of black police and non-sworn police employees decided to meet in 1993 to discuss whether there was a requirement for a distinctly identifiable black platform to articulate their views and concerns within the Metropolitan Police of London. That historical development needs to be placed in the wider context of police and black community relations.

Of considerable significance, for instance, is that until the mid-1960s, black people were not welcome in the Metropolitan Police Service (MPS) and probably most other UK forces. One of the reasons for the opposition by senior police officers appears to have been concern over the reaction of the Police Federation and its members. These concerns would appear to have been justified if we consider the overtly racist treatment some of the early black constables had to endure.

Then a watershed event in bringing race to centre-stage in British criminal justice occurred on the weekend of 10–12 April 1981. Hundreds of mostly black youths rioted in Brixton, South London. In the ensuing disturbances police were attacked with stones, bricks, iron bars, and petrol bombs. Many officers were injured, there was looting, buildings were damaged by fire, and police vehicles were attacked. This was a time of recession, unemployment was high and for black youths it was estimated at 55%. Brixton was not alone and street riots occurred in other impoverished inner-city areas of Britain that summer.

Lord Scarman was appointed by the Home Secretary to hold an inquiry. Scarman's report (1981, p. 2) concluded that 'complex political, social and economic factors' created a 'disposition towards violent protest.' This report proved highly influential. He found loss of confidence and mistrust in the police and their methods of policing. Liaison arrangements between police, community, and local authority had already collapsed before the disturbances. He recommended concerted efforts to recruit more ethnic minorities into the police force, and changes in training and law enforcement. The problems of racial disadvantage and inner-city decline were highlighted and more 'Urgent action' was needed to prevent racial disadvantage becoming an 'endemic, ineradicable disease threatening the very survival of our society.' Positive discrimination to tackle racial disadvantage was 'a price worth paying' (Scarman, 1981, p. 208).

Then in 1983 the Policy Studies Institute (PSI) conducted a survey of Metropolitan Police Officers as part of their 'Police and People in London' report. This publication caused some newspapers to brand the police as 'racist, sexist and drunken bullies,' for there were some overtly racist and discriminatory remarks made by the sampled officers about the black community. In 1984 a serving inspector (Hope, 1984) conducted research into the experiences of black and Asian police officers, comparing a sample of 36 black and Asian officers with 36 white officers. His main conclusions were that negative interaction with supervisors was a particular concern to all black and Asian police officers: black (African and African Caribbean) officers in particular were adversely affected by racism; there was no support for victims of racism, neither by management nor the Police Federation; white officers had no sympathy for, or understanding of, black and Asian police officers' problems.

In 1990 another milestone was reached when the MPS, concerned at the disproportionately high premature resignation rate among black police officers, organized a series of seminars whereby all black police officers in the Met were ordered to attend. The seminars, held away from London at Bristol University, unearthed a wealth of hitherto hidden and unspoken experiences from the roughly 350 officers that attended. Some of the issues arising from the Bristol sessions were: feelings of isolation/lack of support; failure of supervisors to tackle inappropriate humour and behaviour; officers who complained were branded as troublemakers; the perception that career opportunities were restricted – particularly into the Criminal Investigation Department (CID); in effect, black officers were not being used effectively to represent the Service. Furthermore, research (French, 1993) into the voluntary resignation of officers from the MPS concluded that racism does contribute significantly to their decision to resign. It is against this backdrop that black officers throughout the 1970s, 1980s, and 1990s were expected to compete on equal terms, to thrive, to develop, and to become potential leaders of the police service.

The Bristol seminars brought many black officers together for the first time and the feelings of isolation diminished further as many kept in touch through a series of Bristol Reunions. Around this time as well a small number of black civil staff (un-sworn police employees) attended a management development course for 'ethnic minorities.' On return to work they developed an informal network and this network joined with the Bristol Reunion group. Following a number of meetings, the launch of the Black Police Association (BPA) took place at New Scotland Yard (the Headquarters of the MPS) in September 1994. It could be argued that this was an oppositional stance to the dominant occupational culture by black policing professionals who not only cared about their profession but also strongly identified with the plight and frustrations of London's black community.

The aim and objectives of the BPA were and are: 'To improve the working environment for black personnel within the Metropolitan Police Service, with a view to enhancing the quality of service to the public.' Underpinning this aim were six objectives: providing a support network; working towards improving relationships between police and black people; working towards equality of opportunity; helping to improve recruitment and to reduce wastage; assisting policy development; and providing a social network.

Following the launch of the BPA, attention was drawn to racism and discrimination in policing by two inquiries. The first concerned a murder which had an immense impact on policing the capital and elsewhere. There is strong consensus that the public inquiry into the racist murder of the black teenager Stephen Lawrence was a catalyst for change. Indeed, its impact can be compared to that of Scarman's report on Brixton. The public inquiry's labelling of the Metropolitan Police as 'institutionally racist' caused reverberations throughout the UK establishment. Indeed, the BPA's written and oral evidence to the inquiry team is now recognized as being hugely influential (MacPherson, 1999). The oral evidence of the representatives of the MPS Black Police Association focused further on the police occupational culture and the stereotyping of black people.

The conclusions of the MacPherson Inquiry were damning. Institutional racism had never before been acknowledged by a UK government or by any official inquiry. However, MacPherson was unequivocal: the Metropolitan police force was institutionally racist; and the whole criminal justice system had to look to its institutional racism. The implication was that the restoration of the black community's confidence in the police depended on real commitment.

Secondly, the Morris Inquiry (2004) into the MPS's 'professional standards' (covering complaints, discipline, and corruption), was established after the Black Police Association claimed its members were being disproportionately targeted for disciplinary investigations. The MPS had spent millions of pounds investigating two leading BPA activists of corruption and dishonesty but both were cleared. The extensive inquiry concluded:

> There is no common understanding of diversity within the organisation and it is not embedded in the culture of the MPS ... We fear that some of the efforts the MPS has made to promote the message of diversity across the organisation have been counter productive and the organisation may now be seeing the beginnings of a backlash ... Urgent work must be undertaken to build the confidence of managers in managing all aspects of difference. (Brown, 2005)

Since the inception of the BPA in 1994 within the MPS, similar associations have developed in many if not the majority of police forces in England and Wales. This process has undoubtedly been helped by the government's recognition that such associations are crucial in helping the police improve their historically poor relationship with black and other minority ethnic communities. Government support has helped the development of a national umbrella body, the National Black Police Association (NBPA), with funds for offices and resources. Recognizing the success of the Black Police Association in getting the views of minorities represented in senior policy forums, other minority identity-based organizations have developed including the Greek Police Association, Hindu Police Association, Association of Muslim Police Officers, and the Jewish Police Association.

The proliferation of Staff Associations in the MPS is arguably a consequence of the fact that, when approaching 25% of Londoners are from minority ethnic backgrounds, the MPS remains woefully unrepresentative of London's increasingly diverse population. Government targets introduced following the MacPherson Inquiry were designed to ensure that London's police service broadly represented London's diverse communities by the end of the decade. These targets are unlikely to be achieved for at least 30 years. Against this backdrop many minorities in the MPS see representative groups as the only means of achieving a voice in a wholly white, male-dominated organization. In turn, this issue complements the government's objective of inspiring greater minority ethnic community confidence in the police service.

Police unions – buyers or sellers? New Zealand

Here we wish to explore the power relationships between police unions, police commissioners, and their political masters in the context of New Zealand. The argument is that police unions are ultimately sellers of their support and as such, must be very careful to protect their product or the product they sell may well be spoiled. In this situation of power imbalance where police forces and governments are buyers of police association support there is a well-recognized need for them to maintain a working relationship with a group they are not always comfortable with. In turn police union leaders face a dilemma in attempting to be genuine participants in the police reform process while at the same time maintaining the support of their general membership.

New Zealand has a single national police of 7500 sworn officers and 2500 non-sworn or civilian support officers laterally entered into the police at levels as high as deputy commissioner (who is currently an accountant). They police a geographically dispersed population of 4.2 million people: roughly a third of the population are indigenous Maori, Polynesian, or Asian with the rest of European stock. The New Zealand Police Association (NZPA), almost uniquely among police unions, represents *all* police employees, including civilians and commissioned officers up to the rank of assistant commissioner, although a small group of commissioned officers are represented by the Police Managers' Guild. Being a national association representing all staff, the NZPA is able to deal with media and government nationally with one voice. The NZPA adopted a philosophy of establishing itself as a highly credible commentator on policing and the broader law and order issues. The Association is, for instance, regarded as the principle commentator on the gang and organized crime growth associated with the problem and has run conferences and brought experts to New Zealand to speak about both issues.

At the same time the police became involved in an ambitious computer project which failed to deliver its goals and cost millions of dollars. This allowed the government subsequently to place strict financial oversights on the police which reduced the independence of the commissioner. The tendency in New Zealand is one familiar in other countries and jurisdictions where there is an increased 'politicization' of the police chief's role together with the removal of much of his or her power through financial constraints. In New Zealand this created something of a vacuum of power and influence at the top of the police organization and the NZPA has actively filled this space. In an environment where crime and fear of crime are prominent in the media, the President of the NZPA is often given a higher media profile than the commissioner who does not have the same freedom to comment and must be continually wary of any remark that could be interpreted as negative for the government.

It could be argued, somewhat ironically, that the real power of police unions arises from the fact that they are in the best position to benefit from the increased fear of crime; in a sense they are in the 'fear of crime' industry.

Understanding this is extremely important in making decisions on how police unions can be part of the evolution and reform of the policing industry. In general, the power of police unions has been harnessed to provide for improved working conditions and welfare provisions for police officers, from better pay and equipment through to increased numbers. But the NZPA also understands that its power had to be geared to enhancing the development and reform of the police as well. And, to ensure that the membership is supportive of reform means coaching them to understand the case for change. Yet members' satisfaction is probably most strongly allied to how successful the unions have been at improving their working situation. Failure at this level always contains some threat of removal by vote.

There is a potential conflict here for union officials between wanting to retain their elected position and becoming part of any reform process which involves restructuring in a way that impinges on job stability or members' promotion prospects. External reform driven by a restructuring dynamic or by financial constraints is almost inevitably going to result in considerable change to human resource practices and this implies that police unions become involved in reform as concerned commentators extending limited or cautious support or as antagonists and opponents, unless they want to risk the ire of the members.

This dilemma can be illustrated by the current situation in New Zealand. The government has proposed a rewrite of the 1958 Police Act while the new commissioner wants to incorporate considerable changes to the HR provisions to give far more flexibility in employment. The commissioner has requested the support of the NZPA to achieve this. In response, the Association has a full-time appointee to the Police Act rewrite team, is being closely consulted on all aspects, and has a team of practitioners to act as consultants and 'reality-checkers' to the Act. This involvement in legislative and structural change has to be finely balanced with engaging the membership who simply want to know how reform will impact on their interests. To complicate matters pay negotiations are simultaneously taking place. The commissioner is, in effect, in the position of a buyer who must come up with a reasonable offer to satisfy the 'seller,' which is the Association acting on behalf of its membership. The NZPA, while eager to be part of this reform process and in a strong position to be highly influential in doing this, needs to maintain a balance between taking a responsible and even proactive and inclusive approach to reform and to ensuring the majority of its membership is sufficiently reassured to embrace the change process.

One of the major challenges for all police unions in the future, however, will be to maintain their considerable power which results from the fact that they represent almost the entire (if not all) police workforce and from their relative autonomy from political masters. Being forced by members to use their power primarily to improve wages and conditions risks the sort of 'feather-bedding' that has brought about the demise of once powerful trade unions in a number of countries on account of restrictive practices. The fear of crime threat is now in danger of becoming over-used, and some police unions are under pressure to become militant, using industrial action, or threatening it, to leverage pay increases. Police union leaders who resist this path might well be replaced by those who promise a more militant approach to bargaining and who are more narrowly concerned with improving the working conditions of their members irrespective of the changes that are taking place in the broader policing environment. Government, in turn, may feel forced to look for cheaper means of providing security for their citizens such as the Community Support Officers in the UK, discussed earlier in this paper. This 'plural policing,' which is also prevalent in the Netherlands, puts more uniforms on the street for less cost and is attractive to administrators.

For the reasons explored above, it is difficult to imagine police unions actually leading the case for radical change when this will impact on their members' aspirations and material interests. The test for police union leaders will be to understand the changes in the environment in which they operate and to appreciate where their power lies (Burgess, Fleming, & Marks, 2006). Advocating the status quo is not really an option, as it will ultimately consign police unions to irrelevance, and managing that balance between working with the government as purchasers of police reform while not putting an exorbitant price on police member support is the challenge facing more forward thinking police union leaders.

Police reform has become an inevitable, and in some respects even desirable, feature of police organizations. This implies that police union leaders need to have a reform agenda of their own to proactively place before police chiefs and government. The NZPA has already begun to think ahead in this way. In 2004, the NZPA invited academics, experts, and officials from other non-police enforcement agencies to attend its delegates' conference to debate the extent to which their agencies are strategizing to take over more traditional police work. The conference unanimously passed a motion instructing the leaders to 'future proof' the Association in relation to changes in its environment. In order to survive police unions have to maintain their power base as sellers or vendors in the police reform environment and make police management and government realize they are purchasers. Treating the relationship in this manner can ensure that police unions continue to maintain value in their product and that well-planned and relevant reform will serve to maintain that value.

Conclusions

In conclusion, we have argued that there are a range of styles and a variety of functions in police unions across and within societies. We have constructed a rudimentary typology to convey this diversity. But clearly that, in turn, requires further research to flesh out in depth the pertinent differences between the rapidly shifting contexts in various countries and between unions. The Police Federation of England and Wales is, for instance, well resourced because virtually everyone from the lower ranks is a member: the substantial amounts from fees enable it to sponsor campaigns, to advertise, to lobby politicians and stakeholders, and to launch court cases on behalf of its members. This contrasts, say with South Africa, where the two main unions have to compete for members and are nowhere near as well resourced as the Federation (which also receives support from the government). It also stands in stark contrast to the USA where unions are essentially local.

In New Zealand the Police Association represents all police personnel, sworn and non-sworn, and is clearly shrewd at using its bargaining power in a fluid political situation with considerable institutional change on the cards. In the Netherlands the unions not only have a high density of membership but can draw on a still relatively influential trade union movement which means they are taken seriously by police management, the government, and other stakeholders. And in the Black Police Association in the UK we can see a splinter group – which can be compared to other representative bodies based on faith, ethnicity, identity, or gender – which argues that the traditional police union (in this case the Federation) does not adequately pursue its interests. Although the Federation would argue that it has moved substantially away from its traditional WASP style and membership, we can surmise that as police forces become more multicultural their employees will likely demand separate representation for their specific interests. This will continue if they are motivated by feelings of discrimination and exclusion. And there is evidence of how resilient traditional police culture remains (Chan, 1999).

There are, then, a number of key variables – size, strength, resources, militancy, relation to the main union movement, legal status and rights, etc. – which could be used to chart differences between unions and associations. A fundamental one is the union's stance on reform. The papers and discussion at the conference illustrated cogently that certain unions are deeply concerned with responding to external reform, and are a force to be reckoned with (despite legislation weakening union power in some countries), provide an increasingly sophisticated voice for the rank and file, and have adapted to wider social change with some success.

In a number of countries 'reform' has meant government proposals to alter the nature of the police organization through external pressure for results, budgetary discipline, altered recruitment, and new working practices. In Britain the response of the Federation has been somewhat defensive and it has mounted opposition that has led to victories in a number of skirmishes which have successfully thwarted government proposals. This defensiveness is understandable when it comes to reform impacting on jobs, pay, pensions, security of employment, and conditions of work. But as we have shown in this paper, this defensiveness does not make them 'Luddites' or dinosaurs. The unions are often highly enlightened about, and supporters of, institutional change centred on enhanced professionalism, quality of infrastructure, employment of new technology, standards of integrity, welfare provision, and recruitment of minorities. This is definitely the case in the Netherlands where police union leaders are respected as committed and sophisticated partners in the change process. A major dilemma arises when a union wishes to be positively engaged in reform but sees the reform agenda as both distorting the domain assumptions of a policing philosophy, as in attempts in the UK to reducing policing to crime control, and as an assault on the rights and rewards of its membership.

This raises a host of empirical questions that need to be answered. The meeting in Berkeley and this special issue of *Police Practice and Research* will hopefully foster a research agenda which addresses the historical, comparative, and contemporary issues we have raised in this paper. This agenda needs to address change in relation to the police organization, internal and external reform, police unions (including representative associations and special interest groups) with particular regard to internal democracy, employee rights, and voice for all police officers and employees.

References

Adams, R.J. (2006). *The human right of police to organize and bargain collectively.* Paper presented at 'Police Reform from the Bottom Up' roundtable, Berkeley Center for Criminal Justice, University of California, Berkeley, October 12–13 2006.

Albeda, W. (1977). *Arbeidsverhoudingen in Nederland (2nd ed.).* Alphen a/d Rijn: Samson.

Bayley, D.H. (2006). *Police reform: Who done it?* Paper presented at 'Police Reform from the Bottom Up' roundtable, Berkeley Center for Criminal Justice, University of California, Berkeley, October 12–13 2006.

Bayley, D.H., & Shearing, C.D. (2001). *The new structure of policing.* Washington, DC: NIJ.

Blair, I. (2003). *Leading towards the future.* Speech at conference on Future of Policing, London School of Economics.

Brown, J. (2005). *Academic commentary on the Morris Report.* Paper presented at Bramshill Seminar, University of Surrey.

Burgess, M., Fleming, J., & Marks, M. (2006). Thinking critically about police unions in Australia: Internal democracy and external responsiveness. *Police Practice and Research: An International Journal, 7*(5), 391–409.

Chan, J. (1997). *Changing police culture: Policing in a multicultural society.* Cambridge: Cambridge University Press.

Critchley, T.A. (1978). *A history of the police in England and Wales* (Rev. ed.). London: Constable.

Downes, D. (1988). *Contrasts in tolerance.* Oxford: Clarendon Press.

Finnane, M. (2008). No longer a 'workingman's paradise'? Australian police unions in a changing industrial environment. *Police Practice and Research: An International Journal, 9*(2), 131–143.

French, P. (1993). *The voluntary resignation of black and Asian police officers from the Metropolitan Police Service.* London: Metropolitan Police.

Henry, A., & Smith, D.J. (Eds.). (2007). *Transformations of policing.* Aldershot: Ashgate.

Hoogenboom, A.B. (2006). *Operationele betrokkenheid. Bedrijfsvoering Nederlands Politie 1993–2005.* Zeist: Kerkebosch.

Hope, R. (1984). *The experiences of black and Asian police officers.* MSc dissertation, Cranfield Institute.

Juris, H.A., & Feuille, P. (1973). *Police unionism.* Lexington, MA: Lexington Books.

Kwinika, M. (2006). *Police unions and police reform.* Paper presented at 'Police Reform from the Bottom Up' roundtable, Berkeley Center for Criminal Justice, University of California, Berkeley, October 12–13 2006.

Leishman, F., Savage, S., & Loveday, B. (Eds.). (1996). *Core issues in policing.* Harlow: Longman.

MacPherson, Sir W. (1999). *Stephen Lawrence Inquiry.* London: HMSO.

Marks, M. (2005). *Transforming robocops.* Scottsville, RSA: University of KwaZulu-Natal Press.

Marks, M. (2007). Police unions and their cultural influence: Subculture or counter-culture. In M. O'Neill, M. Marks, & A. Singh (Eds.), *Rethinking police culture: New debates and directions* (pp. 229–251). London: Elsevier.

Mawby, R.C., & Wright, A. (2003). The police organisation. In T. Newburn (Ed.), *Handbook of policing* (pp. 169–195). Cullompton, Devon: Willan.

Morris, Sir W. (2004). *The case for change: People in the Metropolitan Police Service.* London: Metropolitan Police Authority.

Newburn, T. (Ed.). (2003). *Handbook of policing.* Cullompton, Devon: Willan.

Newburn, T. (Ed.). (2005). *Policing: Key readings.* Cullompton, Devon: Willan.

Neyroud, P. (2003). Policing and ethics. In T. Newburn (Ed.), *Handbook of policing* (pp. 578–602). Cullompton, Devon: Willan.

Neyroud, P. (2007). Managing the police through a time of change. In A. Henry & D.J. Smith (Eds.), *Transformations of policing* (pp. 213–224). Aldershot: Ashgate.

Nordholt, E., & Straver, R. (1983). The changing police. In M. Punch (Ed.), *Control in the police organization* (pp. 36–46). Cambridge, MA: MIT Press.

Peak, K.J., & Glensor, R.W. (1996). *Community policing and problem solving.* Upper Saddle River, NJ: Prentice Hall.

Police Review (2006, September 1). Police with pride, p. 13.

POS. (1977). *Politie in Verandering.* Den Haag: Staatsdrukkerij.

Punch, M. (2006). *Policing by degrees: Essex police officers' experience of university education.* Groningen: Hondsrug Pers.

Punch, M. (2007). *Zero tolerance policing.* Bristol: Policy Press.

Punch, M., & van Dijk, N. (1993). Open doors, closed circles: Management and organization in the Netherlands. In D.K. Hickson (Ed.), *Management in Western Europe* (pp. 167–190). New York and Berlin: Walter de Gruyter.

Reiner, R. (1978). *The blue-coated worker.* Cambridge: Cambridge University Press.

Reiner, R. (2000). *The politics of the police* (3rd ed.). Oxford: Oxford University Press.

Savage, S., Charman, S., & Cope, S. (2000). *Policing & the power of persuasion.* London: Blackstone.

Scarman, Lord (1981). *The Brixton disorders 10–12 April 1981.* London: HMSO.

Sheehy, P. (1993). *Inquiry into police responsibilities and rewards.* London: HMSO.

Skogan, W.G. (2006). *Why reforms fail.* Paper presented at 'Police Reform from the Bottom Up' roundtable, Berkeley Center for Criminal Justice, University of California, Berkeley, October 12–13 2006.

Waddington, P.A.J. (1999). *Policing citizens.* London: UCL Press.

No longer a 'workingman's paradise'? Australian police unions and political action in a changing industrial environment

Mark Finnane

Centre for Public Culture and Ideas, Griffith University, Brisbane, Australia

The prospects of engaging police unions in a process of police reform is conditioned by the political context and organisational culture that characterises those unions. Understanding the historical formation of unions and the changing nature of their aspirations and interests is critical to appreciating such prospects. The history of Australian police unions, long established and privileged by high levels of acceptance in their political environment, suggests the need for optimism about police union engagement in police reform to be balanced by a realism about the limitations imposed by their primary purpose, to serve the interests of their members.

Introduction

What has been, what might be, what should be, the role of police unions in police reform? To address such questions invites the possibility of both positive and negative appraisal – and historical perspective. Historically the subject is large, but little addressed. Internationally the literature has been dominated until recently by a burst of attention in the 1970s, with much silence subsequently. Robert Reiner's study (Reiner, 1978) of what he called the 'blue-coated worker,' published nearly 30 years ago, remains the exemplary sociological study of police unionisation, not limited in its value to what it says about the particular English context which it addressed. Surprisingly ignored in the USA, the history of police unions has been little addressed since the early 1970s studies of the emergence of a more aggressive police labour movement after decades of constraint (Bopp, 1971; Burpo, 1971; Gammage & Sachs, 1972; Juris & Feuille, 1973). This flowering of work on police unionisation expressed a contemporary recognition that police were increasingly conscious of themselves as workers, bearing rights and interest that they sought to deploy in an environment that encouraged the rise of a plurality of social movements.

None of these works constituted a substantive historical account of police unionisation in the respective jurisdictions and little attention was paid subsequently in either Britain or the USA to this phenomenon. Among academic researchers the present author's monograph on the history of Australian police unions (Finnane, 2002) is unusual in its historical focus on the politics of the police unions although there have been valuable contributions more in the institutional history genre, for example, for New Zealand (McGill, 1992) and the Republic of Ireland (Allen, 1999). In the journal literature there has however been a developing focus on the status of police unions in both policing and industrial relations studies, enabling recent large-scale comparative work across a wide range of jurisdictions (Marks & Fleming, 2006).

In addressing below the relations between police reform and police unions I consider the lessons that might be learned from the history of the cluster of police unions that lie within the Australian jurisdiction. To what degree have police unions been able to contribute to and help shape organisation change – and conversely, how important is their resistance to such change? What consequences have such contributions had for democratic policing agendas? And what role might police unions have in the future in playing a constructive role in reforming police organisations? Such questions have their context in a frame of reference interested in the relations between the organisation of policing and the expectations of democracy – for example, by inviting us to consider the tension between democratic control of an organisation and the 'democratic use of coercive force' (Loader, 2006; Sklansky, 2004–2005).

In confronting such questions I am struck less by the possibilities that they open up than by the limitations that history creates in addressing them. In what follows I draw primarily on the case of Australian police unions, though conscious of the comparative context in which their achievements and practices can be assessed. The value of exploring these issues using Australian data flows from the longevity and remarkable success of police unionisation in that country. For almost a century now police in most Australian jurisdictions have enjoyed a right to organise that once seemed extraordinary to police in other countries. They have done so, somewhat paradoxically, in a country that enjoys (though some might say, suffers) a strong state tradition. The jealously guarded rights of local democratic control that have characterised, and in some views, cobbled policing organisation in the USA, are absent from Australia, where even the smallest police forces, organised in state-wide jurisdictions, are responsible for lands the size of whole countries, and free from the dictates of city or town authorities. As is well known, the Australian polity has its origins in a penal colony, under the control of military governors, whose authority was only gradually whittled away by the Colonial Office ceding legal and then political rights to the free-born and emancipated inhabitants of the colonies. In the Australian colonies collective labour organisation was influential from the late nineteenth century in shaping the state structures for management of workplace conflict – which in turn played an important role in institutionalising the labour unions, enabling and channelling their growth (Macintyre, 2004).

The fabled egalitarianism of Australian political culture, expressed in the early granting of universal male suffrage, was always constrained by high expectations of state control and responsibility for the well-being of the population. In the face of the main security threat faced by Australian settlers during colonisation, that posed by Indigenous resistance and depredations during the nineteenth century, the dominant response was that delivered by a centralised state in each of the colonies. While initial experiments in policing involved some forms of local organisation and functional specialisation, only in Tasmania did these survive past the 1860s and even there only until the end of the nineteenth century (Petrow, 1998). In the Australian police forces the dominant organisational influences were those of both the London Metropolitan Police and the Royal Irish Constabulary. What made Australian policing different from that in the USA was the independence from local control, the subordination of police to the political executive of a larger polity. In this the Australian police forces generally followed the model of policing in Ireland, with its command based in Dublin Castle, a governance arrangement continued into the post-partition Free State (Allen, 1999; Finnane, 1994).

The rapid legitimation of police unions in five of the six states of the Australian Commonwealth proceeded generally from the early ascendancy of the Labor Party in those states (a very strong liberal tradition helped things along in South Australia) (Finnane, 2002;

Fleming, 1995). The pronounced labour union character of some of these bodies was evident in their titles – the Western Australian union for example was from 1926 the WA Police Union of Workers, after the union was registered as a trade union under the state's industrial arbitration framework. In the early days of these police unions there was commonly debate about the relation between unionisation and socialism and there is clear evidence in the early days of the Queensland union of syndicalism and even, among some members, sympathy with the Bolsheviks. Anxiety among some members about the implications of unionisation is reflected in the reassurance conveyed by the Western Australian union executive in 1926 that just because members now belonged to a union of workers it did not follow that they would have to support other workers on strike (Finnane, 2002, pp. 61–62).

In Victoria political conditions were more hostile – and the response of government to the ambitions of police unionisers was to mimic the English (and Irish) solution, a strictly controlled 'representative' association (Allen, 1999; Emsley, 1991; Haldane, 1986; Reiner, 1978). The poor judgment of government and commissioner in resisting a movement that was more readily recognised in the adjacent states became evident during the 1920s and 1930s. Not only was there a police strike in 1923 (though this was effectively a wild cat strike of the mainly non-unionised cadets and junior police (Brown & Haldane, 1998)). At the end of the 1920s aggravation between the Victorian Police Association and the commissioner resulted in further widely publicised political conflict. Yet the fears that unionisation would impact severely on police discipline and effectiveness were scarcely realised by differences in performance between the state bodies. The Victorian police struggled to manage urban crime in the 1920s and were involved in repeated episodes of alleged corruption and abuse of powers such as the use of the third degree in interrogations during the 1930s (Haldane, 1986). On the other hand any argument that unionisation would make policing better was scarcely given support by the mixed performance of police in other jurisdictions during these decades. The unions were defensive in the face of public criticism of police methods, stubborn in their opposition to commissioner discipline, and generally narrow in their preoccupations. This was all predictable enough – pay and conditions were generally poor, hours long, the police organisation hierarchical and command driven. Many commissioners of Australian police forces in the inter-war years were from military backgrounds, and behaved like it (Finnane, 1994, 2002).

It should not be thought that the early legitimacy of Australian police unions entailed their full access to the democratic and industrial rights enjoyed by other groups of organised workers in Australia. But this did not make police unique. In some cases the constraints were those shared by other public servants – for example, in limitations on participation in political activity. In other cases these political disabilities flowed from the distinctive disciplinary codes, and the local norms of policing them, that were characteristic of police organisations – for example, the practice reported in Western Australia in 1957 of charging a police officer involved as an adulterer in a divorce suit with conduct prejudicial to the good order of the force (*WA Police News*, March, May 1957). Yet, by engaging police in the industrial relations frameworks of conciliation and arbitration, the institutional recognition of unions was a powerful weapon in containing and channelling complaints and aggravations arising from police work. In other words, while Australian recognition of police unions spoke volumes for the (male) embrace of the 'workingman's paradise,' this same political recognition was also a conservative restraint on expressions of dissatisfaction or the fomentation of grievances.

The political recognition and institutional legitimation of Australian police unions contributed to the domestication of the occupational status of policing. By bringing police within the institutional frameworks that governed wages and conditions for workers in general, governments invited police unions to contribute to that normalisation of its own members – the process of seeing their work not as exceptional but as comparable to that of others who provided significant service to the community, such as nurses or teachers. From the 1940s and 1950s when police unions began the arduous task of negotiating their way into alliance with the Australian trade union peak bodies, that process was an explicit part of the police unions' political agenda. The long-term effects of becoming fully part of the labour movement were, once again, ambivalent. When neo-liberal economic policies began to achieve their ascendancy from the late 1980s the police unions found themselves no longer treated as exceptional. In Victoria one result was the development of a profound hostility between the police union and the Kennett government which in 1993 stripped away some standard public service employment conditions, such as annual leave loadings (Finnane, 2002, pp. 219, 229). The echoes of that conflict are found more recently in the Australian police unions' appeals to the Commonwealth government to exempt their members from the federal jurisdiction governing employment under the new 'Work Choices' legislation, widely regarded by the union movement as an 'Americanisation' of industrial relations, an ideological attack on the union movement, and certainly entailing significant constraints on organising capacity and industrial coverage (Burgess, 2006; Delord, 2005; Williams, 2005).

How did the Australian police unions employ their relative privilege? Much of the day-to-day work of police unions over time involved direct representation on behalf of individuals. A very significant benefit of the union was and remains its provision to members of legal services, especially in relation to defence against legal actions against the police and in the course of internal departmental proceedings. The uneven legal protection afforded police work, combined with uncertainty about the provision of legal aid by police departments, created a fertile ground for the growth of a collective commitment to self-protection through the conventional structure of a legal defence body. Such services are commonly considered to be a fundamental, though far from singular, reason for the very high rates of unionisation of the policing workforce (Fleming & Peetz, 2005).

Beyond the provision of such services to individual members, the police unions from an early stage became adept practitioners in the art of industrial campaigns, waged not only in the institutional arena of the industrial court, but also in the political arena. From the early 1920s the NSW union engaged a parliamentary representative. Later in the same decade, the Victorian Association tested the limits of political intervention in an election campaign to the point of provoking the ire and retaliation of the Commissioner. I have described elsewhere the characteristics of police union activity over time and across all the Australian jurisdictions (Finnane, 2000). In brief I have suggested that the primary objectives of police union industrial campaigns can be divided into four – direct benefits, delayed benefits, workplace relations, and the policing environment. Their achievements in these domains have been predictably mixed. In the years of the Great Depression, police unions proved unable to withstand the pressures for salary cuts that were applied across the public service. In good times their record was of course better – but probably little better than allowed by the fiscal contexts and comparative gains of other public sector workers. Pension benefits were an important motive for working in the Australian police forces from an early period – and controversy over the level of benefits and access to them was correspondingly a source of aggravation from time to time. In 1923 the limitations on access to retirement benefits was a significant factor in shaping the resentments that boiled over into the Melbourne police strike (Brown & Haldane, 1998). To the extent that promotion expectations may be classified as a delayed benefit then police unions have played an important, if ambiguous, role in influencing the framework of career policing – ambiguous I say because the unions were very frequently the bastions of resistance to the introduction of merit as the dominant criterion for promotion, falling back on the rewards for seniority that all those who stayed long enough in police service could in the last instance expect. The pyramidal structure of career policing with its corresponding salary scales inevitably means that the rewards of promotion to higher levels can always flow only to a minority – providing little reason for a highly unionised workforce to support merit-based promotion schemes.

In the context of our interest in police reform it has been the impact of the unions in the areas of workplace relations (e.g., discipline) and the policing environment (e.g., police powers) that has been more fundamental. These constitute after all the domains in which policing and police practices more affect the public. They are also those domains in which the possibilities of police reform as a process involving the rank and file are expressed. In considering these impacts we need to remember that the police reforms that are the expression of police union activity are not always reforms that can be embraced as democratic in their character, however 'democratic' might be their origin as an articulation of police workers' demands. But I will return late in this paper to the ambiguities of the police role in its Australian (indeed in any) context for the notion of a democratic policing.

In workplace relations the police unions in Australia have generally played a reactive role. This is hardly surprising given their composition and their fundamental responsibilities to protect the working conditions of the membership. To the extent that one characteristic of union organisation has been its collectivist democratic culture, workplace reforms that placed a high emphasis on criteria other than seniority (read longevity of service) were always more likely to be resisted. But historical realities in the end make reactive strategies redundant. When police organisations became too obviously behind the main game (e.g., in responding to the new styles of personnel management) they were forced into change by assertive ministers and governments. When they became embroiled in corruption, as in Queensland in the 1980s and New South Wales in the 1990s, the unions had to give way to political demands for renovation – including such previously challenging notions such as lateral recruitment (Chan, 1997; Dixon, 1999; Finnane, 1988; Lafferty & Fleming, 2000). Without these external stimuli and political directives organisational change in employment patterns and career mobility would have been severely retarded. To the extent that a democratic policing might also be related to an organisational form that fosters diversity in its workforce the role of unions in welcoming or resisting such change demands continuing attention.

Historically the reactive and defensive character of police unions could be particularly evident in resistance to the employment of women. In the Australian context there was little unique in such resistance – union objections to the employment of women on a full participatory basis just continued a cultural pattern that was mandated by government policy and a wages system that undervalued female employment. But the story in fact is more complex. While police *and* police union culture in some places and times were initially unfriendly to the interests of women police, and to the recruitment of more women, there were times (notably in Victoria and South Australia) where the recruitment, equality of wages, and promotion prospects of women police were more openly supported. The motivation to support equal wages was also self-interested – to resist the threat of government employing police at cut rates, a motive also evident in the Victorian Association's resistance after 1945 to the employment of Auxiliary Policewomen. The South Australian Police Association had been successful in obtaining equal wages for the few women constables in 1918 and resisted strongly the Commissioner's attempts in 1952 to reduce female rates to 75%. This was sensible union politics – for another result was that most of the women police now joined the South Australian union, contributing to the diversity of the union (Higgs & Betters, 1987, pp. 127–131). From 1956 the Queensland Police Union (which had strongly opposed the entry of women police in 1930) argued the case for equal pay and later equal powers, after admitting women as full members to its ranks for the first time (Prenzler, 1998). But when a reforming Queensland Police Commissioner started to recruit and promote women in an affirmative drive to change the composition of the force in the early 1970s he provoked strong opposition from a union which became one of his most vocal opponents (Bolen, 1997; Prenzler & Wimshurst, 1997). In contrast the Victorian Association was from the 1950s a strong advocate of the promotion of policewomen, and was ready to see women delegates on the union executive from the 1970s. Most recently the Victorian Association has become, though briefly, the first Australian police union to have a woman as President – appropriately enough in a state which also appointed the first woman police chief, Chief Commissioner Christine Nixon, in 2001.

Another leading dimension of workplace relations in which police unions have historically played an ambiguous role lies in the area of discipline and work performance. The field is broad – and overlaps with the domain of civilian oversight. But in the first place the major tensions have been between police unions and commissioners. If any area demonstrates both the potential and limitations of police unions to influence organisational change it is arguably that of the extent and mode of commissioner powers. The statutory framework of Australian policing gave very substantial authority to the police commissioners, subject to ministerial direction, in disciplining the forces under their command (Moore, 1991). During the decades when police unions consolidated their legitimacy much of their activity was concerned with constraining the powers of such commissioners, particularly those who exercised their powers in autocratic style. Police union secretaries spent much time in direct representations on behalf of members with grievances over their treatment under disciplinary charges. In some places legal defence funds were exhausted in expensive court actions. One response of the unions was to challenge politically the exercise of commissioner powers through seeking statutory change. In the decades when the unions were most dependent on a sympathetic Labor Party, the political climate of the day was crucial. The Victorian Police Association was almost crippled by a hostile commissioner in 1929–30. But it succeeded 15 years later in statutory change to curb the commissioner's powers – at a time when the responsible Attorney-General was a solicitor who had once represented the Police Association in its many battles with the former commissioner (Finnane, 2002, p. 68). In more recent times the authority of commissioners has been generally affirmed or restored by governments especially anxious to ensure that swift action can be taken to address corruption. At the same time the restructuring of employment relations in the Australian public sector has typically resulted in a growth of contract conditions in the upper echelons of police bureaucracies – with a corresponding enhancement of termination powers. In these contexts police unions have had and continue to play a major role in negotiating employment conditions, ultimately through testing the limits of commissioner authority by deploying their considerable financial capacity to fund legal actions.

Discipline and other aspects of workplace relations have understandably been amongst the key concerns of police unions, supplementing the fundamental concerns about pay and conditions. What about the policing environment? This includes not only the statutory and regulatory conditions (criminal and other) that authorise policing business, but the panoply of institutional factors that enable and constrain how police go about their business. The latter range from the size and definition of the police budget through the forms of legal and political accountability and oversight, ranging in turn from courts through ministerial direction and government policy priorities to public inquiries by standing or ad hoc commissions.

From the vantage point of their relatively early gaining of political recognition, the Australian police unions have chosen over time to address most of these areas of the policing environment. At a time when police representative bodies in Britain and the USA were struggling for recognition, Australian police unions were already actively pursuing law reform to boost police powers and engaging in electoral lobbying (Fleming, 1997). In addressing the public context of policing an important advantage of the relative autonomy of unions has been their access to and active use of the media. In some matters they have played a noisy and sometimes effective role in shaping public agendas or institutional approaches – in a well-documented example, the NSW Police Association in 1979 campaigned against the reform of police summary offence powers, reform that significantly affected discretionary charges that police had used for decades in street policing (Egger & Findlay, 1988). But again the story is complex and one must stress the limits to police unions' deployment of their undoubted power to be heard in the public domain. This lesson is a caution to those who express anxiety about the growth of police union power as much as it is to those in police unions who beat up the potential of the unions to agitate in the political arena. In the brief space here I want to consider the historical record of police unions in challenging or seeking to change the policing environment – in areas such as police strength campaigns, law reform, and civilian oversight and inquiry.

In spite of the environmental differences I have stressed, police unions in Australia engaged in political campaigns from the 1960s around law and order issues articulated to employee rights and organisational resources and structures, as in the USA, Canada, and Britain (Bopp, 1971; Burpo, 1971; Juris, 1971; Juris & Feuille, 1973; Reiner, 1978; Stenning, 1994). The law and order election in NSW in 1965, the first in which police numbers became an important bargaining chip, was one fought against a background of police union agitation over the previous three years for an extra 1000 police, a figure the union boosted to 2000 not long before the election, applying ratios drawn from the 1962 UK Royal Commission into Police. Where police unions before 1960 had usually been careful to stress their political neutrality at election time, from 1965 the NSW union, followed by others later, was determined to use its considerable capacity to intrude policing issues into electoral campaigns (Finnane, 2002, pp. 159–174). The results have been mixed – but there are some cases in which the union is likely to have influenced outcomes of contests in particular electorates. And a long-term result has been that law and order agendas have become a permanent feature of the electoral scene: a familiar scenario of policing and penalties auctions (which party will put the most police on the streets and deliver the most criminals to prison for the longest guaranteed times?). In their enthusiasm for political intrigue the executive of one police union in 1995 negotiated a secret memorandum of understanding with the leaders of the opposition political party prior to a crucial by-election. The memorandum covered various kinds of commitments to most of the items on the union shopping list. The subsequent disclosure of this deal has arguably had a sobering impact on police unions, encouraging a greater appreciation of the value of those rules of the electoral game that are meant to respect the values of a democratic electoral system by making transparent the role of key stakeholders and commitments (Finnane, 2002; Lewis, 1999). A more common electoral strategy these days is the questionnaire distributed to the major political parties, with publicity to union members on responses to those issues. Yet both police unions and political parties competing for police backing in hard fought electoral campaigns find it hard to resist the temptation to 'sweetheart deals' that test the limits of transparency. As recently as November 2006 the Victorian state election was marred by allegations of a 'secret deal' between the incumbent government and the Police Association, which had earlier been highly critical of the government's performance on policing matters (Murphy & Hannan, 2006).

In a second domain of activism, police unions have long been interested in putting forward proposals, or demands, for law reform, or in opposing such. The Western Australian Police Union was an early proponent of very restrictive firearms regulation, after four police were shot dead in separate incidents in the late 1920s. Success in this campaign was signalled by the government passing the desired legislation in 1931. In Queensland around the same time the police union was a prominent advocate of reform of the vagrancy and police offences act, seeking and obtaining significant powers for control of criminals moving between states (Fleming, 1997). In these activities the unions were essentially supplementing initiatives long taken from within police departments. But the freedom of the union to publicise demands through the media and to lobby politicians other than the responsible minister was a significant advantage and was used. A correlate was the union's capacity to oppose change. A remarkable case has been well documented – the resistance of the NSW union to liberalising reform of the state's Summary Offences Act in 1979. In a widely publicised campaign the union targeted not just the changes but the minister responsible for the legislation – subsequent evidence provided strong evidence of a police go-slow in the minister's own electorate with a dramatic fall in police charges for the available offences during the year of this campaign (Egger & Findlay, 1988).

The Australian police unions generally did not improve their reputation for more than reactive response during a particularly troubling decade from about the mid-1980s. This period saw a succession of corruption inquiries, coinciding with government reform programs that introduced new management regimes and contemplated a greater role for civilian oversight of police work, including the external review of public complaints (Chan, 1997; Freckelton & Selby, 1988; Lafferty & Fleming, 2000; Lewis, 1999). A combative political environment developed, in which very assertive civil liberties campaigns targeting police behaviour had their mirror in police union resistance to outside scrutiny. When state and Commonwealth governments collaborated to establish a major public inquiry into the deaths of Aborigines in custody (both police and prisons), the Western Australian Police Union attempted by legal action to have the inquiry shut down. Subsequently that union participated more actively by way of a formal submission, although the tenor of the submission raised serious concerns in the Commission about the perceptions held within the police union about the policing of Aboriginal people. In contrast the Commission found more constructive the submission from the peak body, the Police Federation of Australia and New Zealand, and the Commission also formally commended the collaboration of two other police unions in facilitating Commission research on police attitudes and practices (Finnane, 2002, pp. 177–180).

The police unions' response to some other initiatives of these years in civilian oversight and inquiry was patchy. In Victoria in the late 1980s the Police Association developed such a strong animus against a newly established Police Complaints Authority that the body was closed down by the government after a very public campaign by the union (Freckelton, 1988, 1991). This was a not too comfortable reminder of the power of a union which, in combination with the leadership of the Victoria Police, was in virtual revolt against government a decade before, when mass meetings of police had protested Commission of Inquiry recommendations for prosecution of a number of police on corruption charges (Haldane, 1986, pp. 290–292). Learning perhaps from the Victorian kind of experience, and in some cases prodded by forward looking police unions, governments in Australia seeking to introduce civilian oversight have sought a more collaborative approach – seeking to keep alive principles of oversight and accountability while respecting the key role to be played by police departments in the handling of complaints against police.

Reflecting on this bare bones review of the kinds of agendas pursued by the police unions during the last few decades of the twentieth century we must conclude that those unions became very self-conscious players in seeking to shape the policing environment. They did so as an exercise in deploying newly won political freedoms, for participation in industrial and political domains on a scale generally enjoyed by Australian labour unions and unionists for most of the twentieth century. The transparency of their activities could at least be read as a positive sign of their capacity to take part in the political process in good faith – highlighted by the mistake of the Queensland union in partaking in a secretive process for winning government favours, a process widely seen as anti-democratic and not since repeated. There is by now an emerging consciousness in some police unions of the dangers of crying wolf once too often. In a somewhat futile attempt to pre-empt the inevitable, the NSW Police Association President in 2002 launched a 122-page dossier of demands in advance of a looming state election. Seeking to avoid a 'law and order frenzy' as government and opposition parties went to the hustings, the Association's demands were presented as a 'true test of a political party's commitment to law and order – a well resourced, well-remunerated force' (Videnieks, 2002). This attempt to reclaim the moral high ground of a non-political agenda is of course itself a political act. But embedded in this initiative was a recognition that simplistic law and order electioneering had delivered over the years little in the way of longer term security for the work of public police.

Given the histories I have sketched above, what kinds of impacts can we see on police organisations, and what kind of consequences have there been for democratic policing agendas? A critical issue in assessing the impact of police union politics, in Australia and elsewhere, is the question of who runs policing. As I prepared the conclusion to this paper a leading Sydney newspaper was running a story headlined 'Police Seek Right to Issue Orders on the Spot' (2006). This report in fact referred not to the New South Wales Police (the state's department of police) but the NSW Police Association, which had forwarded to the state government a proposal for senior police officers to have the power to issue a domestic violence order. Such a proposal might have its merits, though the media report also carried reservations from domestic violence workers about the wisdom of such innovation. The union's initiative, poorly reported as so often in media reporting of police issues, reflects the frequently prominent role of police unions generally in policy debates about policing. A blurring of lines between police and police union has accompanied this development. In some cases this flows from the negligence (or formal impediments flowing from a perception of their legal position) of police departments in communicating effectively with the media. The value of a union's independence in the conditions that have been won over a long period of time is its capacity to speak generally about policing, in ways untrammeled by convention or formal constraints. There are of course some limits to this independence – but they are those of general law and politics rather than conditions imposed by virtue of the occupation and business of policing. When one union president recently criticised in virulent style the outcomes of a Queensland coronial inquiry into the death of a man in police custody, his aspersions on the integrity of the office of coroner led to a charge of contempt of court, as they might in the case of any other public commentary of this kind (Mancuso, 2006). The more police unions are normalised, that is, the more that political recognition establishes their legitimacy, the greater the capacity of the politico-legal culture to exercise the kinds of restraint required of corporate bodies in open societies.

If democratic ends are served by greater transparency and public debate then the readiness of the police unions to advocate policy or organisational change has been a positive development. The limits of this democratic advantage lie somewhere in that space where polities, however they are constituted (municipal, state, national), need to make choices about what is policing business, and who should do it, and how it should be done. As the industrial representative always of their existing membership, with all the constraints that this imposes, the police union always remains a particular interest. Its priorities reflect a cultural orientation towards a kind of police work historically defined, and a fundamental material investment in the continuity of that work in terms of employment of its members and maintenance of its own organisation. Such organisations require particular kinds of leadership to embrace change, to contemplate the future in ways other than simply defensive. The normalisation of policing as an occupational status that I have argued followed in Australian practice from the early recognition of the unions is threatened now by the very exceptionalism of police unions with their very high rates of industry coverage. Whether this is followed by a retreat of police unions into more defensive modes of approach to the possibility of organisational change remains to be seen (Burgess, Fleming, & Marks, 2006).

Counterbalancing the (necessary) self-interest of the police union, there are signs over recent years of a greater openness to communication and partnership with non-police organisations, agencies, and communities (Burgess et al., 2006; Fleming, Marks, & Wood, 2006). An interesting development has been the police union interest in limiting the use of coercive force in the management of industrial confrontations. In a particularly aggravated nationwide conflict over changing industrial conditions on the waterfront in 1998, police unions played a constructive role in limiting the potential violence of clashes between striking workers and strike-breakers. The sensitivity of this role was highlighted by allegations by a key business leader involved in the dispute that the police were compromised by the affiliation of the police union to the peak trade union organisation (Baker, 2005, pp. 189–190 and generally on these issues). In other arenas, forward looking police union executives have authorised research and policy developments that involve liaison with other unions, community organisations, universities, or government agencies (Burgess et al., 2006). Within police unions themselves one sees some considerable evidence of difference and contradiction over these kinds of developments. Commonly expressed complaints about alleged soft sentencing, legal process requirements, restrictive regulatory regimes that allegedly stop police doing their work, sit alongside commitment to equity in the workplace, interest in the positive potential of community policing and restorative justice and so on. The environment is fluid, the organisations are large (the NSW union for example has 14,500 members currently, for a population of 6.8 million; the Tasmanian one about 1100, serving a population of 490,000), and the scope for diversity of opinion and response on key issues is accordingly great.

In Australia at least, police unions find themselves at a curious crossroads. The constant sense of alarm and threat that one finds in much police union rhetoric is belied by the strength of these unions in terms of resources and coverage of their workers. From police ranks now come politicians, on both sides of politics. The dominant flavour of police union politics may still be labourist – yet probably no other Australian labour union (frequently linked organisationally to the Australian Labor Party), has had the privilege of the current anti-union Prime Minister opening its headquarters, as John Howard did the Police Federation of Australia headquarters in 2003. In spite of this degree of comfortable accommodation with a conservative government, police unions have been prominent in the fight against the Australian government's most recent legislative attacks on the historical privileges of the trade union movement. Police now police the protests in which their own unions and colleagues take part.

Police unions thus try to have it both ways. From the privileged position of being a powerful political and industrial lobby, they have mounted a strong case to be treated as exceptional in seeking exemption from the application of the Federal Government's Work Choices legislation, a neo-liberal economic reform that has significantly affected trade union rights in Australia. Arguing that police are workers and entitled to workers' protections on an equal basis with those in the rest of society, police unions in Australia have made very large gains in the status and conditions attached to being a police officer. They have done so within an industrial relations framework (the Australian arbitration system in its various forms) which over more than a century facilitated the institutional security of the union organisations, including police unions, which were protected by that system.

Yet in spite of these historical differences of the political culture compared to either British or North American jurisdictions, police unions in Australia now look and sound more like police unions in other countries. In 1917 the English *Police Review* looked with envy at the model of police unionisation that had been developed in the more congenial political environment of Western Australia (Editorial, 1917). Today nearly a century later one finds the same kinds of challenges, strategies, and rhetoric adopted in police unions across quite disparate policing environments. Police unions are a seemingly permanent part of the policing landscape – but a recognition that in the last instance they represent only a particular interest (the interests of their current members) is necessary to remind us that not too much should be expected of their role as change agents. Sometimes they will surprise by their commitment and openness to change. On other occasions their resistance will have to be acknowledged as a reality that comes with recognising that democratic processes mean that not all that is thought best at any particular moment can always be readily achieved.

Acknowledgement

This paper draws principally on the author's book, *When Police Unionise: The Politics of Law and Order in Australia* (Sydney, 2002) – where more detailed archival documentation is available. The author acknowledges the support of the Australian Research Council Large Grant Program, 1998–99: A59802635. Thanks are due to Monique Marks, David Sklansky, Jenny Fleming, an anonymous referee, and to the participants of the 'Police Reform from the Bottom Up' Conference, UC Berkeley, 12–13 October 2006.

References

Allen, G. (1999). *The Garda Síochána: Policing independent Ireland, 1922–82.* Dublin: Gill & Macmillan.

Baker, D. (2005). *Batons and blockades: Policing industrial disputes in Australasia.* Melbourne: Circa.

Bolen, J. (1997). *Reform in policing: Lessons from the Whitrod era.* Sydney: Hawkins Press.

Bopp, W.J. (1971). *The police rebellion: A quest for blue power.* Springfield, IL: Charles C. Thomas.

Brown, G., & Haldane, R. (1998). *Days of violence: The 1923 police strike in Melbourne.* Melbourne: Hybrid.

Burgess, M. (2006). Are police protected from Workchoices? *Police News,* 18.

Burgess, M., Fleming, J., & Marks, M. (2006). Thinking critically about police unions in Australia: Internal democracy and external responsiveness. *Police Practice and Research: An International Journal, 7*(5), 391–409.

Burpo, J.H. (1971). *The police labour movement: Problems and perspectives.* Springfield, IL: Charles C. Thomas.

Chan, J. (1997). *Changing police culture: Policing in a multicultural society.* Melbourne: Cambridge University Press.

Delord, R. (2005). Should Australian labour and policing models mirror those of the US? *Police Journal,* 18.

Dixon, D. (Ed.). (1999). *A culture of corruption.* Sydney: Hawkins Press.

Editorial. (1917). The West Australian Police Association. *The Police Review and Official Organ of the West Australian Police Association, 2,* 3–4.

Egger, S., & Findlay, M. (1988). The politics of police discretion. In M. Findlay & R. Hogg (Eds.), *Understanding crime and criminal justice.* Sydney: Law Book Company.

Emsley, C. (1991). *The English police: A political and social history.* Hemel Hempstead: Harvester Wheatsheaf.

Finnane, M. (1988). The Fitzgerald Commission: Law, politics and state corruption in Queensland. *Australian Journal of Public Administration, XLVII*(4), 332–342.

Finnane, M. (1994). *Police and government: Histories of policing in Australia.* Melbourne: Oxford University Press.

Finnane, M. (2000). Police unions in Australia: A history of the present. *Current Issues in Criminal Justice, 12*(1), 5–19.

Finnane, M. (2002). *When police unionise: The politics of law and order in Australia.* Sydney: Sydney Institute of Criminology.

Fleming, J. (1995). Shifting the emphasis: The impact of police unionism in Queensland, 1915–1925. *Labour History,* (68), 98–114.

Fleming, J. (1997). Power and persuasion: Police unionism and law reform in Queensland. *Queensland Review, 4*(2), 59–74.

Fleming, J., Marks, M., & Wood, J. (2006). 'Standing on the inside looking out': The significance of police unions in networks of police governance. *Australian and New Zealand Journal of Criminology, 39*(1), 71–90.

Fleming, J., & Peetz, D. (2005). Essential service unionism and the new police industrial relations. *Journal of Collective Negotiations, 30*(4), 283–305.

Freckelton, I. (1988). Sensation and symbiosis. In I. Freckelton & H. Selby (Eds.), *Police in our society.* Sydney: Butterworths.

Freckelton, I. (1991). 'Shooting the messenger': The trial and execution of the Victorian Police Complaints Authority. In A. Goldsmith (Ed.), *Complaints against the police: The trend to external review.* Oxford: Clarendon Press.

Freckelton, I., & Selby, H. (Eds.). (1988). *Police in our society.* Sydney: Butterworths.

Gammage, A.Z., & Sachs, S.L. (1972). *Police unions.* Springfield, IL: Charles C. Thomas.

Haldane, R. (1986). *The people's force: A history of the Victoria Police.* Carlton: Melbourne University Press.

Higgs, P., & Betters, C. (1987). *To walk a fair beat: A history of the South Australian Women Police, 1915–1987.* Lockleys, SA: Past & Present Women Police Association.

Juris, H.A. (1971). The implications of police unionism. *Law & Society Review, 6*(2), 231–245.

Juris, H.A., & Feuille, P. (1973). *Police unionism: Power and impact in public-sector bargaining.* Lexington, MA: Lexington Books.

Lafferty, G., & Fleming, J. (2000). New management techniques and restructuring for accountability in Australian police organisations. *Policing: An International Journal of Police Strategies & Management, 23*(2), 154–168.

Lewis, C. (1999). *Complaints against police: The politics of reform.* Sydney: Hawkins Press.

Loader, I. (2006). Policing, recognition, and belonging. *The Annals of the American Academy of Political and Social Science, 605*(1), 202–221.

Macintyre, S. (2004). *A concise history of Australia.* Cambridge and New York: Cambridge University Press.

Mancuso, R. (2006). Police Union 'not surprised.' *Courier-Mail,* Brisbane, December 14.

Marks, M., & Fleming, J. (2006). The right to unionize, the right to bargain, and the right to democratic policing. *The Annals of the American Academy of Political and Social Science, 605*(1), 178–199.

McGill, D. (1992). *No right to strike the history of the New Zealand Police Service organizations.* Wellington: Silver Owl Press.

Moore, D. (1991). Origins of the police mandate: The Australian case reconsidered. *Police Studies, 14,* 107–120.

Murphy, P., & Hannan, E. (2006). Former top cops slam Brack's secret deal with union. *The Australian,* November 24.

Petrow, S. (1998). Economy, efficiency and impartiality: Police centralisation in nineteenth century Tasmania. *ANZ Journal of Criminology, 31*(3), 242–266.

Police seek right to issue orders on the spot. (2006, September 15). *Sydney Morning Herald.* Retrieved from http://www.smh.com.au/news/national/police-seek-violence-protection-orders/2006/09/15/1157827160820.html

Prenzler, T. (1998). Concession and containment: The establishment of women in the Queensland Police, 1931–1965. *ANZ Journal of Criminology, 31*(2), 119–140.

Prenzler, T., & Wimshurst, K. (1997). Women and politics in the Queensland police, 1970–1987. *Journal of Australian Studies, 52,* 88–101.

Reiner, R. (1978). *The blue-coated worker: A sociological study of police unionism.* Cambridge: Cambridge University Press.

Sklansky, D.A. (2004–2005). Police and democracy. *Michigan Law Review, 103,* 1699–1830.

Stenning, P.C. (1994). Police and politics: There and back and there again? In R. Macleod & D. Schneiderman (Eds.), *Police powers in Canada: The evolution and practice of authority* (pp. 209–240). Toronto: University of Toronto Press.

Videnieks, M. (2002). We're no political football, say police. *The Australian,* December 5.

Williams, B. (2005). Peril for police in federal IR system. *Police Journal,* 13.

The human right of police to organize and bargain collectively

Roy J. Adams

DeGroote School of Business, McMaster University, Hamilton, Ontario, Canada

The right to organize and bargain collectively is a well-established international human right. It is a right that is, however, withheld from police in several jurisdictions based on the theory that to allow police to unionize may threaten the internal security of the state. The available evidence indicates, however, that the fear and the restrictions flowing from it are of little merit and thus are undeserving of support.

Introduction

The right to organize and bargain collectively is a fundamental human right. What that means, according to the international human rights consensus, is that it is a right that is possessed by human beings solely as a function of their humanity (Howard & Donnelly, 1987). Human rights may neither be created by nor denied by governments or employers or other organs of society. Since police are human beings they have a fundamental right to organize and bargain collectively but it is a right that is neither well understood, nor well protected and enforced in many jurisdictions (Adams, 2006c). Police bargaining rights are commonly withheld or suppressed based on theory and emotional fears that have meager empirical support. There is, moreover, emerging evidence and thought that police are likely to act in a manner more consistent with democratic principles if they are treated with the dignity and respect called for by international human rights norms.

The human right to organize and bargain collectively

The right to organize and bargain collectively is a derivative from the broader right to freedom of association which has been recognized as a fundamental right since early in the twentieth century (Adams, 2006c). Freedom of association was reaffirmed as a fundamental right in the Universal Declaration of Human Rights (UDHR) that was proclaimed in 1948. The UDHR was a very general document that needed to be expanded and interpreted in order to provide useful guidance regarding legitimate rights-compliant behavior to states and other societal actors. Within the international system, the agency with the mandate to carry out that function is the International Labor Organization (ILO).

The ILO is a supra-national agency composed of states and representatives of trade unions and employer organizations (Bartolomei de la Cruz, von Potobsky, & Swepston, 1996). Once a year delegates meet in Geneva to legislate global standards in the form of conventions and recommendations. State members are duty bound to consider those instruments with a view towards making them effective via domestic legislation. But freedom of association, from which the right to organize and bargain collectively is derived, is included in the ILO constitution binding all members to respect those rights whether or not they have ratified the relevant conventions or legislated the pertinent recommendations.

There are two main conventions relevant to these rights: numbers 87 (Freedom of Association and Protection of the Right to Organize) and 98 (The Right to Organize and Bargain Collectively). Although the language of those conventions does not apply directly to non-ratifying countries, the ILO has set up a Committee on Freedom of Association (CFA) whose job it is to interpret the constitutional requirement. It does so by hearing complaints alleging violation of freedom of association. In rendering opinions about such allegations it is guided both by the language of Conventions 87 and 98 and by the jurisprudence that has accumulated over the years as a result of its decisions on past cases. By this process, all member states are, de facto, required to respect and implement the clauses of the two conventions. With respect to the right to organize and bargain collectively, as Rubin (2005, p. 120) notes, there is little difference between the responsibilities of states who have ratified the relevant conventions and those who have not. Over the years the CFA has issued opinions on over 2500 cases creating a rich jurisprudence. Those who want guidance on the responsibilities of the relevant parties in a wide variety of circumstances need only consult this body of jurisprudence.

Key principles

'All workers whatsoever' according to the language of Convention 87, have a right to organize, to select leaders, to develop a program to defend and forward their interests, and to make demands on their employers. In such circumstances employers have a duty to recognize and negotiate in good faith with their employees' representatives with a view towards arriving at mutually acceptable solutions to issues raised. Should negotiations fail the employees have a right to organize a campaign designed to produce concessions including withdrawing their labor in concert – in short they have the right to strike (Adams, 2006a). States have a responsibility to protect and promote these rights and duties and ensure that they are effectively honored.

That is the minimum on which workers everywhere should be able to rely. Needless to say these rights are not universally honored nor effectively protected but possession of rights and their enforcement are separate issues.

Balancing rights

There are many rights that are considered to be human rights and, as a result, in particular circumstances they may collide with each other. In such cases a 'balance' needs to be worked out and, in the international system, the ILO is considered to be the appropriate agency to fulfill that function with respect to labor rights. Thus, for example, all workers have a default right to strike but a strike by workers in certain key positions in society would put at risk the wellbeing of many people. For example, if all nurses or doctors refused to work the result might well be the loss of innocent lives. For people filling jobs considered to be essential for the public welfare the ILO has established that they may organize and bargain collectively but if that process reaches impasse the State should ensure that instead of the strike, they have an alternative dispute resolution mechanism available such as binding arbitration (Bartolomei de la Cruz et al., 1996). In short, the right to strike, which is considered by the CFA to be an essential aspect of the right to organize and bargain collectively, may be withheld from some workers in order to ensure the right of citizens to the uninterrupted availability of essential services. But the ILO's list of essential jobs is short and the continuing right to organize and bargain meaningfully of those in those jobs is protected.

The International Labor Organization and police labor rights

Within the ILO orbit, despite the 'all workers whatsoever' clause in Convention 87, there is one class of employees that states may, without offending their commitment to the Organization, deny entirely the right to organize and bargain collectively: police and the military. The official justification for this exclusion is that unionization might compromise the responsibilities that police and the military have for the 'external and internal security of the state' (Rubin, 2005, p. 126; see also International Labour Office, 1994, p. 27). The ban on strikes that applies to other 'essential' workers is not considered a sufficient guarantee of the required services.

With respect to police, however, there is little evidence that a total prohibition of unionization and collective bargaining is necessary in order to ensure the state's internal security. Police are, in fact, permitted to unionize and bargain collectively in several countries. Police unionism is common, for example, in Europe, Australasia, Canada, the USA, and South Africa (Marks & Fleming, 2006).[1] Many of these countries are among the world's most highly advanced. Permitting police to organize in these countries, obviously, has not compromised the internal security of the state.

The South African case is notable in that it is a country in transition in which the authorities might be expected to be more apprehensive about the supposed hazard of independent unionism than those in countries more settled politically. However, a robust police union movement has not destabilized the South African state but has, it appears, become part of an emerging democratic culture (Marks & Fleming, 2006).

The Canadian case

The situation in Canada is of special note because it provides a naturally existing test of the validity of the concern. Police generally across the country are permitted to organize and bargain collectively. In some provinces police are permitted to strike but in others impasses are required to be settled by reference to conciliation and arbitration (Forcese, 1980; Kinnear, 1998). The one exception is the Royal Canadian Mounted Police (RCMP) (Lynk, 2006; MacKay, 2003). The RCMP is a federal police force but also provides police services to several provinces and municipalities on contract. About half of RCMP officers are assigned to municipal policing duties but while their counterparts are permitted to organize and bargain, they are not (Kinnear, 1998).

A Federal Government Order-in-Council issued in 1918 (P.C. 1918 – 2213) forbade members of the RCMP from becoming 'a member of or in any wise associated with any Trades Union Organization …' Contravention of that regulation was 'cause for instant dismissal.' The rationale for the exclusion was a fear that unionization would result in 'divided loyalty' between officers' allegiance to their fellow members and their required obedience to superiors. The government wanted to ensure that the officers remained loyal and obedient to their commanding officers. This fear was of particular concern in relation to labor unrest. The government was concerned that the officers might refuse to obey a command to subdue labor uprisings (MacKay, 2003, p. 18).

The period in which the Order was issued was one of serious labor unrest in several countries. Inflation stemming from the cost of World War I eroded the purchasing power of workers who organized in protest. In some countries labor demonstrations grew into general revolution and the fall of monarchies in Russia, Germany, and the Austro-Hungarian Empire (Adams, 1995). In the USA the Seattle General Strike and the Boston Police Strike of 1919 and in Canada the Winnipeg General Strike, which also occurred in 1919, were all interpreted by some observers as radical events that might spark similar widespread social upheaval (Juris & Feuille, 1973; Schrag, 1992). Although the Winnipeg General Strike came after the Order-in-Council of 1918, in conjunction with the Boston Police Strike, it no doubt helped to perpetuate the fears that gave rise to the Order (Kinnear, 1998). In Winnipeg city police joined the strikers and put themselves under the command of the strike committee. Although little violence and disorder occurred in that case, in Boston the strike resulted in broadly publicized looting and violence (Schrag, 1992). The combination of these events helped to cement in the minds of policymakers fear of an unlikely conjunction of events that would result in general disorder putting at risk the security of the state.

In the 1960s and 1970s, public sector employees in Canada grew militant and pressured governments to extend full collective bargaining rights to them and most were successful. Within the RCMP a movement began to form a union but it was not successful (Forcese, 1980). The 1918 Order-in-Council had been reinforced in 1945 with the adoption by Parliament of the *Rules and Regulations for the Government and Guidance of the Royal Canadian Mounted Police Force of Canada*.[2] In 1967 the *Public Service Staff Relations Act* granted bargaining rights to most federal employees but explicitly excluded members of the RCMP (Lynk, 2006). In response to a growing consensus that public sector employees have a right to organize and growing pressure from within the ranks of the RCMP for representation, Order-in-Council 1918 – 2213 was rescinded in 1974. However, instead of replacing it with genuine, independent collective bargaining similar to that of other essential workers and provincial and municipal police officers, it was replaced instead by a Staff Relations Representative Program. The program which provides for consultation between government officials and RCMP representatives is entirely controlled and regulated by the government (Lynk, 2006). Although it has been accepted by many RCMP officers (MacDougall, 2000), it provides for no impasse resolution devise. In short, it does not meet ILO independence standards and members of the RCMP continue to agitate for genuine, ILO-compliant legislation (see, e.g., *Delisle v. Canada*, 1999; Kinnear, 1998; Adams, 2007b).

Although fears about the possible ill effects of 'divided loyalty' continue to provide the justification for the government refusal to recognize the right of RCMP officers to ILO-compliant unionization,[3] 'divided loyalty' is not an issue with respect to unionized provincial and municipal police. Although there have been many actual and threatened police strikes, the breakdown of civil order has not happened or has been quickly restored when it has occurred such as during the Montreal Police Strike of 1969.[4] Since the events in the post-World War I era there have been few incidents in which the 'security of the state' might credibly have been said to be seriously threatened (Forcese, 1980; Lynk, 2006).

The inevitable conclusion from these considerations is that the rationale for the denial by government of the right to organize and bargain collectively of police officers is without empirical support. A set of circumstances might conceivably appear in which the worst fears of police unionism opponents would materialize. But the same might also be said about the radicalization of any class of workers. Labor-inspired revolutions occurred in Russia, Germany, and Austria in the World War I era, and in more recent years in Poland and South Africa, not because of the disloyalty of the police and military but rather because of mass labor uprisings against fatally flawed governments. Good government, responsible to the general welfare, would appear to be the best defense against labor unrest and social upheaval. Even if police services are deemed to be essential (and that case has not been convincingly made) there would appear to be no substantial reason why police cannot be effectively regulated in a manner similar to other essential workers – that is, by permitting them to organize and bargain collectively but substituting binding arbitration for the right to strike. The suppression of the human right of police to independently organize and bargain collectively stems largely from emotional fears based on imagined scenarios that are unlikely to materialize.

In North America the quashing of the rights of police to organize and bargain collectively is made easier as a result of conventions under which collective bargaining is regarded as an ordinary political issue rather than a human right (Adams, 2006b). Although the right, as discussed above, has been heralded internationally as a human right on the same plane with the right to equality regardless of color, sex, or religion, the right to freedom from forced labor, the right of children to freedom from exploitation, the right to a fair trial, the right to vote, and other fundamental rights, in Canada and the USA it has not been recognized as an equivalent human right.[5] Despite having promised solemnly in the international arena to protect and promote collective bargaining as a human right both Canadian and American governments remain formally neutral regarding its exercise. Nor do they object when employers actively oppose unionization and collective bargaining as they would if voices were raised against employment equity or in support of child or forced labor (Adams, 2006b).

Their position with respect to the exercise of the right to organize and bargain collectively stems from a conception of the employment relationship that is, as I have recently argued, at sharp odds with the conception inherent in the work of the ILO and the international human rights community (Adams, 2006a, 2006b). In North America the default employment relationship is an individual one between the employee or prospective employee and the employer, commonly an enterprise of some size. The enterprise is seen to have a right to offer the prospective employee terms that may be accepted or rejected. The employee may also negotiate for terms better than those offered but, as many observers have noted, the bargaining power of the worker in most instances is likely to be much inferior to that of the corporation and thus the negotiations are likely to be very one sided. But there is another, less often remarked, problem with this default conception. The human resource policies of nearly all enterprises of any size are, today, rationalized and standardized. Terms and conditions are applied to classes and thus cannot be individually negotiated. For example, in most cases every employee covered by the firm's pension plan is subject to common regulations and may not individually negotiate variations.

With respect to unionization, the dominant corporate attitude in Canada and the USA is that if, in the words of Wal-Mart's *Manager's Toolbox for Remaining Union-Free*, employees are satisfied with the way that they are being managed, there is no need for a union (Adams, 2005). In short, the availability of unionization is like an insurance policy against bad management. If managers treat employees with respect and provide them with fair and equitable conditions they should not turn to an outside intermediary to represent their interests. The relationship between management and employees is conceived of as a unitary one. There is a single social system in which those involved have different, but not adversarial, roles. When the union enters, this social system is shattered to be replaced by a whole new adversarial regime. An 'outside organization' is said to come between management and workers. To unionize is to engage in a sort of rebellion against the established order. It is conceived of as a radical rejection of managerial competence.

This vision has taken such firm root that, although surveys indicate that the large majority of workers want workplace representation, many are unwilling to act on that desire for fear that the result will be worse employment relations. In 2003, in the USA, the Hart survey organization asked a sample what they believed was the 'biggest disadvantage to having a union.' Some 38% of the respondents said 'having worse relations between employees and management …' (Freeman & Rogers, 2006, p. 17).

The ILO's vision is entirely different from the one promoted by management interests. From the ILO's perspective, collective bargaining is a necessary element of all democratic, human rights respecting societies. It is the economic counterpart to political democracy and thus collective bargaining for all workers for whom it is relevant should be society's goal. Working under rules unilaterally imposed (even if they are substantively acceptable) is, it is hypothesized, also bad for political democracy. Being compelled to function within autocratic structures on a daily basis may well make workers more likely to tolerate non-democratic processes in society as a whole. One study of the relationship between unionization and political participation in the USA found a positive link between union membership and likelihood to vote (Radcliff, 2001). With respect to police specifically, the case has recently been made by Marks and Fleming (2006) that unionized police are more likely to respect the rights of citizens and less likely to resort to tactics that offend basic rights.

In addition to fostering acceptance of undemocratic political practices, working within autocratic enterprise governance systems also compromises one's dignity. One's material welfare as well as sense of self-worth is closely connected to one's salary, benefits, job security, promotional opportunities, and personal relationship with fellow workers. If all of those features of one's life are removed from one's control then one is in a position that is not much advanced from that of slaves or serfs (Adams, 2006c). In such circumstances, it has often been remarked, labor is treated not as human but rather as a commodity in the production process. Although a benevolent employer or market forces may result in acceptable material rewards the personal indignity of being subject, unilaterally to the will of another, to be regarded as a thing, adheres. One assertion behind the idea of collective bargaining as a human right is that such a status is unacceptable in any decent society. Human dignity requires that human beings maintain control of their lives; it requires that they do not acquiesce to situations in which key aspects of their lives are unilaterally imposed upon them by others. Human beings in respectful relationships naturally negotiate issues of mutual concern. From this perspective, the absence of collective bargaining in any employment situation is prima facie problematic. The goal of any society that embraces the notion of collective bargaining as a human right is near universal collective representation. However, in both Canada and the USA as well as many other countries, conventions have taken hold that justify autocratic enterprise governance and thus weaken democratic norms.

Conclusion

If a strong global norm is to be established in support of respect for human rights then the default behavior with respect to any group of citizens must be compliance. Only in those situations where clear evidence of a clash of rights exists may constraints be legitimately applied. With respect the right of police to organize and bargain collectively, that evidence does not exist. Instead, the outlawing of police unionism is based on theory and emotional fears that are poorly supported by the empirical record. The formal justification for treating police differently from other 'essential' workers is that independent police organization may compromise the stability of the state. That justification is apparently based on imagined scenarios that the record indicates are highly unlikely to occur. There are very few examples of situations where police, organized or otherwise, have failed to uphold the integrity of the state. Instead, the empirical record suggests that treating police with dignity and respect by recognizing and bargaining in good faith with their chosen representatives is good public policy. Both theory and available evidence suggests that doing so may well strengthen rather than weaken democratic norms.

Acknowledgement

My thanks to Monique Marks and an anonymous reviewer for helpful comments on earlier versions of this paper. The final result is, of course, entirely my responsibility.

Notes

1. In its 1994 survey of the state of Freedom of Association in the world, the ILO mentioned that legislation in all of the following countries permitted police to unionize and bargain collectively: Australia, Austria, Belgium, Côte d'Ivoire, Denmark, Finland, France, Germany, Iceland, Ireland, Luxembourg, Malawi, Netherlands, New Zealand, Niger, Norway, Portugal, Senegal, Spain, Sweden, Tunisia, UK, and the USA (Rubin, 2005, p. 126). However, the classification of some of these countries is questionable. For example, the Police Federations in the UK are established and closely regulated by law and would not seem to meet the ILO test of independence. In the US State Department's annual review of human rights some of the African countries on the list (Senegal, Côte d'Ivoire, Malawi) are identified among those who legally forbid police unionism.
2. *Rules and Regulations for the Government and Guidance of the Royal Canadian Mounted Police Force of Canada* (1945) 79 *Canada Gazette* 1577, s. 31(a).
3. As a result of the *Delisle v. Canada* decision (op. cit.) the Commissioner of the RCMP in 2003 removed the explicit prohibition against officers being members of independent associations and associations have formed in British Columbia, Ontario, and Quebec (Lynk, 2006, pp. 27–28 and 73). However, with government approval, RCMP management continues to recognize the SRR as the exclusive mechanism for establishing terms and conditions of employment (Lynk, 2006, p. 73). As a result, as Lynk notes 'While these groups show that the mere act of coming together in association can and has occurred to some extent, they also show how very far they are from any meaningful freedom of association, particularly when judged against other police associations and unions' (2006, p. 73). The legal situation changed substantially in Canada in 2007 when the Supreme Court interpreted the Canadian Charter of Rights and Freedoms as containing a right to bargain collectively that applies directly to governments. Subsequent to the decision, the RCMP management once again rejected a request from an independent association of RCMP officers for recognition for bargaining purposes. In response the association has filed a court case that has not yet been settled (see Adams 2007b).
4. Disruption and rioting did result from a police strike in Montreal in 1969 but order was quickly restored. See http://archives.cbc.ca/IDC-1-71-1805-12238-10/on_this_day/conflict_war/twt. Moreover, the strike was a wildcat strike which means that it occurred without the sanction of either law or internal union requirements. Throughout history, wildcat strikes have frequently occurred in situations where there was no official union or bargaining procedure in effect. Thus, although outlawing unions might make the occurrence of a wildcat strike less likely, it is not an effective method of prevention.
5. In law the situation changed significantly when in 2007 the Supreme Court of Canada recognized collective bargaining to be both a constitutional right and a human right. In a decision generally unexpected by the legal community it overturned 20 years of jurisprudence during which the Court deferred to legislatures on labor issues (see Supreme Court of Canada, 2007 and Adams 2007a).

References

Adams, R.J. (1995). *Industrial relations under liberal democracy.* Columbia: University of South Carolina Press.

Adams, R.J. (2005, Autumn). Organizing Walmart, the Canadian campaign. *Just Labour, 6/7,* 1–11.

Adams, R.J. (2006a). America's 'Union-Free' Movement in light of international human rights standards. In R. Block, S. Friedman, M. Kaminski, & A. Levin (Eds.), *Justice on the job: Perspectives on the erosion of collective bargaining in the United States* (pp. 215–230). Kalamazoo, MI: W.E. Upjohn Institute for Employment Research.

Adams, R.J. (2006b). *Labour left out: Canada's failure to protect and promote collective bargaining as a human right.* Ottawa: Canadian Centre for Policy Alternatives.

Adams, R.J. (2006c). *Labor's human rights: A review of the nature and status of core labour rights as human rights* (Working Paper No. 36). Human Rights and Human Welfare. Retrieved from http://www.du.edu/gsis/hrhw/working/index.html

Adams, R. J. (2007a). Court puts collective bargaining into the constitution. *Straight Goods,* June 27.

Adams, R. J. (2007b). Collective bargaining at the RCMP. *Straight Goods,* December 19.

Bartolomei de la Cruz, H., von Potobsky, G., & Swepston, L. (1996). *The International Labor Organization, the International Standards System and basic human rights.* Boulder, CO: Westview Press.

Delisle v. Canada (Deputy Attorney General), [1999] 2 SCR 989.

Forcese, D. (1980). Police unionism: Employee–management relations in Canadian police forces. *Canadian Police College Journal, 4*(2), 79–129.

Freeman, R.B., & Rogers, J. (2006). *What workers want* (Updated ed.). Ithaca, NY: Cornell University Press.

Howard, R.E., & Donnelly, J. (1987). *International handbook of human rights.* Westport, CT: Greenwood Press.

International Labour Office. (1994). *Freedom of association and collective bargaining – General survey.* Geneva: ILO.

Juris, H.A., & Feuille, P. (1973). *Police unionism.* Lexington, MA: Lexington Books.

Kinnear, D. (1998, March 26). *Comments made to the Standing Committee on Human Resources Development and the status of persons with disabilities.* Parliament of Canada. Retrieved from http://www.parl.gc.ca/infocomdoc/36/1/hrpd/meetings/evidence/hrpdev22-e.htm

Lynk, M. (2006). *Examination of the employment rights and industrial relations status of the officers of the Royal Canadian Mounted Police ('RCMP').* Expert affidavit sworn February 22, 2006 in support of an application challenging the constitutionality of the exclusion of members of the Royal Canadian Mounted Police ('RCMP') from Canadian federal public sector labour relations legislation, and certain other statutory provisions that impede the constitutional freedoms of association and expression, and the right of equality. Retrieved from www.legaladvocates.ca/rcmp.html

MacDougall, K. (2000). Nonunion employee representation at the Royal Canadian Mounted Police. In B.E. Kaufman & D. Gottlieb Taras (Eds.), *Nonunion employee representation, history, contemporary practice, and policy.* Armonk, NY: M.E. Sharpe.

MacKay, R. (2003). *The Royal Canadian Mounted Police and unionization.* Parliamentary Research Branch, Library of Parliament, Canada.

Marks, M., & Fleming, J. (2006, May). The right to unionize, the right to bargaining, and the right to democratic policing. *Annals of the American Academy of Political and Social Science, 605,* 178–199.

Radcliff, B. (2001). Organized labour and electoral participation in American national elections. *Journal of Labor Research, 22*(2), 405–414.

Rubin, N. (2005). *Code of International Labour Law.* Cambridge: Cambridge University Press.

Schrag, Z. (1992). *Nineteen nineteen: The Boston Police Strike in the context of American labor.* AB thesis, Harvard University, Boston. Retrieved from http://www.schrag.info/research/chap1.html

Supreme Court of Canada, Health Services and Support-Facilities Subsector Bargaining Ass'n v. British Columbia (2007). 283 D.L.R. (4th) 40 (S.C.C.).

Why reforms fail

Wesley G. Skogan

Institute for Policy Research, Northwestern University, Evanston, USA

Police reform is risky and hard, and efforts to innovate in policing often fall short of expectations. This chapter examines sources of resistance to change in policing. Some are internal, including opposition to reform at virtually all levels of the organization and among special units. The position of unions vis-a-vis change is highly variable, particularly if proposals do not threaten working conditions and officer safety. Politicians and other potential opponents of change lurk in the vicinity of policing, and reformers need to bring them into the process as well. The public must understand how the investment they have in policing will be enhanced, and not threatened, by reform. If new strategies require the cooperation of other service agencies (as, for example, for problem-solving policing) the heads of those bureaucracies must understand they are partners in their city's program, not victims of empire building by the police. At the top, city leaders must match the commitment of chiefs and other police executives to change, if reforms are to survive leadership transition.

It is necessary to be clear-eyed about the difficulties of innovating in police organizations. Because of widespread enthusiasm for innovations, such as community and problem-oriented policing, third-party policing, 'lever-pulling' policing, and evidence-based policing among academics and the informed public, it could appear that reform comes easily.[1] In fact, it is hard, the political risks involved are considerable, and efforts to change the police often fall far short or fail.

This chapter outlines some sources of resistance to innovation in policing. It is not just focused on bottom-up reform, or the role of police unions. In fact, the article by Bayley in this issue concludes that most innovations in policing have come from the outside. Usually the plan has been crafted by academics or consultants, and often the proposed programs come with the support of politicians who are trying to deal with one or another public outrage over police affairs. I summarize what I have gleaned about obstacles to change in police organizations in 11 categories. Many of them reflect processes internal to police agencies. These I mostly attribute to the career and bureaucratic interests and managerial outlook of the parties involved. At the top, executives worry about keeping their jobs and the rank-and-file working hard and out of trouble. Sergeants may not want to stray from what they know how to do in order to keep out of trouble. Street officers do not want to be plagued by out-of-touch programs that add to their workload and give them tasks that lie outside their comfort zone. Elite units such as detectives frequently are able to avoid getting involved, while union leaders keep a careful eye on their strategic situation vis-a-vis management. Others obstacles are probably endemic to public sector organizations: these include problems of interagency coordination, the competing demands of differing constituencies, and the inability of the police to measure their success in the absence of a profit-and-loss statement. External to the police are community and political forces that can stymie change as well.

I do not know the relative frequency with which these obstacles loom large, but I have run across numerous examples of each of them without looking too exhaustively. I have learned about them in my own research on community-oriented and problem-solving projects, plus studies of narcotics operations. This article also incorporates what I have read and gleaned in conversations with police and researchers in hotel bars around the world. Any reform agenda will face formidable obstacles, for the length of the list—it is a long one—is testimony to the difficulty of managing change in police agencies.

Resistance by mid-level and top managers

Resistance does not just come from the bottom of police organizations; revolts by mid-level managers have defeated community-policing projects in several cities. Managers near the middle of the organizational hierarchy saw authority being taken from them and pushed to lower levels in the organization, as part of decentralization schemes. Opportunities for promotion for middle managers may be limited by shrinking management layers and the flattening of the formal rank structure that sometimes goes along with efforts to decentralize for neighborhood-oriented policing. When Chicago abolished its highest civil-service police rank—captain—a lieutenant (the next level below) told me that he felt as if he had been 'kicked in the teeth.' Police managers typically are command-and-control oriented and feel most comfortable when everything is done by the book. When it was broached that foot officers might carry cell phones rather than rely on their portable radios, so that they could remain in contact with citizen patrols, local merchants and others on their beat, Chicago's chief of patrol killed the idea. 'How will we know when they screw up?' was his rhetorical question. Instead, he wanted all communications with officers in the field go through the 911 Center, when they were tape-recorded for future investigation.

Discussions of policing reform also often feature modern management terms, such as 'employee empowerment.' This also makes senior managers very nervous. They worry about laziness, corruption, racial profiling, and excessive force, and they do not trust rank-and-file officers on any of those dimensions. Departments struggle to keep control of their field force. Most police officers work alone or with a partner, and the top brass know little about what they do out there except what they report on pieces of paper that they sometimes fill out to document their activities. Police routinely encounter opportunities to engage in a laundry list of problematic activities, and the usual way that executives respond is to tighten the management screws to rein in officer discretion. However, the reforms of choice today—including problem solving and community policing—celebrate the exercise of discretion, administrative decentralization, reducing hierarchy, granting officers more independence, and trusting in their professionalism. At the same time, it is revelations of misconduct, not rising crime rates, that are likely to cost police executives their jobs, so they remain risk averse.

Resistance by managers and even other top executives often results in innovative policing units being run from the chief's office. Or, to avoid the entrenched bureaucracy, they may be housed in a special new bureau. In one large city, a new chief who was brought from out of town to initiate community policing found that he was unable to get the uniformed patrol division of the department to do anything about it, from the top down. They were there before he came, and they expected to be there when he left. Hence, he created an entirely new chain of command in the department. A special community-policing bureau was set up with a parallel hierarchy. It controlled teams of neighborhood officers, who worked outside the supervision of the rest of the department. It was headed by a director he recruited from another city, so that she would be free of the entrenched politics of the department.

Forming separate units, often staffed by volunteers, may be an attractive change strategy because reforms can be put into the field quickly, seemingly without the necessity of confronting resistance by established units. A risk of this strategy is that officers who serve in these units may not be seen as 'real police.' Officers with community assignments can easily appear to have easy lives. They are frequently interviewed on television, and they are invited to attend conferences in other cities. Sometimes they are free to choose their own work hours, and too often they decide that they are really needed on their beat 9–5, Mondays through Fridays. This was the shift time of choice for New York City's C-POP officers (e.g., McElroy et al. 1993). What they do gets labeled 'social work' by other officers. They become known as 'empty holster guys.' Morale flounders, and some of the best officers will try to transfer out. Where I was doing field work in Texas, community officers had flexible shift schedules, they were given a cell phone, and they took a patrol car home with them every night. When I quizzed a community officer what the rest of the department thought of them, she replied, 'They really hate us.'

Resistance by front-line supervisors

In the first experimental year, when the program was still fragile, I often overheard Chicago's community policing manager warn his team, 'We're not going to let the sergeants kill this!' Sergeants have direct control over what street officers do on a day-to-day basis. One observer identified sergeants as most officers' 'real employer' (Muir 1977). Herman Goldstein (1990: 57) notes, 'However strongly the head of an agency may elicit a different style of policing, the quality of an officer's daily life is heavily dependent on how well the officer satisfies the expectations and demands of his or her immediate supervisor.' Sergeants interpret the operational meaning of official policies at the street level, so when roles and rules are up for grabs, they have to have a clear vision they can support if change is really going to occur there.

Sergeants present problems. First, when programs are new, sergeants are new to it as well. They do not know from their own experience how the job should be done, or what works. Like others in the department, they have to learn skills and new roles from the ground up. Because they are the 'transmission belt' that translates the policies of higher-ups into action, it is important that they represent organizational policies. If they actually believe in them that would help too. This matters even in traditional command-and-control organizations, but many contemporary innovations in policing call for significant decentralization, pushing both authority and responsibility for decision making deeper into the organization. There, sergeants are the facilitating management layer. What Chicago's change manager sensed was what our survey data revealed: at that layer of management, support for community policing was very thin. On questions gauging their support for collaborating with the public and engaging in problem solving, sergeants scored very close to the rank-and-file, and both groups were largely convinced that it could never work (Skogan and Hartnett 1997).

Resistance by rank-and-file officers

Efforts to implement policing reforms have sometimes failed in the face of resistance by ordinary officers as well. Enthusiasm by public officials and community activists for innovations in policing encourages its detractors within the force to dismiss reforms as 'just politics.' They see them as passing fads, something dreamed up by civilians for the police to do. Police are skeptical about programs invented by civilians. This is partly a matter of police culture. American policing is dominated by a 'we versus they,' or 'insider versus outsider' orientation that assumes that the academics, politicians, and community activists who plan policing programs cannot possibly understand their job. Police are particularly hostile to programs that threaten to involve civilians in defining their work or evaluating their performance. They do not like civilians influencing their operational priorities, or deciding if they are effective. Police on the street grouse about 'loud mouths' in the community who are active because they want police to provide them personal service, and groups and organizations that want police to support or defend their economic and social interests. Outsiders must be 'gimmie guys,' for why else would they be taking such an interest?

There is also resistance to change when—and because—it requires that officers do many of their old jobs in new ways, and that they take on tasks that they never imagined would come their way. Reforms of the day ask them to identify and solve a broad range of problems, reach out to elements of the community that were previously outside their orbit, and put their careers at risk by taking on unfamiliar and challenging responsibilities. A difficulty with these expectations is that they frequently lie outside the traditional roles for which they were selected and trained, which they have honed through years of practical experience. Police would prefer 'to do what they signed up for'—usually a combination of crime fighting and emergency service. As Thacher indicates in this issue, police claims to professionalism are based on their experience and judgment rather than to the abstract and technical skills of many occupational groups, and as a result they are loath to enter uncharted waters. Street cops also rightly fear being assigned additional duties and paperwork while still being held responsible for handling their old workload.

In my experience, translating the 'fundamental principles' of initiatives like problem solving and community policing into actual practice is another difficulty. Abstract concepts must be turned into lists of practical, day-to-day activities and then enshrined in enforceable orders to which officers in the field can fairly be held accountable. To a degree many outsiders find hard to fathom, little is supposed to happen in police departments without General Orders detailing how it is to be done. Of course, the troops have actually to go along with those orders, and the emphasis should always be on the 'para' in these 'paramilitary' organizations. As Hans Toch points out in his contribution to this issue, the view that police departments are efficiently hierarchical and bureaucratic does not reflect how the daily work gets done. This is why sergeants are so important. From their perspective, officers typically hear about new programs when they are announced at city hall press conferences, and they feel that most initiatives are adopted without their input. They are resentful when 'the community' is consulted about internal police business and they are not. Officers who have survived previous policing reforms often derisively recall the acronyms that designated those projects and can recount the forces that inevitably led to their failure.

Voluntary overtime programs are obviously attractive in this environment. For years, many departments paid volunteer officers some extra money for conducting community-oriented projects. They were to do community policing *after* their day of 'real' police work is done. No one had to do it, but there was extra money in it. However, not only may officers be tired by the end of the day, but it seems unlikely that they would really do things differently during that extra two or three hours. I once studied a narcotics team paid to do 'community-oriented narcotics policing' for an extra three hours, four days each week. There was a great deal of federal money for the program, but I found that the officers did not have the slightest idea how to do 'community-oriented narcotics policing.' It was not just that they received no training. They all worked undercover out of a secret office, dressed in rough clothing, and believed they could not reveal themselves to the community. The whole program was a good example of a bad idea dreamed up by civilians, in this case from Washington, DC (Skogan and Annan 1993).

Resistance by special units

Specialized units such as detectives are often threatened by department-wide programs that require them to change their ways. For example, detectives may be required actually to exchange information with uniformed officers, and not just suck it into their 'black hole,' and they might find debate opening about their effectiveness. I often describe Chicago's detectives as 'the biggest, toughest and best-armed gang in town,' although in truth there are several bigger and better-armed street gangs. Often special units have special relationships with politicians that protect them. It can take political connections as well as the active support of friends and relatives on the force to become a detective, and politicians will move to protect them if they are threatened with unwanted change. What the politicians get in return goes unstated.

In my experience, detectives have used their elite status in the organization to avoid getting involved in programs like community policing. In Chicago, a succession of chief detectives has pursued the same avoidance strategy, which is to smile warmly at the mention of community policing and suggest that detectives are planning to get involved soon. There are many other nooks and niches in the organization where police who did not like the city's program could also hide out and get ahead, including the organized crime division, the narcotics unit, and various roving squads of plainclothes tactical officers. Their anonymity and disconnection from any community contact helped them 'take heads' and 'kick ass' with relative impunity, in the name of good, aggressive policing. Because the ultimate measures of good police work remains making arrests and seizing guns and drugs (see 'Measuring What

Matters' below), those are the jobs that everyone wants. Vacant positions in the department are always in the uniformed patrol division, where community policing has been effectively sequestered.

Resistance by police unions

The extent to which resistance by police unions is an issue varies highly from city to city in the United States. The states vary in the extent to which police can be represented by unions and can effectively threaten job action, but in many big cities they are a force to be reckoned with. In Chicago, the major police union endorsed community policing, and stayed focused on wages, benefits, working conditions, and officer safety. In the mid-1990s, the union even formed a community-policing committee whose members started showing up national conferences. However, in other places unions decided to attack the program. In a West Coast city the union protested strongly against the idea. They charged that it was just 'social work,' and that the planned training program was intended to instill 'political correctness' in police officers. They threatened to keep officers from appearing at community-policing training. As a compromise, they agreed to tolerate one day of training, in place of the three-day training sessions that had been planned. At the time they were hoping to move to a four-day workweek, which they later achieved. In the East, the head of one police union stormed into a meeting of police commanders to announce that a new policing experiment they were about to launch would 'never happen.' Having national level unionization might not help. In one European country, the chief of the second largest city told me there would never be anything like 'community policing' anywhere, because the national union simply would not allow it.

A crucial issue can be the match between the demands of a new program and rules stipulated in the contract between the union and the city. These contracts bind the parties to work rules, performance standards, and personnel policies that can run counter to organizational change. Almost everywhere contracts between cities and police unions affect the ability of department managers to make decisions about staffing. Frequently they grant officers the right to choose assignments based on seniority. This can limit the ability of department managers to determine which—and even how many—officers work in a district, what shift they will be assigned to, and perhaps their specific job assignments. For example, in Chicago officer's district assignments are decided almost completely by seniority. It can be impossible to put them where managers want them (based on their ability to speak an immigrant language, for example) or to keep officers assigned to a beat if they want to work somewhere else.

Along with their many friends and family members, organized police groups can also be a formidable force in local electoral politics. This inhibits politicians from pushing them too hard in directions they do not choose to go. In Chicago, all officers are required to live in the city itself, where their political strength and cohesion have neutralized the local prosecutor, county sheriff, and others who might delve independently into their affairs. Their families, friends and fund-raising efforts have also captured the support of several state legislators from suburbs that are close in but outside the mayor's sphere of influence. State senators and representatives can be counted on to make an end run around city legislation and administrative actions at the capital. There, downstate legislators who care little about the details of Chicago government and its budgetary problems are happy to go along with efforts to negate the city's attempts to control staffing and spending.

Competing demands and expectations

Police managers and city executives also have to find the officers required to staff new programs. Community policing is particularly labor intensive, and may require more officers. Finding the money to hire more officers is hard, so departments may try to scavenge them from existing units. This can bring conflict with other powerful police executives and politicians who support the current arrangement. Police also face 'the 911 problem,' for their commitment to respond to calls as quickly as possible dominates the resources of most departments. Chicago, for example, receives more than five million 911 calls each year, and sends a patrol car in response to 3.1 million of them. In some cities, community policing encountered heavy political resistance when the perception arose (encouraged by its opponents) that officers previously devoted to responding to 911 calls were being diverted to this social experiment, leaving (it was claimed) the community at risk. Houston's first attempt to do community policing was defeated by this claim (Skogan and Hartnett 1997).

Hence, police executives try to look for ways to implement new programs more cheaply. One important organizational function that often gets shortchanged is training. Training is expensive and officers have to be removed from duty—or paid overtime—to attend. During the early 1980s, one Western city tried to run a neighborhood-oriented program with no training at all; they hoped that officers (who were doing it as an overtime assignment) would guess what to do from the name of the project. More recently, officers in another large city received one day of training; in another major agency it was two days of training. This for a project that is supposed to revolutionize policing.

Inability to 'measure what matters'

One problem facing both community and problem-solving policing is that it is hard to document what officers are doing or if they are being effective. The problem-solving component of community policing shifts the unit of work from individual incidents to clusters of problems, and those are harder to count. It is also hard to evaluate whether problem solving is effective, and to determine whether individual officers are doing a good or a bad job at it. The public often wants action on things that department information systems do not count at all. As a result, both individual and unit performance is hard to measure and to reward. However, the thrust of New York City's CompStat and other new 'accountability processes' in police departments is that measured activities get attention and unmeasured accomplishments do not get much attention, even if the unmeasured activities matter very much. Top-down management and their relentless focus on recorded crime statistics almost inevitably reinforces the most traditional conceptions of policing (Weisburd et al. 2003). CompStat may be the most important obstacle to reform in contemporary policing.

Like many American cities, Chicago has adopted a CompStat system of its own. In a new book I call this 'CompStat, Chicago Style' (Skogan 2006). As in New York, the process focuses on traditional measures: the number of crimes, arrests, guns seized, and calls for service answered. The focus on reducing crime inevitably presses the organization toward reliance on those numbers. Away from police headquarters, managers think that the accountability process undervalues the 'intangibles' that are community policing's hallmark, including community satisfaction, public involvement in crime prevention projects, and the formation of police–community partnerships. They lament that the city's CompStat system forces them to stray from community policing. One told me, 'When [community policing] started, it wasn't supposed to be this numbers thing, and now it's totally a numbers thing.' Another critic noted, 'This is mission-oriented policing, more traditional . . . This is top-down management, stats driven.' At the public meetings held every month all over the city, residents complain about teen loitering, graffiti, noise, and loose garbage in the alleys (Skogan 2006: Table 4.3), but action on these is not prized in accountability sessions. In Chicago, as elsewhere, important things that are not being measured elude the accountability process, which is driven principally by objectives that can be measured by the department's information systems. Over time, organizations almost inevitably shift their attention to what they can measure, and this pressures them to revert to traditional policing practices.

Failure of interagency cooperation

Adopting community and problem-solving policing inevitably means accepting an expanded definition of police responsibilities. When the public becomes involved in setting priorities, a new set of issues that previously fell outside the police mandate will be high on their list. In Chicago, the public is concerned about burglary and robbery, to be sure. However, at the meetings described above they also express a great deal of concern about abandoned cars, rats running loose in the alleyways, dilapidated buildings, homeless people sleeping in the parks, missing street signs, burned-out street lights, and runaway youths squatting in abandoned buildings. Although police can note that abandoned cars are a high-priority problem, they have to turn to other city agencies to get them towed away.

However, for a long list of familiar bureaucratic and political reasons other municipal agencies usually think that community policing is the police department's program, and not theirs. They resist altering their own professional and budget-constrained priorities, and their five-year master plans. Making inter-organizational cooperation work can be one of the most difficult problems facing innovative departments. When a chief of police in Boston was new, he assured me that he could handle change in his department. His biggest fear was that his mayor might not deliver the city's other agencies, and that they would not provide the kind of support that community policing requires. In my experience, if community policing is the police department's program, important parts of it will fail. Community policing must be the entire city's program.

To make this work, bureaucratic obstacles must be overcome by police headquarters and the city administration. Problem solving takes sustained, government-wide commitment to the program, and many American cities do not succeed in developing this commitment. In some cities, officers assigned to community work develop lists of individual contacts in other city service agencies whom they feel they can call on if they really need help. A neighborhood officer I interviewed in Texas relied on his brother-in-law, who worked for the appropriate city agency, to get cars towed in his zone. There and elsewhere, newcomers to the job have difficulty getting anything done. To make a formal request in some places requires the police chief to write a memo to another agency head. Before Chicago's program began, police officers predicted that the coordination of city services with their problem-solving efforts would not work. Based on bitter experience, they expected that other agencies would continue to be as unresponsive as in the past, and they complained about it loudly. But soon the mayor made his expectations about the new program forcefully clear to his agency heads; if they did not cooperate, they would lose their jobs. City hall staff members developed a computerized management system for coordinating responses to beat officers' service requests and monitoring how responsive the service agencies were. Service delivery turned out to be one of the most successful components of the program during its early years, but it was not easy (cf. Skogan et al. 1999).

Public unresponsiveness

Ironically, sustaining public involvement in policing matters is difficult. The two groups may not have a history of getting along. Especially in disadvantaged neighborhoods, police may be perceived as arrogant and brutal rather than as potential partners. Residents may fear that more personal attention from the police could result in harassment and indiscriminate searches. Nothing in the past has prepared the public for new approaches to policing, and they are unlikely to understand the goals or tactics associated with new modes of policing. When they do hear about it, there may be no reason for residents to believe it. In poor neighborhoods the past is too often strewn with broken promises. Residents are accustomed to seeing programs come and go in response to political and budgetary cycles that are out of their control, and they can rightly be skeptical that community policing or any other promised reform will be any different. Organizations representing the interests of community members may not have a tradition of cooperating with police. Because their constituents often fear the police, groups representing low-income and minority areas may be more interested in monitoring police misconduct and pressing for greater police accountability to civilians than in becoming closely identified with them.

Civic participation is also generally difficult to sustain in worse-off places. Poor and high-crime areas are often not well endowed with an infrastructure of organizations ready to get involved in civic projects. Crime and fear stimulate withdrawal from community life. Residents easily view each other with suspicion rather than with neighborliness, and this undermines their capacity to forge collective responses to local problems. Because they fear retaliation by drug dealers and neighborhood gangs, programs requiring public meetings or organized cooperation may be less successful (Skogan 1988). In Chicago, there was discussion of potential retaliation for cooperating with police or attending beat meetings at 22 per cent of the meetings we observed (Skogan 2006). As a result, areas that need the most help usually find it hardest to get people involved.

In the case of community policing, police executives have learned that if the public is going to take a significant role they will need educating. Civilians will not know what they can newly expect from the police, nor what they themselves can contribute to solving neighborhood problems. Like police themselves, uninformed citizens are likely to define their expectations of policing in traditional terms, expecting more patrols, fast response times, and arrests to solve their problems for them. It will be their instinct to demand more of the same in response to almost every issue. At Chicago's community meetings, the most common complaint lodged against the police (at 31 per cent of meetings) concerned the speed with which they answered calls, and the second (21 per cent) was that there were not enough of them on patrol (Skogan 2006: Table 45.3). Sophisticated concepts and a new set of jargon are involved, so police reform requires aggressive marketing before many voters and taxpayers will understand what is being accomplished.

Nasty misconduct diverting public and leadership attention

Investments that police make in innovation are always at risk. In the United States, community policing is a legitimacy building strategy. Everyone is aware of the deep division in the country around policing issues. Whites are highly satisfied while African-Americans are dissatisfied, and the gap between the races has not changed much over the past 40 years. There is evidence that the seemingly endless recurrence of highly publicized acts of police violence affects public attitudes, reversing occasionally improvements in public opinion. Community policing promises that police will accommodate the public and not just the other way around. However, when use of excessive force or killings by police becomes a public issue, years of progress in police–community relations can disappear. The same is true of revelations of widespread or deep police corruption.

Nasty misconduct can also undermine reform efforts because department and city leaders lose their focus on managing innovation. The mayor of Chicago once remarked to me that he has to think about his police department every day. He hates that, because he has many other things to worry about. However, he knows that managing change in large organizations requires his focused attention. Nasty misconduct causes city and department leaders to lose their focus, and it diverts the attention of the media from the unnewsworthy aspects of police reform.

Reform may not survive leadership transition

Police everywhere spend a great deal of time (a lot of it on-the-job time) debating what the tea leaves tell them is going on amid the shifting power alliances downtown. How long is the chief going to hang on? Who are the heirs apparent, and do their views differ from the incumbent's? Whose stock is rising and falling, and whose views must to be attended to or can safely be ignored? The difficulty is that divisions downtown are almost inevitable in transitioning organizations. This slows everything down, as uncertainty over the future course of the department will be read by many as a rationale for cautious inaction until the situation is clarified.

Uncertainty is multiplied when a new chief or even mayor arrives, for they may have even more new ideas. When leaders come to office, they want to do new things. They want to make their own mark, and can have little interest in picking up the unfinished projects of the people they replaced. The old police chief in one mid-sized city I know struggled for more than a decade to build a new community policing program. However, when he retired, his replacement (who came from another city) had no interest in it at all, and the program was disbanded virtually overnight. Another city elected a new mayor in 1999, one who ran on a tough 'law and order' platform. His predecessor had committed the city to community policing, and had selected a new police chief from out of town to inaugurate the program. The new mayor fired the chief at their first meeting. A deputy chief who was present at the meeting stood and promised to push a 'zero tolerance' strategy that the mayor found more appealing. The mayor promoted him to chief of police on the spot. He also instituted a 'New York style' management system in every city agency, to drive progress against the measures that mattered to him.

If reforms are to persist, the astute change manager has to ensure that they are the department's and even the city's project, not just their own. If they can build public and political support for reform, its budget may survive when money is tight and resources are hard to come by. Political support, and deep support from the community, is also a tool for beating back dissidents within the department when necessary. If it is the city's and the community's program, perhaps their potential successors will also think reform is a good idea, or at least one that candidates must promise to support in order to get the job.

This was the situation in Chicago in late 2006, after 14 years of community policing. In 2003, the city's major newspaper created a crime scare during a period when the mayor was choosing a new chief of police. Politically, the cheapest and most immediate response he could make was to anoint a candidate from the detective squad committed to tough enforcement. The new chief in turn reorganized and refocused the department on guns, gangs, and homicides. Soon commitment to the department's community policing program withered. Most districts lost their community-policing managers, lieutenants who were instead put in charge of flying squads. All of the department's slack resources were rounded up to staff them. Police hoping to get ahead organizationally gravitated toward crackdown units, for they are the focus of the top brass. Headquarters accountability reviews, which used to include community-policing activities and goals, were scaled back dramatically to make time for discussion of homicide patterns. Activities that better fit a recentralized management structure driven by recorded crime have become what matters. The only thing that protects the shell of the program that remains is that it was politically infeasible to shut it down, so deeply are the beat-oriented parts of community policing woven into the political and organizational life of the city's neighborhoods. There it lurks, waiting perhaps to be resurrected when a crisis of legitimacy again haunts the police, and they have to rediscover community policing in order to rebuild again their credibility with the community.

Note

1. For a discussion of the potential and pitfalls in these and other recent innovations in policing, see the chapters in Weisburd and Braga (2006).

References

Goldstein, H., 1990. *Problem-oriented Policing*. New York: McGraw-Hill.

McElroy, J.E., Cosgrove, C.A., and Sadd, S., 1993. *Community Policing: The CPOP in New York*. Newbury Park, CA: Sage.

Muir, W.K., 1977. *Police: Streetcorner Politicians*. Chicago: University of Chicago Press.

Skogan, W.G., 1988. "Community organizations and crime". *In*: M. Tonry and N. Morris, eds. *Crime and Justice: An Annual Review*. Chicago: University of Chicago Press, 39–78.

Skogan, W.G., 2006. *Police and Community in Chicago: A Tale of Three Cities*. New York: Oxford University Press.

Skogan, W.G. and Annan, S., 1993. "Drug enforcement in public housing". *In*: R. Davis, A. Lurigio and D. Rosenbaum, eds. *Drugs and the Community*. Springfield, IL: Charles C. Thomas, 162–174.

Skogan, W.G. and Hartnett, S.M., 1997. *Community Policing, Chicago Style*. New York: Oxford University Press.

Skogan, W.G., Hartnett, S.M., DuBois, J., Comey, J.T., Kaiser, M., and Lovig, J.H., 1999. *On the Beat: Police and Community Problem Solving*. Boulder, CO: Westview.

Weisburd, D. and Braga, A., 2006. *Police Innovation: Contrasting Perspectives*. New York: Cambridge University Press.

Weisburd, D., Mastrofski, S., McNally, A.M., Greenspan, R., and Willis, J., 2003. "Reforming to preserve: Compstat and strategic problem solving in American policing". *Criminology & Public Policy*, 2, 421–456.

Enduring issues of police culture and demographics

Jerome H. Skolnick

Center for Research in Crime and Justice, New York University School of Law

I address two issues about police and policing that David Sklansky has raised in two important papers one (as yet unpublished) on what he calls 'the police subculture schema' (Sklansky 2007); the other about the impact of the new demographics of law enforcement (Sklansky 2006). The two are clearly related in the following questions: What aspects of police culture are enduring? How and in what ways has police culture been impacted by the new demographics? Have the new demographics increased police relations with the black and brown communities?

Policing as an occupation

Are occupational groups like aboriginal tribes with their distinctive languages, traditions, rules, understandings, and behavioral injunctions? If put that way, of course not. However, occupational groups do develop understandings about how to interpret conduct, retain loyalties, express opinions, use or abuse authority. These occupational 'rules' are rarely, if ever, written. Unlike formal ethical codes, violators of informal rules cannot be brought before a board of authorities to interpret and enforce violations. Such understandings may be expressed as George Will has done regarding baseball's code governing 'such matters as when it is appropriate to pitch at, or very close to, a batter; when and how to retaliate for that; which displays of emotion are acceptable and which constitute 'showing up' an umpire or opposing player, what sort of physical contact, in what sorts of game situations (breaking up a double play at second, trying to score when the catcher is blocking the plate) is acceptable' (Will 1991).

Police respond to a profusion of unwritten rules about such matters as how and when to back up a partner with force, how to respond to someone who challenges police authority, and a myriad of other situations that grow out of the distinctive features of the police assignment. However, is there something larger about the role and practice of policing—anywhere in the western world—that supports a claim about universal, stable, and lasting features of the culture of the police that must be taken into account in any attempt to reform the police.

One is surely that being a police officer is a defining identity, almost like being a priest or a rabbi. 'The day the new recruit walks through the door of the police academy,' the former New Haven police chief James Ahern wrote, 'he leaves society behind to enter a profession that does more than give him a job, it defines who he is. He will always be a cop' (Ahern 1972). Paradoxically, this identity may even be even more powerful for police who are of a racial, religious, or gender minority. In some circles, a Black police officer is considered a race traitor. Black police understand this potential, and meet it with different reactions. Some view themselves mainly as police, or professional police. Others, like the NYPD's '100 Blacks in Law Enforcement Who Care' and the 'Latino Officers Association' identify themselves as champions of minority rights, and publicly and actively make reform demands on the higher authorities to take various actions, especially to affirmatively promote minorities. Some turn against the job, leave, and develop counter identities, as anti-police.

Affirmative action in hiring and promoting minorities and women has been a widespread reform; and as Sklansky's (2006) paper asserts, it has brought necessary changes to police departments. However, the issues of race and gender in policing are delicate, complex, and can be the third rail of police reform. Because American cities tend to have sizable populations of people of color, mayors and police executives have had to be responsive to the demands of those communities. At the same time, police executives must deal with a variety of communities who are sensitive to different issues. Hence, when we think about police reform, we cannot ignore the politics of police reform. And what may seem like reform to one group—like community-oriented policing (COP)—may appear to be 'soft on crime' to another. Some police executives, like some politicians, are able to finesse these problems. Others are not.

Years ago, I asserted that working cops develop a 'working personality' derived from three enduring features of the police role—the exercise of authority, which is comparable to the role of the schoolteacher; the exposure to danger, which generates perceptual tendencies similar to those of the combat soldier; and the pressure to produce, which mimic the compulsions experienced by the industrial worker (Skolnick 1993). And police—especially police on patrol—are suspicious as they patrol the streets. Police are supposed to register the normal, and the abnormal, and to stick together and support each other on the job. In that sense, police on patrol will always be blue. We won't be able to, nor should we, seek to change that feature of patrolling, but we can teach police how to use their authority so as not to seem officious and insensitive to the concerns of the people they police. COP and problem-oriented policing (POP) are reforms that address these issues. The NYPD, under Ray Kelly, is not tied to a COP or POP label, but 'community outreach' is part of the philosophy of the department, and resonates with the idea of COP.

The capacity to use force is, of course, another necessary, enduring, and potentially troublesome feature of the police enterprise. 'Whatever the substance of the task at hand,' Egon Bittner, a superb ethnographer, wrote, 'whether it involves protection against an undesired imposition, caring for those who cannot care for themselves, attempting to solve a crime, helping to save a life, abating a nuisance or settling an explosive dispute, police intervention means above all making use of the capacity and authority to overpower resistance' (Bittner 1970: 40). Bittner appreciated that police do not actually use force very often. 'But,' he concluded, 'there can be no doubt that this feature of police work is uppermost in the minds of people who solicit police aid or direct the attention of police to problems' (ibid.). In sum these features—identity, danger, authority, the pressure to produce, suspicion, the capacity to use force—are enduring aspects of the police occupation. And the most serious complaints against police are claims that police used excessive force.

James Fyfe taught me to appreciate that protection of life is the most important obligation of police—and that the most important part of police training is to teach cops how not to employ more force than is necessary. This of course implies (a) that there is a body of knowledge about how to employ force; and (b) that police are motivated to use force minimally and properly.

The political disposition of the police

Mark Baker, who interviewed more than a hundred cops for his book on police and their lives, concluded that police lean to the right politically and morally. 'They advocate the straight and narrow path to right living,' he writes. 'They believe in the inviolability of the marriage vows, the importance of the family, the necessity of capital punishment' (Baker 1985: 211). However, the cops he interviewed did not necessarily abide by apple-pie-and-motherhood values. At least half the married male police officers whom Baker interviewed told him about their girlfriends and mistresses (something I was introduced to in research with police who told me about 'beat wives'—girlfriends who resided in the beats cops were assigned to patrol).

After a few years on the job, the cops interviewed by Baker developed a distinctive hierarchy of wrongfulness: 'dead wrong, wrong, but not bad, wrong but everybody does it.' Skepticism, cynicism, mistrust of outsiders—all are traits observers of police apply to them and that they apply to themselves. However, Baker's book was published in 1985. New research, especially ethnographic research, is needed to find out whether and where these observations are still current. Is there is more variation than Baker reported? Probably. Urban police, more racially and culturally diverse than they were two decades ago, more educated, may be different. But how, where, and how significantly remains to be seen.

The code of silence

The feelings of loyalty and brotherhood sustaining a silence code unquestionably protect cops against genuine threats to safety and well-being. John Kleinig (2000) in his ethical analysis of the silence code, compares the culture of policing to norms found in ideals of friendship and family. Police are obliged to back up each other, protect each other, and follow each other into situations of grave danger—as, for example, we saw on 9/11 when police followed one another into crumbling buildings to try to save those trapped by the terrorist attack.

However, the code of loyalty and brotherhood can also protect the interests of police who violate the criminal law. An unrecorded code has been noted as a feature of policing across continents, wherever commissions of inquiry have investigated police corruption. Major investigations into police misconduct in the United States—the Knapp (1972) and Mollen (1994) Commissions in New York and the Christopher Commission in Los Angeles (1991)—have all singled-out 'the Code' as an obstruction to their inquiry into police corruption or excessive force. So has the Fitzgerald inquiry in Queensland (1989), the Wood Royal Commission in New South Wales (1997) and is discussed by Maurice Punch in his studies of scandals in New York, London, and Amsterdam (Punch 1985).

Community norms and expectations regarding police and race

Norms about police use of force have shifted dramatically since the beginnings of the civil rights movements. Police of the Deep South of the 1930s were routinely brutal to 'Negroes,' as they were trained and expected to be by the communities in which they served. 'It is part of the policeman's philosophy,' Gunnar Myrdal wrote, 'that Negro criminals or suspects, or any Negro who shows signs of insubordination, should be punished bodily, and that this is a device for keeping the Negro in his place' (Myrdal 1944: 541). Arrested Negroes were routinely beaten in police wagons, even when they were safely locked up. This was thought to be both a deterrent and a just desert, 'vengeance for the fears and perils the policemen are subjected to while pursuing their duties in the Negro community' (ibid.).

How different were police above the Mason–Dixon line, the oft cited cultural boundary between the North and the South? The South of the 1930s was legally segregated, a caste society, while the rest of the nation was de facto segregated in schools, housing and economic class, even in universities, a pattern that the 1968 National Advisory Commission on Civil Disorders, popularly known as the Kerner Commission, called 'institutional racism.' Northern elite university administrators and faculty in 1968 were rarely bigoted—racial epithets were severely frowned upon—but administrators, faculty, and students were overwhelmingly white, custodians black.

The difference between institutional racism and bigotry is nicely illustrated in the work of William Westley, of the University of Chicago, who observed police in Gary, Indiana in the 1950s. Westley reported that no white policeman he came in contact with 'failed to mock the Negro, to use some type of stereotyped categorization, and to refer to interaction with the Negro in an exaggerated dialect, when the subject arose' (Westley 1951: 168). Were the Gary police unrepresentative of bigoted police of that era? The Gary police were likely more typical than exceptional, based on a variety of research from that era, especially research associated with or sponsored by the President's Commission on Law Enforcement and the Administration of Justice, the Kerner Commission, and the National Commission on the Causes and Prevention of Violence.

What about the Oakland, California, Police Department, the most studied police department on the west coast, which maintained a so-called 'legalistic' style of policing in the 1960s? James Q. Wilson reported that Oakland's legalistic style—with its high level of enforcement activity as expressed by aggressive preventive patrol, could be experienced as 'harassment' by Blacks (Wilson 1968: 190). Indeed, Wilson reported that every Black citizen interviewed for his study claimed that police harassed Blacks, a charge Wilson dismissed as a misperception, a side effect of the policing style, rather than a consequence of racism (ibid.).

However, did Wilson appreciate how bigoted many rank-and-file Oakland police of that era could be? When I studied the 'legalistic' Oakland police circa 1964, the Oakland chief issued a remarkable directive in this increasingly non-white city ordering all officers—all of whom were white but one—to avoid saying the following words 'in the course of their official duties.' The words were: *boy, spade, jig, nigger, blue, smoke, coon, spook, headhunter, junglebunny, boogie, stud, burrhead, cat, black boy, black, shine, ape, spick, mau–mau.*

However, of course, it is one thing to issue a directive, and another for it to be followed. The Chief understood that defiantly racist cops would be literalists—if told they were forbidden to use the 'N' word, they would find ways to substitute another pejorative expression. And the Chief understood that if the police were to be 'legalistic' in enforcement, that is, aggressive about enforcing the criminal law (and unlike the police in Eastern departments, relatively incorruptible) they should not be, or even be perceived to be, bigoted. A legalistic style combined with racism can be an explosive mixture, and very nearly was in Oakland—and as it was in the 'legalistic' Los Angeles police department in 1965.

Of course, not all the white police were bigoted, but enough were to generate charges of racism within non-white communities. Actually, despite the Chief's memorandum, I rarely contacted encountered police who mocked Blacks. I knew of them, but rarely rode with them. And I did meet some who, like William K. (Sandy) Muir's professional police, were sensitive to minorities and their interests (Muir 1977). In contrast to Westley's uniformly outspokenly racist police, the Oakland police of the 1960s and 1970s were a mixed bag. Besides, even those who were intransigently racist weren't stupid—by that time they understood that, unlike Westley's police, community support for racism was declining (within the white as well as the non-white communities). Consequently, it was imprudent to utter racial epithets that outside observers could overhear.

Restrictions on the use of force

Studies of the race riots of the 1960s usually found that the spark that set off the riot was police use of excessive force. That does not mean that the conduct of the police was the only factor behind the riots. The America of the 1960s was indeed institutionally racist and sexist—there were few black (or female) auto salespersons bank tellers, or executives in major corporations. Labor unions, especially craft unions, were mostly white. And, as in Oakland, there were few blacks and no women police.

Even as I maintain that police have a discernable *culture* flowing from the nature of the job, police *behavior* is strongly influenced by the underlying values—and politics—of the community that finances the police department and pays their salaries and benefits. Sandy Muir, who also studied the Oakland police, deeply appreciated how informal use of force norms played out in the street. These norms, Muir suggested, achieve paradoxical results—thus, *the stronger ones' reputation for being mean, tough and aggressive, the less iron-handed one actually has to be* (ibid.: 101–126).

Furthermore, Muir asserted, even when iron-handed law enforcement proves effective in general, it also invites retaliation by those who are *not* intimidated by it. Abusive police must then raise the force ante, employing ever more severe violence to continue to seem formidable. This, for Muir, generated a competing paradox: *Police who rely on coercive force to make the world a less threatening place make it more dangerous place for themselves and for other cops* (ibid.: 110). Those who are being policed do not distinguish among blue uniforms. All cops come to be defined as brutal, and thus appropriate targets for retaliation.

Muir saw how police who are gifted with maturity, empathy, and interpersonal skills—and who weren't racist—could escape from the trap of relying on the threat of force. He had seen in his observations of police how some accomplished cops could intuit how to handle even the most difficult and potentially explosive situations. He believed that appropriate 'training and enhanced language skills' could diminish police violence. I think that's likely to be true, provided that communities appoint police executives who are able to motivate police to use force minimally and correctly (Muir 1980: 48).

Police management

Muir was influenced—as I was—by a remarkable and controversial Oakland Police Chief, Charles Gain. As a white officer, Gain advanced partly because of his skills and intelligence, and partly because he was supported by the increasingly sizeable and influential Black community. Just as Myrdal's and Westley's police reflected the norms of their communities, Gain's ascension to be the Oakland Police Chief, and his policies, reflected the increasing political influence of the Black community. However, Gain, as Chief, was caught between a recalcitrant rank and file, a somewhat white racist dominated police union, and an increasingly radicalized Black community—especially with the rise of Oakland's own, the armed Black Panther party. As the influence of the Panthers grew across the nation, Oakland became an ideological center of Black militancy. Yet, Oakland never experienced a full blown race riot like those that devastated Newark, Detroit, and Los Angeles.

Did Charles Gain's innovative policing philosophy—combining professionalism, respect for the rule of law, and sensitivity to minorities—prevent a race riot; or did the presence of organized Black militancy serve as an outlet for the grievances felt by the Black community? Perhaps each contributed, in different ways. Nevertheless, its worth tallying some of Gain's innovations, years before 'community policing' became a recognizable strategy for urban policing.

Some of the Gain innovations, which we might want to consider as an agenda for police reform:

> He took internal affairs investigations very seriously.
> He cracked down on those uttering racial slurs—he included telling racist jokes, and gave out 10- or 15-day suspensions for such behavior.
> He enlisted a civilian chief administrator, just as O.W. Wilson, Gain's guide, had enlisted Herman Goldstein in Chicago.
> He introduced a family crisis unit, a juvenile diversion program, a consumer fraud unit, and a landlord–tenant investigation program.
> He recruited Hans Toch and others to develop a program in conflict resolution and peer review of 'critical incidents.'

His most significant and controversial innovation—for its time—was his pre *Tennessee v. Garner* policy on use of deadly force. He told me (when I interviewed him in 1968 for the 2nd edition of *Justice Without Trial*) that this was his most severe trial as police chief. Police shootings were happening regularly, he said, and they were driving him to distraction and insomnia:

> "Attempted burglary of a Laundromat was the typical occurrence," he said. "The police would have reasonable cause to believe we'd seen a perpetrator, chase him on foot, know

that we couldn't capture him on foot and we'd discharge fire on him . . . that sort of thing was going on during a two to three month period."

"It got so that I wasn't sleeping at night . . . I would lay awake until four o'clock in the morning, waiting for the next shooting, These shootings occurred with enough frequency, so that either they were shooting and missing or injuring and killing.

"So finally one day, I think it was the 9th of July, I came to work and there had been another one. By two o'clock in the afternoon, I decided I had had it. I was tired and I knew I had to put the restrictions into effect" (Skolnick 1993: 255).

The restrictions forbade shooting unless the officer's or another's life was threatened. He told me that when he presented his policy, he received no counsel or support from any of his subordinates, but that the City Manager backed him; and that without the City Manager's support he could not have instituted the new policy. The rank-and-file police strongly objected, and the newly formed police union rewarded him with a vote of no confidence.

By the close of 1968, Chief Gain ordered that, in addition to the restrictive deadly force policy, he had instituted, the Oakland Police Department was going to operate within the rule of law. Unlike other police executives who attacked the decisions of the Warren Court—especially *Miranda v. Arizona*—he believed and argued that the police should respect law, not only criminal statutes, but also decisions moderating or restricting bearing on police behavior.

Many rank-and-file cops considered him to be an intolerably authoritarian taskmaster. Some of the officers retired, others resigned. He understood that his insistence on adherence to legal rules was not necessarily absorbed or appreciated by the officers. He didn't care, or at least said he didn't. 'This policy works to achieve behavioral conformity. It is difficult to determine whether attitudes had changed,' he told me. Within the Department, a substantial number—likely a majority—of the officers believed that Chief Gain's management style had undermined department morale.

His critics asserted that police feared to use their authority to investigate crime, for fear of overstepping legally and politically correct bounds. They feared departmental reprisal, they said, and vacancies opened. When Chief Gain resigned in the fall of 1973, his successor, George Hart, organized a retirement dinner. More than 800 persons, representing every segment of the community—including a couple of U.C. Berkeley professors named Muir and Skolnick—attended. The most fulsome accolades were by representatives of minority groups. The Police Association representative was properly polite, but scarcely effusive.

The infusion of black, hispanic and female officers

By 1973, 69 African-Americans, 19 Mexican-Americans, five Chinese Americans, seven Philippine-Americans, and others of non-white ancestry, including Native Americans and Hawaiians joined the Oakland Police Department. There was a white social club, and a separate black one. All, however, joined an 'Association' that was de facto a union, unaffiliated with any major national union.

David Sklansky's (2006) paper does a nice job of showing changes by race, ethnicity, and gender in police departments across the United States. However,

Edward Conlon, the Harvard educated author of *Blue Blood,* quotes one officer as saying 'over time and in the main, cops tend to think like other cops.' We need more ethnographic research to learn whether this is true of most Black, Latino, and perhaps female police working in contemporary police departments. Susan Martin's *Breaking and Entering* distinguishes between *police*women and police*women* (Martin 1980). *Police*women think they should be as fearless as men, especially when other police are endangered. They criticize the less successful female officers—the police*women* for accepting 'a more limited police role.' Is this patterning of women policing still true?

Police unions

The rise of financially and politically powerful police unions has been, on the whole, an impediment to police reform. And the unions resist being studied. Although we can count good studies of patrol police and detectives, we have no in-depth studies of police unions. Perhaps that is because unions typically defend cops who are accused of misconduct, and lawyers are involved. Perhaps it is also that police unions are usually, like the old craft unions, composed of political conservatives. Nevertheless, as I'll illustrate below, when minorities are increasingly part of the dues paying police force, the unions are obliged to represent the interests of black as well as white officers.

The story begins with the assault on Abner Louima, a Haitian immigrant. A police officer, Justin Volpe, had been struck while trying to subdue a crowd, and believed that Mr. Louima had hit him. On the way to the 70th precinct for booking, four police officers administered street justice. They took Louima out of the car and beat him, presumably to teach him a lesson of compliance. This part of the Louima incident, which suggests a more usual retaliation (called, among officers a 'tune-up') than the one Justin Volpe was to administer, has not played a prominent part of the story because of the later sadistic violence to which Mr. Louima was subjected.

Later that night, after Louima was booked in the 70th precinct house, officers did not protest when they saw him being marched to a holding cell with his pants down. Nor did they protest when, after another officer and Volpe took Louima to the precinct bathroom, Officer Volpe brandished a broken broomstick with blood and feces and shouted 'I took a man down today.'

Louima was hospitalized to prevent his death, and the story of his brutal assault began to appear in the media. Several demonstrations, involving thousands of protestors, were held outside the 70th precinct. Five days after the beating Mayor Giuliani and Police Commissioner Howard Safire reassigned the white Commanding and Executive officers and 10 white officers. During the next weeks, the NYPD transferred 22 Black officers, several of whom were Haitian-American, to the 70th precinct. At the time, the community served by the 70th precinct was 40% Black, 38% White, 14.3% Hispanic, and 6.9% Asian.

In 1999, The P.B.A., which had provided legal counsel to the white officers who had brutalized Louima, sued the City of New York on behalf of the 22 Black and Black-Hispanic officers who were transferred to the 70th precinct without their consent. The judge who presided over the case (*Patrolmen's Benevolent Assoc. of the City of New York v. City of New York*, 74 F. Supp.2d 321) noted that race-conscious hiring or promotion programs in police organizations are typically challenged by white applicants alleging 'reverse discrimination.' This case was 'unique.' Never before had Black applicants sued to prevent a transfer based on their race. The Black and Hispanic officers prevailed, on grounds that under the 'strict scrutiny' demanded that, where race is an issue, the City bore the burden of justification; and it could not meet that high standard.

This case, an offshoot of the original Louima case, raised questions that students of police, and police reformers, have been struggling to answer since the race riots of the 1960s. As a general matter, how much affirmative action in policing is appropriate, useful and lawful? Can police managers properly use race as a criterion in making their assignments?

As discussed above, cities across the nation have adopted race-conscious hiring and promotion programs, mostly after they were ordered by courts to do so. These, along with other factors, have resulted in the hiring of substantial numbers of minority and female police officers in cities across the country (see Sklansky 2006). Are affirmative action programs still needed in cities, like New York, where whites constitute a minority (35.0%) of the population?

Aggressive 'broken windows' policing and COMPSTAT

In the 1960s, aggressive policing sometimes generated race riots. However, aggressive policing has worked in New York City in the twenty-first century to reduce crime and, in the Bloomberg administration, has done so mostly to the satisfaction of minorities. I suggest four reasons why:

One, aggressive policing works best when it is combined with fast and efficient information technology, e.g. COMPSTAT.

Second, 'broken windows' policing reduced crime in the Giuliani administration, but minorities still did not trust the police to be unbiased. The Louima and Diallo cases are well-publicized examples of minority community mistrust. Even William Bratton wrote op-eds in *The New York Times* critical of the overly aggressive policing style of his successors.

Raymond Kelly was also critical of the NYPD's aggressive policing in those years. When he became Commissioner he retained COMPSTAT, which had been institutionalized in the NYPD, but the tone of the meetings changed emphasizing counseling over 'gotcha' criticism. On the whole, the Bloomberg administration was more concerned with community acceptance and internal acceptance. That tone is reflected in its still aggressive, but not quite so confrontational, policing. Kelly recruited James Fyfe to be Commissioner of Training (who reported directly to Kelly, who supported him in his effort to train police to the highest standards). Kelly instituted other reforms, perhaps the most notable of which was, instead of distributing graduates of the police academy to the city's 76 precincts, he sent them to those experiencing the highest crime rates. (The NYPD, with more than 37,000 uniformed officers, is the nation's largest police force.)

In New York City, the areas with the highest crime are populated mainly by Blacks and Hispanics. This usually results in more stopping and searching, especially of young Black males. Statistics provided by the police department to the City Council in early February 2007 showed a fivefold increase since 2002 in the number of stops to more than 500,000 (Baker and Vasquez 2007). Nevertheless, police stops of black and brown, and especially of black, males remains a touchy issue, and most especially when the stops result in a 'frisk.' To the police, the stops are a necessary and effective means of controlling serious crime, especially crime involving guns.

To those who are innocent, stops are felt to be intrusive and humiliating. The most recent data (which I requested from the NYPD and was sent to me in early February 2007) showed a noteworthy distribution of population and crime victimization in New York City. Whites (2000 Census) constitute 35.0% of New York City's population, Blacks, 24.5%, and Hispanics, 27.0%. However, Blacks constitute 60.0% of murder victims and 69.9% of murder suspects. Blacks comprise 70.3% of shooting victims and 74.5% of shooting suspects. The police say that those being stopped resemble people who have been identified by victims or witnesses and that there is no racial profiling. The Rev. Al Sharpton has said he plans to file a class action lawsuit over the police stops (Vasquez 2007).

Police size

The numbers of police in New York City have made a big difference in the NYPD's capacity to police aggressively. Five thousand or more police were added to the NYPD in 1993 at the end of Mayor David Dinkins' administration. Kelly was Dinkins' police commissioner and well understood the importance of numbers. Bratton had those numbers at the beginning of his tenure and Kelly has them, more or less, now.

There is another problem challenging the NYPD's capacity to police aggressively. Although the last NYPD class to graduate from the police academy had a majority of non-white males and women, the class was half the size of what the NYPD believed it needed and was prepared to hire. Just to keep pace with attrition, the NYPD needs to hire more than 3,000 police officers a year for the foreseeable future. However, an arbitrator ruled in August 2005 that the salaries of new officers be dropped dramatically, from $40,658 to $25,100, a nearly 40 per cent reduction, to fund a 10.25 per cent raise for all officers over two years (Seifman 2007; Skolnick and Smith 2007).

In recent years, the NYPD has recruited its best educated and most diverse officers ever. However, the mandated pay cuts to recruits have curtailed the department's previous success in recruiting, as has the competition from better paid suburban police agencies. How this will play out remains to be seen. However, when young NYPD cops are paid less but are required to do the same assignments as their colleagues, resentment may grow, and morale suffer. Worse, some may regard subsistence level salaries as an incentive to engage in corruption, a regular NYPD problem in previous years, but absent—so far—in the Bloomberg–Kelly years.

West coast police agencies, like L.A.'s and Oakland's, pay much higher salaries than the NYPD, but have ratios of police to population less than one-third the NYPD's. Oakland and Los Angeles can boast competent police executives, but nevertheless experience high homicide rates. Correlation does not necessarily indicate causation. However, a shortage of sworn police complicates a police department's ability to be as responsive to crime rises as the NYPD. Yet, cities on the west coast, where police compensation is relatively high, are also experiencing declining interest in the policing. The era of affirmative action in hiring and promotion may be coming to an end, and a new era of a shortage of qualified applicants may be just beginning.

References

Ahern, J., 1972. *Police in Trouble*. New York: Hawthorne Books.

Baker, M., 1985. *Cops: Their Lives in Their Own Words*. New York: Fawcett.

Baker, A. & Vasquez, E., 2007. Police report far more stops and searches. *New York Times*, 3 February 2007, A1.

Bittner, E., 1970. *The Functions of the Police in Modern Society*. Cambridge: Oenschlager.

Kleinig, J., 2000. *The Blue Wall of Silence: An Ethical Analysis*. Occasional Paper XIII. The Center for Research in Crime and Justice, New York University School of Law.

Martin, S.E., 1980. *Breaking and Entering: Policewomen on Patrol*. Berkeley: University of California Press.

Muir, W.K., Jr., 1977. *Police: Streetcorner Politicians*. Chicago: University of Chicago Press.

Muir, W.K., Jr., 1980. "Power attracts violence". *Annals of the American Academy of Political and Social Science*, 452, 48–52.

Myrdal, G., 1944. *An American Dilemma: The Negro Problem and Modern Democracy*. New York: Harper.

Punch, M., 1985. *Conduct Unbecoming: The Social Construction of Police Deviance and Control*. London: Tavistock.

Seifman, D., 2007. NYPD's blue over lack of recruits. *New York Post*, 6 May 2007.

Sklansky, D.A., 2006. "Not your father's police department: Making sense of the new demographics of law enforcement". *Journal of Criminal Law and Criminology*, 96 (3), 1209–1243.

Sklansky, D.A., 2007. "Seeing blue: Police reform, occupational culture, and cognitive burn-in". *In*: M. O'Neill, M. Marks and A. Singh, eds. *Police Occupational Culture: New Debates and Directions*. Amsterdam, The Netherlands: Elsevier.

Skolnick, J.H., 1993. *Justice Without Trial. 3rd Underpaid Cops: NYPD's Low Rookie Pay Endangers City's Future* ed. New York: Macmillan.

Skolnick, J.H. & Smith, D., 2007. "Underpaid cops: NYPD's low Rookie pay endangers city's future". *New York Post*, 9 May 2007.

Vasquez, E., 2007. Numbers show how police work varies by precinct. *New York Times*, 5 February 2007, B1.

Westley, W.A., 1951. The Police: A Sociological Study of Law, Custom, and Morality. PhD dissertation. University of Chicago.

Will, G., 1991. *New York Review of Books*, 10 June 1991.

Wilson, J.Q., 1968. *Varieties of Police Behavior: The Management of Law and Order in Eight Communities*. Cambridge: Harvard.

Police and social democracy

William Ker Muir

University of California, Berkeley, CA, USA

Good patrol officers develop their beats by teaching their publics about living in a free society. The patrol sergeant is in the best position to demonstrate to his officers how to be an effective civic educator.

I

A word with pleasing overtones, like democracy, attracts a host of meanings. There is representative democracy, with its unique features of a widespread franchise, periodic elections of key government officials, and majority rule. Representative democracy gives an electorate a weapon to threaten termination of incumbents' political careers. (A variation of representative democracy is direct democracy, where the voters themselves resolve key issues by majority rule.)

Political democracy, on the other hand, is about the protection of the individual and his freedom of action. In that sense, it is the near opposite of representative democracy and its rule by majority. Political democracy's emphasis is on institutional devices to counter governmental power with power, particularly with checks and balances and procedures of due process.

Cultural democracy, a third meaning, signifies deliberation among numerous parties. Key to cultural democracy is the moral norm that talking and persuasion will trump command and force in the making of a community's significant decisions. (Its opposite is hierarchy.)

Fourth, and finally, social democracy means equality—not a material equality, but a moral one, in which the 'self-evident truth' is that all persons are 'created equal'—that all individuals share a sameness in their capacity for self-government. In the words of Jefferson, all men and women possess a 'moral instinct,' consisting of the capacity for empathy and a desire to matter to others. (Social democracy's opposite is aristocracy, with its distinction between superior and ordinary people.) Social democracy was the feature of American life that struck Alexis de Tocqueville so forcefully when he visited America in 1831–1832. His insight into the different consequences of social democracy and aristocracy—the prodigious energies, individual pride, and generous public-spiritedness of democratic societies in contrast with the lassitude, submissiveness, and selfishness of aristocratic ones—has proven ever more prescient with each passing decade.

II

All four meanings of democracy have application to the activities of police. With its focus on the relationship between public officials and a city's police department, for example, representative democracy raises the question of the degree to which the police should be overtly engaged in partisan local elections. In engaging in partisan politics, police (like judges) jeopardize the appearance of even-handedness. However, we also know that government employees in general (and schoolteachers, garbage collectors, fire departments, mass transit workers, and clerks in particular) are invariably the best organized and most zealous elements of an electorate; their numbers and organization give them disproportionate influence with elected officials. Consequently, if the police refrain from participating in the electoral contests of their city or state, they (and the public they protect) are likely to be slighted in the battle for a city's limited resources. The representative democratic question is, how can police harmonize their need to be both partisan and above politics?

As for political democracy and its concern for individual rights, the issue is two-sided. One key question is the relationship between the administration of the department and its non-managerial members. How appropriate is a policeman's Bill of Rights? Under what circumstances can it be enforced productively, so that the individual *officer* can be treated fairly without injuring the 'general welfare' (i.e., the department's ability to protect the citizenry)? Is an aggressive police union essential to its functioning? (Here, one thinks of some of the deleterious effects of public school teacher unions, even after admitting their necessity). The mention of police unions suggests another important electoral democracy issue, how to prevent oligarchy? Most industrial unions do not tolerate internal disagreement; union leaders are notorious for suppressing opposition. Unions virtually always are one-party regimes. The question is, how best to contain this oligarchic tendency in police unions? By encouraging the formation of rival unions within a department? By nurturing rival parties within a single union? For more on this topic, see Seymour Martin Lipset, James Coleman, and Martin Trow, *Union Democracy.*

The flip side of a police officer's rights are the rights of the citizen, including those suspected of or charged with criminal activity. Police have always defended their own rights, but have been less inclined to champion the rights of the accused. Whether future developments in reinforcing the rights of police can take place in a manner that enhances support for the rights of the ordinary citizen is an intriguing question.

What about cultural democracy? Cultural democracy has direct application to any organization that, like an army, a fire department, or a police department, exposes its members recurrently to personal danger. In this connection it is useful to recall the observation of Chester Barnard, author of the classic book on management. In his *The Functions of the Executive*, he makes the startling remark that the quintessential 'democratic' institution is an army engaged in battle. Barnard is speaking of democracy in the cultural sense, and his point is that leading a fighting unit into combat requires persuasion and inspiration; a frightened or uncertain group of men can always refuse to go forward. Similarly, a leader of police—especially the sergeant who is responsible for a patrol squad—must talk, not command, his officers into being brave—into being so courageous as to be willing to sacrifice their lives. It is the patrol sergeant who must find ways to coax, train, and persuade the individuals in his or her unit to act bravely and with creative initiative amidst danger. In this respect, how to train sergeants to be leaders of officers that will act courageously when put 'in harm's way' is the key cultural democratic issue.[1]

III

Today, the most innovative forms of community policing highlight the fourth meaning of democracy—social democracy. Here, the central issue involves the relationship between law-enforcement officers and the public they police, particularly the poor and undereducated of our cities.

While preventing crime, the best police are simultaneously trying to explain and exemplify the very meaning of self-government and enlightened self-interest—inspiring neighborhoods to solve their own problems without relying solely on governmental imitative, teaching the values of civilization and its intolerance of bullies, and conferring honor on those who try to improve things.

Police call this motivating and teaching function 'developing one's beat.' As a general matter, teaching police how to develop a beat is not attempted in police academics. Rather, those skills—those social-democratic skills—are handed down by good sergeants and veterans talking to rookies on the job.

In the department I studied 30 years ago, however, several formal devices were instituted to enable the teaching of developing a beat. One was officer participation in management matters. The Chief established two programs—review boards in connection with gun discharges and abuse complaints—in which peers sat in judgment. In deliberating on what went wrong and went right, officers learned from each other and more often than not what they learned was philosophy concerning notions of human nature, the good society, and the nature of the good policeman. In addition, the department collaborated with psychologist Hans Toch and others in cultivating 'agents of change.' The program, involving officers with evident leadership abilities but who also had been involved in a disproportionate number of troublesome incidents, really was an extended seminar on the police role in a free society. (The program lasted an entire year and took place during off-duty hours.)

Some departments provide sergeants a great deal of latitude in shaping up their squads. I attempted in *Police: Streetcorner Politicians* to describe what one remarkable sergeant (whom I called Robert Peel) did to convince his men that people in 'inner cities' did not differ in their human nature from people in other walks of life. He was able to demonstrate that individuals, whether rich or poor, are both flawed and also long to earn the respect of others. Furthermore, because people, despite their imperfectness, want to be 'worthwhile,' they can be entrusted to govern their own lives—*under certain circumstances*. This intensely felt need for dignity, Peel taught, was the 'hot button' that astute police could exploit in crises.

More importantly, his explanation of human equality made his officers' beats more understandable to them. They began to see the value of 'talk' and to grasp the means by which they could explain to their 'publics' the rules of the game—what was expected of them in a socially democratic society and what they could expect in return (*Police: Streetcorner Politicians*, pp. 184–187). Sergeant Peel raised questions among his men and precipitated systematic discussion on three topics: first, about how the police department functioned as a system of collaboration; then, about the meaning of 'manliness' (with insights on what it meant to be human); and, finally, about how the city worked.

As a political scientist, I suppose I'm unduly sensitive to the omission of an explanation of our socially democratic American society in the training regimes of our police departments. There is virtually no discussion of the miracle of American democracy. I don't mean the teaching of the nuts-and-bolts of representative democracy. I mean the social-democratic ideas of Hamilton (and his recognition of human imperfection) and Jefferson (and his recognition of the 'moral instinct' universal in the human race). It is the coupling of these seemingly contradictory traits in our natures and the devices in our society to accommodate them both that make self-government possible.

The ideal police academy course on democracy would deal with the topics of anarchy and its moral and economic consequences, the consequences of police being too weak (the emergence of private warlords) and too strong (tyranny of the kind described in the case of *Brown v. Mississippi,* 297 US 298 [1936]), the notion of balance of power in our government (separation of powers and checks and balances), the importance of free markets, and the conditions under which law, religion, and education make Americans a virtuous people.

The obvious objection to teaching democratic philosophy to sergeants *is* its irrelevance to the police task. Police—and patrol officers, especially—work in dangerous and desolate circumstances, amidst terrifying anger and tragic despair. The perils of their work and the misery they encounter hardly amount to a receptive environment in which to educate the citizenry. Mastering skills necessary to control events in strangers' homes and ominous neighborhoods is so important (and so difficult) as to make learning how to teach civics seem downright silly. Yet, my five years of experience with the Oakland Police Department convinces me of both its practicality and its benefits.

As for practicality, the lever—the factor of opportunity—is the patrol sergeant. Supervising a half dozen or so (often) young officers, he can make the time to teach his squad about the origins, singularity, and importance of our country's socially democratic ideas.

The benefits to the sergeant's squad would be increased understanding, effectiveness, and pride in their profession. The benefits to citizens I'd have to guess at, but I'd bet the ranch that they would become less angry, more cooperative, and more filled with self-respect.

Training sergeants to be civic educators of their patrol officers (who in turn would 'develop their beats') is not an idea that will spread like wildfire. Departments will object that, with their limited resources, they cannot expand efforts to train patrol sergeants in this seemingly impractical sphere. I am optimistic, however, because I've seen how such efforts pay off. Moreover, multi-department programs (like the Police Corps[2]) that train individual sergeants chosen from a number of departments obviate the need for each department to create and fund classes for its officers alone.

IV

My favorite story is of the wayfarer who comes on three workers at a construction site. When the stranger asks each of the workers what they're doing, one responds,

'I am piling stones.' The second answers, 'I'm building a wall.' And the third says, 'I am building a cathedral.' The point of the story is that connecting our daily activities to a noble and enduring object is the secret of satisfaction and motivation. To see one's policing duties within the overall context of this nation's remarkable socially democratic experiment elevates the notion of the policing profession and makes sense of the demands we make of the well-intentioned men and women who enter it.

Notes

1. Why sergeants are sovereign in police departments is the subject of a short discussion in my *Police: Streetcorner Politicians*, pp. 235–248 and 264–266.
2. The Police Corps, the brainchild of Adam Walinsky, has recently lost its federal funding and (so far as I know) is now out of business. However, Walinsky is a vital and inspiring resource for anyone interested in innovations in policing.

Index

Page numbers in *Italics* represent tables.
Page numbers in **Bold** represent figures.

academic research 100
accountability processes 150
Action Review Panel 37
Adams, R.J. 136–42
African America community 92
agencies 165
Ahern, J. 156
American Bar Foundation 82
Annual Report of the Seattle Police Department (2002) 32–3
ANOVA/MANOVA procedures 46
Australia: jurisdiction 124; police unions 123–33; political culture 124
Australian Federal Police (AFP) 2–3
Australian National University (ANU) 62
Australian Research Council 59–60
Auxiliary Policewomen 127

Bacon, F. 74
Baker, M. 158
Barnard, C.: *The Functions of the Executive* 168
Bayley, D.H. 16–24, 54; American policing 94
Berkeley Conference 5, 90
Berry, J.: *et al* 106–21
Bevir, M.: and Rhodes, R.A.W. 60
Birzer, M.L. 63
Bittner, E. 81; policing practice 82; situated knowledge 80
Black militancy 161
Black Police Association (BPA) 117; development 115–18
Black Police Officers Association 108
100 Blacks in Law Who Care (NYPD) 157
Blue Blood (Conlon) 163
Boston Police Strike (1919) 139
Bradley, D.: *et al* 61
Bratton, W. 164
Breaking and Entering (Martin) 163
Bristol University 116
British Association of Women Police 114
Broken Arrow Initiative 6–7

Broken Arrow Police Department (BAPD) 43; Citizen Crime Survey 46; employee differences **47**; management 110; survey results comparison *48, see also Leadership Team*
Brown, J. 117

C-POP officers 146
Campbell, D. 79
Canada 138–41
capacity governance model 65
CAPS program 93
Chicago: community meetings 153
Christopher Commission Report 96
Citizen Complaint Review Board (CCRB) 98
Citizens Subcommittee 54
civic participation 152
civil rights leaders 98
civil rights movements 159
civil service systems 92
civilian review boards 95
Code of Silence 31
collaborative knowledge production 67–9
collaborative projects 69
Colonial Office 124
Commission of Inquiry 130
Commission on Law Enforcement and the Administration of Justice (1967) 16
Committee on Freedom of Association (CFA) 137
community: activists 90; forms 169; norms 159–60; policing 150–1, 154; work 151–2
community-oriented policing (COP) 17, 39, 157
community-policing bureau 146
COMPSTAT 17, 150–1; 'broken windows' policing 164–5; reform 33–4
computerized management 152
conduct 101
Conlon, E.: *Blue Blood* 163
Conservative administration UK (1992–1997) 113
correlation 165

craft knowledge 22
Crime Commission (1967) 98
crime control 110
crime rates 46
Criminal Investigation Department (CID) 116
cross-jurisdictional variations 102
culture 156–65; change 67, 109–11; democracy 167

data-driven policing 32–3
de Groot, A. 81
de Tocqueville, A. 167
debunking studies 19
decentralization 31–2, 145
decision-making 42; team operations 44–5
DeLord, R. 42
democracy: control 124; electoral system 129; meanings 168; policing 1
democratization 32
demographics 156–65; change 9
Detective Branch 110
Diamond, C. 79
Dinkins, D. 165
discipline patterns 101
discretionary behaviour 30
dispute resolution 137
Dutch Public Union (NPB) 112

employee representative groups 107
employment relationship 140
ethical codes 156
executive leadership 53
external accountability 21

Fairness and Effectiveness in Policing (report) 88
Federal Government 133
Federal Government Order-in-Council 138
federation of trade unions (FNV) 112
Finnane, M. 123–33
fiscal crises 102
Fleming, J. 67–8
focus groups 65
Force Options Research Group 35
force restrictions 160–1
Foster, J. 62
front lines research 74–84
fundamental responsibilities 127
The Functions of the Executive (Barnard) 168

Gain, C.R. 37
Gay Parade 111
General Orders 147
Geva, R.: and Shem-Tov, O. 63
global norms 141
Goldstein, H. 19, 62, 146

Google (website) 99
Grant, J.D.: and Toch, H. 36
Great Britain 3, 112–15; policing 115
Great Depression 126
Greenhill, N. 62–3

Hart, G. 162
Hart survey organization 141
Heckman, J. 77
Herbert, S. 96
Hill, F. 33
HM Inspectorate 114
hot-spots policing 17
Howard, J. 132
human rights 136–42

industrial campaigns 126
industrial democracy 112
industrial paradigm 79
Industrial Revolution 106
innovation 101
institutional security 133
institutions: change 120
international human rights 136
International Labor Organization (ILO) 1, 136; labor rights 138
international networks 8
Israeli Police 63

jurisprudence 137

Kelling, G.L.: and Moore, M.H. 18
Kelly, R. 157
Kerlikowske, G. 32–3
Klockars, C.B.: *et al* 31

labor: demonstrations 139; revolutions 139
labor legislative networks 8
Labor Party (Australia) 128
labor relations 94
labor rights 137
labor unions 160
labor-management cooperative (LMC) projects 42
Latino Officers Association 157
law-and-order conservatism 13
Lawler, E.E. 40
Laws, D.: and Rein, M. 75
leadership 39–55; implementing 45
Leadership Team 43; assessment 45; effects 46; member responsibility 49
legislation 149–50
LEMAS report (2003) 91
Levi, M. 99
Lipset, S.M.: *et al* 168
literal warfare analogue 29

Local Police Departments (LEMAS report) 91
Locke, E.A. 53
London Metropolitan Police 113, 124
Los Angeles Police Department (LAPD) 96; Rampart scandal 97
Louima, A. 163

McCulloch, P. 78
MacPherson Inquiry 118
management 94, 161–2; paradigms 61; strategies 40
management committees 23
management-union decision-making 50
managerial strategies 4
Manager's Toolbox for Remaining Union-Free (Wal-Mart) 140
Manpower Demonstration Research Corporation 77
Marks, M.: and Sklansky, D. 1–13; and Wood, J. 64
Martin, S.: *Breaking and Entering* 163
Melbourne police strike 126–7
Metropolitan Police Service (MPS) 115
military organizational attributes 29
misconduct 97; investigation 95, 101–2; investigation examples 158
Montreal Police Strike 139
Moore, M.H.: and Kelling, G.L. 18
moral analysis 83
Morris Inquiry (2004) 117
Muir, W.K. 160, 167–71; *Police* 169
municipal agencies 151
Murphy, C. 2
Murphy, L. 29
Murray, J. 2
Myrdal, G. 159

National Academy of Sciences 88
National Advisory Commission on Civil Disorders 159
National Black Police Association (NBPA) 117
national level unionization 149
National Policing Plan 114
National Research Council 20
National Symposium on Police Integrity (1996) 96
neo-liberal economic policies 126
Netherlands 111–12; society 112
New Labour Government 114
New Public Management (NPM) 110
New Scotland Yard 117
New South Wales Police Association 108
New York City 146, 164–5; crime reduction 33
New York Police Department (NYPD) 157

New York Times 164
New Zealand 118–20
New Zealand Police Association (NZPA) 118
Newton-Smith, W. 74
nexus policing project 58–70; methodological practices 67
Nixon, C. 128
non-union employee associations 97
North America 140; jurisdictions 133
Nozick, R. 76; rationality 78

Oakland Police Department 36, 162
occupational groups 156
officer infusion 162–3
officer misconduct 35–7
Organisational Development Standing Committee 68
organizational changes 18
organizational culture 10
organizational democracy 27–8
organizations 23; agency and change 60–1; attributes 28; initiatives 39
Ospina, S.: and Yaroni, A. 42
outsider role 23–4
Oznowicz, R. 34

parliamentary organization 28–30
participatory action research (PAR) 59
participatory management 11
participatory reform 35
Peer Review Panel 36
pensions 102
Police Act (1919) 113
Police Act (1958) 119
Police Administration (Wilson) 92
Police and Civil Rights Union (POPCRU) 7–8
Police Community Support Officers (PCSOs) 114
Police of the Deep South 159
Police Executive Research (PERF) 19
Police Federation of Australia and New Zealand 130, 132
Police Federation of England and Wales 112–15
Police (Muir) 169
Police Officers Bills of Rights (POBR) 95
Police Practice and Research (journal) 13
Police Review (magazine 1917) 133
Police Subculture Schema 59
police-academic partnerships 63
police-community relations 89, 102
Policing (journal) 12–13
policing literature 58
Policy Studies Institute (PSI) 116
policy-making 6

politics: corruption 30; democracy 141, 167;
directives 127; disposition 158; recognition
131–2; risks 144
practical purpose 82–3
Pride Parade 111
problem-orientated policing (POP) 17
problem-solving policing 150–1
Professional Standards Unit of the
Metropolitan Police 108
professionalization 90; movement 92
profit-and-loss statement 145
program assessment 76–9
program improvement 76–9
public concern 89
public employees 99
public policing 9
Public Service Staff Relations Act (1967) 139

Quality Leadership initiative 41
quasi-military rituals 30
Queensland colonial inquiry 131
Queensland Police Union 128

racial profiling 89
racial relations 102
Rampart scandal 97
rank-and-file 22–3
rank-based authority 3
rationality 77
reactionary model 108
reconfiguration 35
reform 16–24, 144–54; cooperation 151–2;
demands and expectations 150; leadership
transition 153–4; process 118; public 152–3;
resistance 145–50; roster 17
reform agenda 145
reformers 92
regional networks 8
Rein, M.: and Laws, D. 75
Reiner, R. 106; blue-coated worker study 123;
Police Federation of England and Wales
113
relationships 69
representative democracy 167
research 75–83
research agenda 11–13
Reuss-Ianni, E.: *The Two Cultures of Policing*
80
Rhodes, R.A.W.: and Bevir, M. 60
routine management 101
Royal Canadian Mounted Police (RCMP)
138
Royal Irish Constabulary 124

scholars 100
science 74; human interests 83; knowledge 75
Scotland 27

Seattle General Strike 139
self-regulation 21
sergeants 146
Sex Discrimination Act (1976) 114
Shared Leadership (SL) 41; civilian
employees 51–3; community-oriented
policing 50–1; intervention outcomes 45;
interview data 49; investigative activities
52; organizational process 47; productivity
51; workforce indicators 46
Shearing, C. 3
Sheehy Inquiry (1993) 113
Shem-Tov, O.: and Geva, R. 63
signs-of-crime policing 17
silence code 158
Simon, H. 81
situated knowledge 79–82
Sklansky, D.: and Marks, M. 1–13; police
department changes 162–3; Police
Subculture Schema 59
Skogan, W.G. 144–54
Smith, J. 77
social democracy 167, 167–71
social scientists 109
social work 149
socialist movements 106
South Africa 3; capacity governance model
65
South African Police Force 3
South Australian Police Association 127–8
specialized units 148
Steinheider, B.: and Wuestewald, T. 39–55
strategic innovation 20
street wisdom 34–5
structural change 109–11
subculture 96–7; norms 102
Summary Offences Act (1979) 130

Tasmania: University of 62
Tasmanian Institute of Law Enforcement
Studies (TILES) 62
Texas 146
Toch, H. 27–37; and Grant, J.D. 36; police
departments 147–8
training 170
Transit Safety Division 66–7
Trojanowics, R. 19
The Two Cultures of Policing (Reuss-Ianni)
80

Uniformed Patrol Branch 110
uniforms 28–9
Union Democracy (Lipset *et al*) 168
union-management relations 101
unionization 90; patterns 106–21
unions 7–9, 95–6; activities 102; contracts 93;
innovation impact 93–4; neglect 88–103;

police-community relations 98–9; typology 107–8
United Kingdom (UK): Royal Commission 129, *see also* Great Britain
United States of America (USA) 4; Civil Rights Act 21; community policing 153; Justice Department 90; reform paradigm 24; reforms 16, 24; society 170
Universal Declaration of Human Rights (UDHR) 136
universal knowledge 79–82

Victim Support Team (VST) 35
Victoria Police 62
Victorian Police Association 125, 127
Volpe, J. 163

Wal-Mart 140
Walker, S. 88–103
Warren Court 162
watchdog model 108
Weisburd, D.: *et al* 31
Western Australia Police Union of Workers 125
Western countries 7
Western societies 107
Westley, W. 159

Wilson, J.Q. 159
Wilson, O.W.: *Police Administration* 92
Winnipeg General Strike (1919) 139
Wisconsin Police Department 41
Wood, J.: *et al* 58–70; and Marks, M. 64
Work Choices Legislation 133
work counsel models 43
workplace decision-making 5
World War I 139
Wuestewald, T.: and Steinheider, B. 39–55

Yaroni, A.: and Ospina, S. 42
youth service delivery 64

Related titles from Routledge

Innovative Possibilities: Global Policing Research and Practice

Edited by Les Johnston and Clifford Shearing

This book brings together observations that reflect upon the state of police and policing across the globe and associated forms of policing scholarship. A wide range of international authors look at:

- a review of the nature of the relationship between policing research and practice with the Victoria Police in Australia
- how the National Improvement Strategy for Policing (NISP) in Britain is developing and how research is being used to design, define, monitor, and develop its strategic interventions using a series of case studies
- the complex American terrain of the police in the USA, including how crime statistics are used to rationalize, justify, and account for their actions
- a comprehensive review of research on police reform in Latin America during the last two decades
- the complex and diverse social terrain in Africa which needs to be understood in relation to its plural policing landscape
- the historical development and current status of police scholarship in China, together with the emerging issues arising from it

The overarching concern of these reflections is with bridging the deep-seated tensions that exist between scholarship and practice within policing across the globe. This book was originally published as a special issue of *Police Practice and Research*.

February 2011: 246 x 174: 136pp
Hb: 978-0-415- 61835-9
£80 / $125

Available from all good bookshops

Related titles from Routledge

Policing: Toward an Unknown Future

Edited by John Crank and Colleen Kadleck

The enclosed papers are the culmination of a project Dr. John Crank and Dr. Colleen Kadleck carried out assessing issues facing the police into the early 21st century. The papers are future oriented, in the sense that they anticipate trends visible today. Everywhere, the contributing scholars found that the organizational concept, practice, and function of the police was undergoing transition. Yet, the seeming state-level hardening of the police function was ubiquitous. Two themes were noteworthy. On the one hand, in developing or 'second world' countries, police face endemic problems of corruption, organized crime, and drugs. Police, in response, are undergoing centralization and intensification of law enforcement activities. In countries with first world economies – Canada, the United States, and Australia – contributors discovered trends toward expansion of the police function, a trend described by Brodeur as toward 'high policing'. It reflects the growing reliance on surveillance for crime control and for the tracking of minority, indigenous, and immigrant populations in crime prevention efforts. The results suggest that governments, sometimes encouraged by their citizenry, seem increasingly to rely on the police to deal with a broad array of social as well as criminal problems.

This book was originally published as a special issue of *Police Practice and Research*.

February 2011: 246 x 174: 160pp
Hb: 978-0-415- 61818-2
£80 / $125

Available from all good bookshops

Related titles from Routledge

Police Responses to People with Mental Illnesses
Global Challenges

Edited by Duncan Chappell

Community police frequently encounter people with mental health illnesses, and these interactions are often sensitive and demanding; yet despite this, surprisingly scant attention has been given to the development of empirically tested and established best practice approaches to managing this important aspect of police work. *Police Responses to People with Mental Illnesses* seeks to reduce this gap in knowledge by providing an international overview of some of the latest initiatives in the field, and the challenges still to be confronted in many places in overcoming cultural and associated barriers to protecting the rights of the mentally ill.

This book was originally published as a special issue of *Police Practice and Research: An International Journal.*

November 2011: 246 x 174: 112pp
Hb: 978-0-415-69937-2
£80 / $125

9647579